11 S 11D

KING ALFRED'S COLLEGE
WINCHESTER

To be returned on or before the day marked
below :—

1 OCT 1990

30. APR 97

PLEASE ENTER ON ISSUE SLIP:

AUTHOR GRICE

TITLE Rogues and vagabonds

ACCESSION No. 71428

ROGUES AND VAGABONDS

or The Actors' Road to Respectability

ROGUES AND VAGABONDS

or The Actors' Road to Respectability

by

ELIZABETH GRICE

TERENCE DALTON LIMITED
LAVENHAM . SUFFOLK
1977

Published by
TERENCE DALTON LIMITED
ISBN 0 900963 78 6

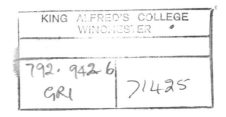
Text photoset in 10/12pt. English

Printed in Great Britain at
THE LAVENHAM PRESS LIMITED
LAVENHAM   .   SUFFOLK

CONTENTS

INDEX OF ILLUSTRATIONS

For Neville, who was wary of
"that factual book"

ACKNOWLEDGEMENT

Rogues and Vagabonds has brought me many friends as well as professional help from far and wide. It has even given me the excuse to loiter with intent in two of my favourite counties, Norfolk and Suffolk.

I am especially grateful to Pamela, Lady Troubridge for allowing me to see her late husband's excellent collection of provincial playbills; to Geoffrey Snagge, who afforded me a day's hospitality while I studied the manuscript diary of his forbear, Thomas Snagg; to Sybil Rosenfeld, whose scholarship has been a guide; to Kitty Shaw (née Fisher) and her cousin Caroline Fisher-Carver for their kindness in making the rich Fisher Collection available to me; to E. A. Goodwyn and Clive Palne for their notes; to Peter Northeast, who was a valuable scout; to Moira and Jonathan Field for their help with the Fisher Circuit; to Dr Paul Schlicke for his enthusiastic support; to Alick Williams for guidelines; to Dick Condon, Manager of Norwich Theatre Royal; to Michael Dibdin; to Raymond Mander and Joe Mitchenson.

I was fortunate to have the expert help of the staffs of the Suffolk Record Office in Ipswich and Bury St Edmunds, the Colman and Rye Libraries of Local History in Norwich, the Norfolk Record Office, Cambridge Record Office, The Cambridgeshire Collection, King's Lynn Central Library, Ipswich Museums, Birmingham Public Library, the British Reference Library and the Enthoven Collection.

Tim Scorer took endless trouble to photograph much original material at Norwich and Ipswich. Evelyn Clarke gave me a roof over my head within sound of Norwich Cathedral chimes while I worked in that splendid city. Many have indulged me with theatre talk quite beyond the call of friendship and my family have been patient beyond expectation. My sister Sue slaved to complete the typescript in time. To all, warm thanks.

Elizabeth Grice,
Henham, Suffolk.
July, 1977

William Hogarth's "The Laughing Audience", 1733. It shows a typically rowdy scene in a corner of the theatre. Two gentlemen in the boxes fight openly, an orange seller tugs at the sleeve of one of the beaux trying to attract his attention away from a rival fruitseller; people in the pit respond boisterously to the performance; the three figures in the foreground are members of the orchestra trying to concentrate on their wind instruments.

CHAPTER ONE

Lewde and Ungodly Spectacles; or,
The Players Under Fire

"Most of the present stage entertainments sap the foundation of all religion, as they naturally tend to efface all traces of piety and seriousness out of the minds of men; but . . . they are peculiarly hurtful to a trading city, giving a wrong turn to youth especially— gay, trifling, and directly opposite to the spirit of industry and close application to business." John Wesley, 1764.

NOTHING now compares with the hubbub of the eighteenth century stage, least of all today's theatre. It was capable of representing at one time or another the entire gamut of social encounter, from a street brawl to a drawing-room soirée. No theatre-in-the-round could suggest its intimacy, and audience participation as the twentieth century feebly knows it is an exercise in restraint beside the irreverent vigour demonstrated by playgoers two hundred years ago. Perhaps the only contemporary scenario remotely resembling it is the House of Commons in rare fettle at a controversial debate. The disrespectful ferment, idiosyncratic conventions and sheer boisterousness of Georgian theatrical experience is unmatched in modern terms.

Henri Misson, a French visitor writing of his travels through England in 1719, reported that there were two London theatres, "one large and handsome, where they sometimes act Operas, and sometimes Plays; the other something smaller, which is only for plays". In the smaller of the two, a commotion of Hogarthian vulgarity assaulted his eyes and ears, the kind of colourful anarchy which persisted in country theatres long after London audiences had learned discretion.

The auditorium was seething. Public ebullience bordered on outright disorder; squabbles in the pit, congestion in the galleries, the actors a natural target for fruit peelings and nutshells. The theatre pit, as Misson saw it, was raked like an amphitheatre and crammed with baize-covered backless benches. "Men of quality, particularly the younger sort, some ladies of reputation and virtue, and abundance of damsels that haunt for prey, sit all together in this place, higgle-piggledy, chatter, toy, play, hear, hear not. Farther up, against the wall, under the first gallery, and just opposite to the stage, rises another amphitheatre, which is taken up by persons of the best quality, among whom are generally very few men. The galleries, whereof there are only two rows, are filled with none but ordinary people . . ."

This was theatre of the people, undignified by the concept of culture; theatre in the raw. Fine women flocked there wearing masks to protect their reputations lest they should be identified frequenting unacceptable houses of public amusement and, at the other end of the social scale, stage-struck young men gathered at "spouting clubs'' to recite dramatic parts, while young women were cut off without a farthing for supporting them. When the playwright Thomas Dibdin included Arthur Murphy's cautionary farce about a besotted young actor in his 1815 collected edition of plays, he was quite unable to resist commenting that "The Apprentice" "was very properly levelled at the prevalent, and, it may be said, dangerous passion which then (1756) existed, and, in spite of the moral of this well-written farce, does still exist, amongst young people possessing stronger inclination than ability to attempt the stage as a profession".

The play's hero, Dick, is accused of the ultimate defection—he has been attending a spouting club, "a meeting of 'prentices and clerks, and giddy young men intoxicated with plays . . . they all neglect business and think of nothing but to become actors''. Dick's father, Wingate, typifies parental outrage:

> "Ay, that damned Shakespeare! I hear the fellow was nothing but a deer-stealer in Warwickshire. I never read Shakespeare. Wounds! I caught the rascal myself reading that nonsensical play of Hamblet where the prince is keeping company with strollers and vagabonds."

But the opposition to plays and players was no mere domestic issue. It was political. From the rollicking scene Misson described, no ignorant observer would have smelled persecution; yet such gatherings, steadily proliferating in towns and villages all over the country, were generally illicit or at best allowed by the local magistracy on sufferance.

At the beginning of the eighteenth century, "legitimate" drama was confined to the stages of two London theatres, Covent Garden and Drury Lane. These theatres were the only ones licensed by royal patent to perform plays—a monopolistic system introduced by Charles II in 1660 to keep drama in check, politically and morally. Everywhere else, actors lived precariously, sometimes hounded by the authorities, sometimes treated with indulgence or even covert patronage. In large provincial towns, the art of survival had to be perfected to a fine degree: Bath, Bristol, Edinburgh, York and Norwich were places where the battle for acceptance and respectability was fought early and with honours.

It was not until the last quarter of the sixteenth century that players and playwrights were branded as an evil influence instead of being treated merely as a nuisance or an extravagance. Companies of actors who played when and where they could were seen as beguiling a sheeplike populace with material likely to undermine authority, whether of Church or State. By 1572 these "mad spouters of plays" were so numerous that an Act was passed (and had to be reinforced twenty-five years later) denouncing them and all their ilk. Fencers, bearwards, common players and minstrels not belonging to any baron of the realm were labelled collectively and indiscriminately as rogues and vagabonds.

Without a magistrates' licence they were strictly out of bounds, undesirables. Outbreaks of the plague in 1578, 1591, 1602 and 1625 conveniently reinforced every

"Acting off the Stage: The well-fed Magistrate listening to the request of the half-famished Player to perform in a Barn." from Pierce Egan's *Life of an Actor,* 1825

political argument for limiting theatrical gatherings, especially in hot weather; and the Puritanical movement was gaining sufficient weight to add appreciably to the anti-stage posturings of fearful ministers of state and outraged moralists of other persuasions, Quakers and, later, Methodists chief among them.

The famous Norfolk-born jurist, Sir Edward Coke, complained bitterly in his *Charge at Norwich* (1607) that "the country was troubled with stage-players" much as it might be troubled by vermin. He spoke out against them from the bench, reserving special spleen for the provincial actors who were daring to play without either commission from the nobility or licence from the authorities.

"Theatricals" in Norwich formed a strong branch of popular entertainment with obvious potential as a political vehicle. Drama mattered, therefore it could be dangerous. There was a common belief that it had a direct effect on the lives and morals of the people. A contemporary commentator on the mid-eighteenth century scene claimed: "On the virtues, and manners of a people, depends the prosperity of a state; these will be influenced by the theatres; the concern is therefore of a public nature; and the government only can be entrusted with the care of them."

More narrowly, popularity was equated in the municipal mind with disruption and laxity. The Norwich guardians were perturbed by the immense following plays attracted in the city and voiced their fears to London. On 21st January, 1623, a letter from the Privy Council was sent in reply to "Our very loving friends the Mayor and Justices of the City of Norwich" forbidding players, tumblers, dancers and "that sort of vagrant and licentious rabble".

William Prynne, a notorious Lincoln's Inn barrister of corrosive Puritan views, shortly afterwards published his *Histrio-mastix, The Player's Scourge* (1633) hoping to persuade citizens that stage plays were "sinfull, heathenish, lewde, ungodly Spectacles, and most pernicious Corruptions; condemned in all ages, as intolerable mischiefs to Churches, to Republics, to the manners, minds and souls of men". It was exactly the sort of vilification to convince players that they had something exceedingly well worth fighting for. To have their profession struck off as unlawful, infamous and "misbecoming to Christians"—along with dancing, dicing, health-drinking, smoking and bowling—was a guarantee of mettlesome defiance.

During the Civil War of 1642, drama was further blacklisted. It threatened the common weal, luring the "meaner sort of people" away from their labours and putting giddy thoughts into their heads. Most actors supported Charles I, while the Parliamentarians pressed through legislation to demolish or close playhouses, convict and publicly whip actors and to fine spectators five shillings for every offence of attendance. This edict of Lords and Commons was to be read out in all towns and churches in the land and "especially in the County of Essex" where plague casualties had been high. The plague scare was a transparent excuse for Puritan bans on sports, plays and other assorted diversions likely to promote "lascivious Mirth and Levitie".

It was little wonder that when Charles II came to the throne the Restoration theatre was shrunken and enfeebled, except in small pockets of unrelenting activity. William Davenant and Thomas Killigrew hardened their monopoly of the two legitimate London theatres which, though gradually eroded as royal patents began to be granted later to certain provincial playhouses, was not finally broken until the Theatre Regulations Act was passed in 1843.

Absurdly, Covent Garden and Drury Lane, both of them unwieldy and often ill-managed, were the sole official providers of drama. If minor theatres were to perform plays they were forced to resort to subterfuge. Music was the commonest camouflage: unlicensed theatres would advertise and charge for their "concerts" but consented to throw in "the rehearsal of a play" or "Specimens of Rhetorick" for nothing. A few songs or a spot of fiddle-scratching were often all that stood between theatre managers and prosecution. A new genre, the burletta was devised precisely to circumvent the law. As a musical rhyming drama it was a safe programme item, and consequently singers and dancers were as much in demand as straight actors. Besides, as Thomas Dibdin claimed: "a good song, in a village, is thought of more by the audience than all the acting on the stage".

Managers of touring companies practised obsequious routines to win over the mayor and magistrates of the town in which they hoped to find quarter. They sent forward their most presentable member to ask permission to play in a barn or booth or inn yard. In a climate of suspicion and intolerance, however, respectability was a hard-won thing. For some, it was never won at all. Companies of comedians who tried their luck in Norfolk and Suffolk in the early eighteenth century usually found that local magistrates would turn a blind eye to their plays masquerading as music lessons, or some such cover. But the extent of their blindness was not to be relied upon; it was as likely to depend on whether the magistrate had had a good lunch, on his whim, as much as on whether the petitioning players could boast aristocratic backing.

A strong anti-stage faction continued to snap at the heels of the actors, inveighing against them as a "malignant evil". Among the most self-righteous of the pack were those who believed that even if the authorities failed to exterminate them, God himself would intervene. When 80 of the 140 people at a puppetshow were burned to death in a barn in Burwell, Cambridgeshire, on 8th September, 1729, it was instantly interpreted as a manifestation of divine retribution; when an actor was struck down in full spate, it was considered the only proper fate for corrupters of the public conscience. "Should we not think that man a scandalous libertine who should keep a set of plays in his house?" asked the Reverend John Duncan, of Wimborne Minster, in 1787.

The privations of actors outside the patent houses were exacerbated by the Licensing Act of 1737 which attempted once and for all—entirely unsuccessfully—to put some backbone into the previous prohibitions. Two controls were introduced: control of theatres and censorship of the plays acted in them . . .

> ". . . every person who shall for Hire, Gain, or Reward, act, represent, or perform, any Interlude, Tragedy, Comedy, Opera, Play, Farce or Other Entertainment of the Stage or any Part or Parts therein, in case such Person shall not have any legal Settlement in the Place where the same shall be acted, represented, or performed, without Authority by virtue of Letters Patent from His Majesty, his Heirs, Successors, or Predecessors, or without licence from the Lord Chamberlain of His Majesty's Household for the time being *shall be deemed to be a Rogue and a Vagabond* within the Intent and Meaning of the said recited Act, and shall be liable and subject to all such Penalties and Punishments . . ."

In theory the Act took away the power of mayors and local justices to license players, and not until 1788 was another Act passed restoring these powers. In practice, however, all the old dodges were perfected, and new evasions contrived. Plays in the provinces continued to be staged under the winking eye of local justices (despite the fact that the Act vested no such authority in them), buttressed by popular enthusiasm and open patronage from "genteel" families. The players, instead of being crushed under the new legislation or cowed by religious opposition, wore their restrictions lightly. They developed a combative strategy and a purposefulness which was to carry drama through to a golden age. Troupes of actors crossing from shire to shire to catch what support they could, began to form themselves into regular companies, adopting and consolidating their favoured towns into circuits, graduating from barns and booths into specially-built playhouses, and applying with varying success for the status of royal patent.

Between 1768 and 1788, patents were granted to eight major provincial theatres. Among the first of the new wave of eighteenth-century playhouses were those at Bath, Bristol, York, Norwich, Ipswich and Edinburgh. As one of the "richest and biggest Cities in the Kingdom" with a good dramatic pedigree, Norwich was a natural headquarters and by mid-century it was accepted as a close and coveted stepping-stone to the London stage.

Auditioning for the country stage.   from Pierce Egan's *Life of an Actor*, 1825

CHAPTER TWO

Actors on the Road; or,
The Snaggs of being a Strolling Player

"Working in the trade is very different from seeing the finished performance before the curtain, where all is dressed and polished for the show. In the morning all is gloom, negligence and hurry . . . actors in their great coats and dishevelled hair, yawning out their parts and hasting it over to get out of the house, to walk, talk and be admired . . . actresses muffled, and drawling out their words with simpers and affectation The general bustle is to get over the confinement of the drill." Thomas Snagg (1746-1812)

A GREEN room writer of the eighteenth century claimed that the life of an itinerant player was so tough that only two kinds of people could persist in it—the stage-struck and those who from indolence or obscurity could expect nothing better. It was a hard training school demanding stamina, a thick skin and, since most of the distance between towns had to be tramped, a good pair of legs. Members of an outfit such as the Norwich Company of Comedians, who developed a wide and largely unpoached circuit with a profit-linked touring system of strategic importance were favoured compared with the more aimless strolling companies; but some of their trials were not dissimilar and many of the Norwich troupe's actors had started out on the strollers' rough road. Some of the cruder showmen and performers deserved their shabby reputation: they were the "rogues and vagabonds" of the Act, notorious for thieving, loose living and brawls. They gave the whole profession in the provinces a bad name. "The stigma attached to the profession is by no means just," complained the provincial player, Thomas Snagg (alias Wilks), "for though there are dissipated and idle members there are likewise prudent and honourable."

The aim of all touring players was to outwit the authorities or cajole them into granting permission for performances. With characteristic irreverence, Snagg described the usual way of applying for a licence to perform. The manner of taking a town, he said, was by application to the magistrate or mayor of the place "which, if he listens to, his answer generally is: 'If I find your Company regular and orderly I shall not take notice of it.' As there are specific Acts of Parliament against strolling players, a Justice cannot give his permission, though in many towns the theatres belong to the Corporation, or the Town Hall is let for hire."

When Snagg decided in 1771 that he and a fellow actor, George Stevens, would cut themselves loose from the apron-strings of the Norwich Company and set up a "burletta company" of their own, he discovered that to hatch such an "egg of improbability" was impossible without the support and goodwill of the mayoralty.

William Hogarth's satirical view of the sale of benefit night tickets. Actors often sold their own box and pit seats and places on the stage. Top London actors could stand to earn £150-200 during the winter season and probably as much again from their benefit nights after house charges had been deducted. Spiller's prospects, however, look none too good: his bills are weighing heavily in the balance against his ticket sales.

Author's collection

They chose Yarmouth for the venture, "being a populous Sea Port and the residents a play-admiring audience". But the mayor viewed them as some sort of revolutionary band, the Norwich actors objected to their presence, and they were debarred from renting the theatre. As Great Yarmouth's permanent playhouse was not built until seven years later, "the theatre" was housed in the town chamber, specially equipped for the scheduled visits of the Norwich Company.

Despite the inauspicious start, the profligate Snagg refused to consider his scheme doomed. He was not lacking in cash and so he hired a piece of ground, planning to build a temporary theatre of wood and canvas. Large bills were posted advertising a burletta, "The Mad Captain", which Snagg confesses was a piece pirated from an obsolete farce, dressed up with local jokes and songs for the occasion. But he was condemned to learn one of the hardest lessons of the untried theatrical entrepreneur. It was blazing June, 1772:

> "The sun and fine weather were playing such captivating beams against our flimsy productions that the folks thought it pleasanter and more healthful to walk and enjoy the sea breezes than to pay and be shut up to hear our

contemptible warding, for we had neither name, merit nor interest to support us."

The dispirited players returned to "plain comedy". In his raffish memoirs, *Recollections of Occurrences*, Snagg said tersely of their failure: "In short, we decamped like a dog who had burnt his tail." The *débâcle* was softened to some extent by an impromptu invitation to perform at a small town near Harleston in Norfolk. "To make good our retreat we accepted, received permission from the Judge of the District, or at least his word to overlook us as vagabonds, formed a respectable strolling company and played to overflowing houses." Respectable or no, the troupe soon lost what sporadic support they had and Snagg was thankful to relinquish his managerial dignities at the end of a disastrous season.

Snagg's career, touching on East Anglia at many points as it did, was a much better than typical progression from stagestruck amateur to an actor of status in the provinces, and his memoirs are probably the most vivid and detailed account we have of the vicissitudes of country actors in the eighteenth century. Being a cocksure London boy, Snagg contrived to be auditioned by Garrick at the age of nineteen. He sucked a new-laid egg to help him articulate clearly, but his performance was embarrassing. "You may, in time, *do*", pronounced the great man. Unquenched, the theatre-bitten youth enlisted himself in 1765 on the pay-roll of a London company bound for Manchester, perfecting the regulation actor-gentleman's garb in all its flamboyant detail: green travelling coat, buckskin breeches, white waistcoat, broad gold-laced hat, a nice pair of summer boots, and a black silk stock and bow at the neck. The result of fussing over these niceties was that he missed the players' coach and was forced to pursue the party alone on horseback at breakneck speed. He caught the coach up at Newport Pagnall and, two days after his departure from London, arrived in Manchester with "a jumbled and sore bottom". In Manchester he secured a decent furnished room with a small family, paying half a guinea a week, dinner and tea included.

Every company in the country prickled with petty jealousies arising out of the actors' sense of insecurity or self-importance. Not surprisingly, Snagg's greenness was resented by seasoned members of the company who, under a system of equal division of profits, saw their shares diminished by his arrival. Instead of the usual share of proceeds, he was offered what was likely to be the lower form of emolument—a salary of a guinea a week and a vague promise of a benefit night. At least it prevented mutiny at a time when even candle-ends had to be split among a company to keep squabbling to a minimum.

In the event, this arrangement was probably the safest form of pay: receipts totalled £20, the town had recognised the piece as the mediocre offering it was, and Mr Lee, the manager, had scarcely enough money to meet the salaries. "I jogged on discontented in my towering expectation in a cloud of little parts", Snagg recalls. It was the story of a thousand other small-time players.

A dice-throw eventually awarded Snagg a benefit night at Manchester. He played the Prince of Wales in "Henry IV"—to rows of empty benches. "There arrived a whimsical and perhaps fortunate accident to save my credit and account for empty benches," he consoled himself. "The Reverend Mr John Wesley came unexpectedly to Manchester and preached in a square near the playhouse in the open air. As he entertained his congregation gratis I acted to hardly anyone but to those who had taken tickets before."

Snagg's wanderings over the next year took him to London, back to Manchester and then to join Mr Herbert's strolling company in Lincoln. With £12 in his pocket, he tramped across the Pennines accompanied by a King Charles spaniel called Pompey who sickened and died before the trek was over. In one penny-pinching little inn Snagg paid 1s 8d for a trout. His next supper consisted of cold boiled beef and good brandy. He afterwards mounted a broken old ladder to "a sort of Cockloft (they had told me I was to have a very good warm bed in their *upper rooms*), where the bed, I believe, was chaff, the blankets a sort of coarse frieze, and the sheets were linen." Lincoln finally brought him £14 11s 6d at the end of two months.

Lincoln, Sheffield, Mansfield, Bridgnorth, Wellington. Snagg's itinerary was a patchwork of hope and disappointment culminating in an attempt to make his fortune in Ireland. "Worn to a rush" by seasickness on the voyage, Snagg was so ill that he had to be transferred ignominiously into a smuggling vessel and deposited like a piece of driftwood on the beaches of Deal.

Unable to face the dishonour of returning empty-handed to London, Snagg prepared for what he called "a flying movement to Norwich". It was a severe winter and the Norwich coach creaked along treacherous roads for two days. Arriving at Bury St Edmunds to break the journey for sleep, he was astonished to find the Norwich Company under "Mr Crough" (probably William Henry Crouse) already in the heat of action. Lamenting the waste of his paid-up fare to Norwich, Snagg decided to cut his losses (the coach book-keeper at the *Five Bells* at Bury refused to refund him) and introduce himself the following morning. He knew two of the comedians and was handsomely received—to the extent of being offered a share. The players, he found, were "as respected in the towns as the inhabitants themselves".

Inns were frequently the *pied-à-terre* of touring players unless they were able to afford private lodgings. In either place, rehearsing a part could be a noisy business unappreciated by fellow lodgers. Snagg took to the fields around Bury rather than make himself the laughingstock of waiters and chambermaids. "I most opportunely discovered a delightful covered cowhouse where I thought I might bellow like any bull without the least disturbance to anyone," he said. To his embarrassment, he was discovered by an inquisitive cowherd and a few days later, in full spate, saw "a knot of boors, cottage wenches and clodpoles" gaping at him from behind a beech tree.

"A play actor!" they yelled. "By God, clap him, clap him, clap him"—which they did, "with hands not of the most delicate mould".

He had as yet had no pay from the Norwich manager and was down to his last shilling. "All circumstances being maturely weighed," he said, summing up his financial position, "the getting to Ipswich appeared the most eligible, as I might in that town raise the wind by depositing some trifles as a forced loan, procure private apartments and lie *perdu* till I had joined the corps, when I should enter into regular pay."

He took a 21-mile cross-country route, on foot, and reached Ipswich at sunset in a day. On his arrival, Snagg was in a none too presentable state. He confronted a pawnbroker with his gold watch only to receive the dusty answer: "Here, Sir, we never buy things from people we don't know." For a little over three guineas, however, he surrendered his watch, two gold seals and a mourning ring. Stung by the harshness of the deal, he left in disgust and headed for London. In no time at all, he fell in with Josiah Foote, and was invited to help Foote establish himself in Exeter. Throughout his life Snagg maintained a vigorous disrespect for his betters and his *Recollections* dented many reputations. He referred to Foote as "a Thespian butcher", an epithet not far wide of the mark: "I was introduced to the resident manager, Mr Foote, with his apron, sleeves, and steel, who absolutely sold steaks and beef in the morning at his stall and cut up Richard and Macbeth at night on the stage, though he was considerably more in character at the chopping block and selling than at blank verse and acting."

Snagg was a stranger to stability like most others who had, as they put it, "smelt the lamp". Footloose as ever, he toured Sheffield, Grantham, King's Lynn, Swaffham, Wisbech, Boston, Spalding, Peterborough and Newark-on-Trent with his "old troop of Jolly Companions"—the Lincoln contingent, now operating under Mrs Herbert since the death of her husband. The circuit nudged boundaries with that of

"Suiting the Action to the Word: Interior of an Hedge Ale House contiguous to the Theatre (ie. Barn). Mr Plausible Screw's Company refreshing their Memories. Plausible 'laying it on thick' to the companion of Proteus respecting the fine figure of the stage-struck Peregrine and his promising talents as an actor".
from Pierce Egan's *Life of an Actor*, 1825

the Norwich players, here and there actually overlapping. It was while Snagg was at Fakenham in Norfolk, following King's Lynn Mart, that Richard Griffith, actor-manager of the Theatre Royal, Norwich, made a bid for him. The stroller was pleased and flattered:

> "The parts, prospects and advantages pointed out to me were not to be withstood. I embraced the proposals and joined the Norwich Corps at Ipswich on 8th June, 1771."

He reports that from the whole summer circuit (taking in Woodbridge, Norwich, Colchester and Bury St Edmunds) receipts were £2,374. Snagg's own benefit night at Yarmouth raised a respectable £30 17s.

> "As living at this time was reasonable, I really saved money out of my salary of a guinea and a half per week, for I boarded and lodged comfortably for half a guinea per week."

Snagg was fortunate to have landed with a company which had abandoned the sharing system in favour of salaries and could be relied on to give its players a fair wage. In many circuits, the iniquities of "sharing" were notorious. Most theatrical companies in the country at this time practised the system, the theory being that each performer, usually irrespective of merit, took a cut of the profits after expenses had been deducted. The manager's allotment was generally two shares for clothes, two for scenes, one for himself, one for his wife and one for each child that performed. As principal beneficiary of the scheme, the parsimonious manager incurred a great deal of bad feeling. Ruthless managers would push their youngsters on to the stage almost as soon as they could walk or lisp out a few words, for the sole purpose of netting another share.

The anonymous author of *The Green Room Book* expands on further examples of rapaciousness, practised by Mr Stanton, manager of a so-called sharing company in Staffordshire: "The expense of scenery and dresses, and the deficiencies of bad houses he throws into a fund called the stock debt; and if he is an adept he takes good care that the sum may always be very large; so that when the company is successful, he is sure to pay it off. By this business, in the course of a number of years, Mr. Stanton has amassed a tolerable fortune."

Most principal actors—including those at Norwich until the 1750s—played on shares, dividing the profits between them each day. There were never more than 12 shares, so they were often sub-divided into two or four parts. The owner of a share, whether actor or proprietor of the house, could lease part of his share to another actor who was charged a certain "rent" for it and thereby entitled to play in the company and receive his daily portion. The sharer, when he came into the company, paid a lump sum into the general stock. Untried or inferior actors were paid a weekly salary of between six and ten shillings by the sharer.

Because of the paucity of the week-to-week financial rewards, actors' benefit nights were an essential supplement to their income. They occurred usually once a

Miss Goward, later Mrs Keeley, was soon taking the parts of lively soubrettes at Covent Garden. Here she is playing opposite Robert Keeley the man she was to marry. Blanchard, Bartley and Mrs Faucit, all one time Norwich celebrities, are in the cast.

To avoid scandalising his near and dear ones too much, Thomas Snagg took the stage name of Wilks. Here he is pictured as Jessamy. "When the character of Jessamy was first allotted to me," he wrote, "I remonstrated against it as I had never been in the habit of playing in that cast of the fops and the success arose from the extravagance I adopted absolutely through dislike of it; but as I found the audience were pleased I followed the stream and endeavoured to swim with it. I have heard people where I have sat unknown in a public tavern declare they knew me and that I was just the character I represented on the stage. In short, so many stories were uttered of me and my exploits, though all fake, that I believe it heightened curiosity and was of service."

T. G. Snagge

season (though minor players might miss out altogether) and depended entirely on the support an individual could enlist from the townspeople. Many of them would tramp miles knocking on doors and thrusting playbills into the hands of passers-by. There was something degrading about the practice but it was not until late in the eighteenth century that touting for ticket money—or the promise of it—was abandoned in favour of more discreet advertisement. Some actors found the method suited their personal style, however. When John Bernard, in his itinerant days, sought out his friend, Scott, hoping he might be able to secure him a position at Braintree, he found the actor delivering playbills in a suit of blue and gold and carrying a gold-headed cane.

In most regular companies, the benefits were meted out according to superiority, the highest salary taking the first, and so on. Those on the same rate had their benefits determined by the dice—"sometimes per favour, especially a pretty female may have secret interest with the Manager", Snagg divulges. On benefit nights, the actors received merely a part of their takings, the manager appropriating the rest for "costs" unless it was the most desirable kind of all the variations on benefit nights, the "clear" benefit, essentially the prerogative of a top star, when the management paid all charges.

John Bernard poured scorn equally on the sharing system and on benefits. At Westbury-under-the-Plain, Wiltshire, he was faced with "the usual prospect of playing six weeks for my amusement, and taking a benefit at the end for the remuneration of my butcher and baker. This mode of living upon a six or eight week's credit and receiving a surplus of coppers on a particular night seemed to me a curious peculiarity about the County Comedian. Yet it was pretty generally the case in all sharing companies, from the inadequacies of the receipts to meet more than the 'ordinary expenses' viz. Manager, room, lights, bills, fiddler, and scene-shifter".

The amount deducted by the management on benefit nights varied widely. In Norwich until 1776 it was about 20 guineas. The proprietors conducting the Theatre Royal would have liked to raise it to 25 guineas and proposed as much but were eventually forced by an outraged company to reconsider and the following year settled for £24. There were three benefit nights a week.

Tate Wilkinson, the famous York circuit manager, took a trip to Norwich at the end of the 1787 York season and acted for several nights with the company, being given a clear benefit on the last night. Later, he wandered to King's Lynn to play a week there for what he understood to be another clear benefit. When Wilkinson came to settle his bill on his last night, 5th May, the manager, William Scraggs, presented him with a receipt showing a deduction of £7 for "expenses". Wilkinson had enjoyed a clear benefit in the full sense of the word in Norwich the week before; as manager, he had both given and received them all over the country in his time and he was much too wily for Scraggs's prevarications. "At last," he reports, "with grumbling, hesitation and great unwillingness, the money so detained was returned, and though not given with all the heart, I took it with kindly acceptance, having given it up as lost, well knowing, in money matters, delays are suspicious as well as dangerous."

Managers throughout the profession were a motley, baffling species with little recognisable general ethic. Many of them were patently dishonest; others simply had to resort to a certain cunning to make ends meet. If the Norwich circuit was better served than most country towns in its style of management, it was partly because Norwich was a confident, expanding city with willing patrons. By and large, a town got the manager and the theatricals it deserved.

John Bernard, who forsook a sensible job for the "wild and diversified paths" of drama, stumbled across the nadir of provincial drama in Brentwood, Essex, where his friend John Scott was then playing. He describes being ushered into a room fitted up as an inn—paper wings, hoop chandelier stuck with tallow candles, superannuated scenery, a fiddler, a lamplighter and a company of five, the first and worst of whom was the manager himself. Manager Penchard had held on to his position for fifty years, fondly believing that he was still the only person capable of playing juvenile leads. He was miserly, gouty and heavily wigged. "He had gout in his legs, Shakespeare in his Head and money in his heart."

Bernard was treated to the spectacle of Penchard as Plume, a young gallant in "The Recruiting Officer" by George Farquhar. "All the business of the character," commented the young actor sourly, "consisted in his taking snuff and producing and putting away a dirty pocket-handkerchief. As he could neither exit nor enter, when his scene was over, the curtain was lowered, and he was wheeled off."

But eccentricity was by no means the prerogative of obscure theatre managers. Fox, the Brighton manager, was said to combine twenty occupations without being clever in one (a pretty general characteristic of country managers). He was, Bernard reports, actor, fiddler, painter, stagehand and tailor, besides being check-taker and bill-sticker on occasions.

In 1774 while John Bernard was performing with a strolling company in Dedham, Essex, fate (as he supposed), or more likely Richard Griffith, manager of the Norwich circuit, guided two bulky city aldermen, Gay and Day, part-proprietors of the Theatre Royal, Norwich, to the front row. The gentlemen were impressed. They sent a servant round with a note inviting Bernard to "sup at the inn". They told him they liked his work and invited him to join the Norwich group for its ensuing season at Ipswich. Three days later Griffith had hired him to "play the fops and light comedy at a salary of thirty shillings a week, in the theatre which ranked next to Bath, out of the metropolis". News of the engagement—and especially of its impromptu manner—circulated fast. Gay and Day were driven away by a flood of applications from aspiring actors.

Bernard left strolling without regrets. It had, he said, taught him two things: resourcefulness in overcoming obstacles and discretion in controlling money. The transition from irregular to regular acting was crucial to his progress. "If my reader cannot enter into my feelings at this sudden change and unexpected elevation, from the lowest to within one of the highest rounds in the dramatic ladder," he said, "it is useless for me to describe them."

A leaf from the inventory of the Ladies' Wardrobe at Norwich in 1784. Entry 79 is a "Country Stuff dress, white trimmed with Blue, Jacket, Coat and Long Sleeves"; 94 is a "Black Stuff Jacket and Petticoat trimmed with Ermine" and 105 consists of "2 Mermaids Jackets, Yellow trimmed with Green". Several of the items are described as old, very old or worn out.

Norfolk County Libraries

CHAPTER THREE

Seedbed of Drama; or,

Norwich—a Nursery for Great Actors

*"Genius exalts him [the actor] to his sphere; but when there,
Science must uphold him. A system, and a system only, can
enable him to tread midway in air between the heaven of fancy
and the earth of fact . . . He holds the spectator's illusion in his
grasp, but which, like glass, is so delicate and brittle that it is
sure to shatter if he lets it fall."* John Bernard, 1774

*"Though the city of Norwich is not the most theatrical town in
the kingdom, yet that audience to any piece that is well received
will bear a more repeated acting of it than any other town of the
size whatever."* Tate Wilkinson, 1790.

BY THE mid-eighteenth century, Norwich had status. As a cathedral city at the
centre of its county and with widening influence over its whole region, it was a
thriving place to be. The potential theatre-going population was steadily expanding
through the influx of those who, directly or indirectly, depended for their livelihood
on the healthy worsted industry. By 1750, the population had reached 36,240.

The commercial prosperity of Norwich was mirrored in the progress of its
resident company of comedians—a professional, respected and comfortably-off band
with better than average wages and popular headquarters at the *White Swan* inn.
Newcomers to the company were impressed, quick to recognise its standing in the
community. What struck them most was the deference with which the company was
treated in every town it visited and the mutually tolerant relationship which had
matured between local magistrates—who had no business, after all, to be kindly
towards the players—and the Norwich theatre manager. At some towns when the
season was drawing to a close, the town clerk would even send a note of congratulation
to the troupe; and by 1804 relationships had progressed along such a friendly path
that Lord Chedworth was recorded as having left legacies of between £13,000 and
£14,000 to members of the company.

To understand how Norwich became one of the top five or six provincial circuits
in England one needs only to glance back over its honourable dramatic tradition.
Companies of actors fought for patronage in the late seventeenth century and the
contest resolved itself into a struggle between Thomas Doggett and John Power. The
Court of Mayoralty eventually decided that the troupes could play consecutively but
were not to visit the city at the same time. This judgement did not please everybody.
Humphrey Prideaux, Bishop of Norwich, could not condone the Duke of Norfolk's

A theatre for all towns — or very nearly. Between 1730 and 1850, a period roughly co-incident with the rise and fall of the Norwich Circuit, East Anglia was populated with theatres more thickly than it had ever been before, or ever will be again. Those built by the Norwich Company were the grandest, the Fisher theatres the best loved and the makeshift theatres in small towns and villages ensured that nobody need be beyond easy walking distance of a play.

sponsorship of Doggett, nor could he square the court's lenient attitude with the need to keep the people at their work and free from the disrupting influence of rogues and vagabonds. "The D[uke] of N[orfolk] hath been here", he complained, "and some will have it that his only business was to fix Dogget [sic] and his players here, who have now their stage up at ye Duke's places, and are helping all they can to undoe this place wch on ye decay of their weaveing trade, now sinks apace. But I suppose his Grace had some other designe on this journey than for ye sake of these varletts."

After 1700, Doggett left the field to Power (whose company also appeared to be visiting Bath and Bristol). Sybil Rosenfeld (*Strolling Players and Drama in the Provinces 1660-1765*) suggests that Power's was the company which attracted the patronage of the Duke of Grafton (the Grafton seat is at Euston in Suffolk), and acted in the early eighteenth-century under the name "The Duke of Grafton's men, servants to the Lord Chamberlain".

When Thomas Ager succeeded Doggett as head of the Norfolk troupe (with the famous actor Keregan in his train) there was another clash in Norwich—this time between the Norfolk and Grafton factions.

Other competitors were eager to capture the Norwich drama-base, too. In 1721 the Duke of Richmond's Servants played at the *King's Arms* and Henry Tollett, a puppeteer, sailed to East Anglia from Rochester claiming to lead "the Completest Company that ever Stroled". After a tussle for supremacy between Tollett and "Mr Keregan's Company of Comedians", Keregan retired to ply the circuits of Canterbury and York. During Norwich Assize week, a company from the Dublin theatre—including William Penkethman, "flower of Bartholomew Fair"—chanced its hand with "an entire Sett of New Scenes never before put up". Mrs Bedingfield entertainingly described her visit to the fitted-up room they had equipped for theatricals in the *White Swan*:

> "The house was too small for the actors; but a trap-door opened, and four of the company fell in—one a particular man, who was high-sheriff last year, fell upon a pretty woman, and liked his situation so well, that they could not get him out."

Pattern of the Norwich Company's movements between the seven major towns on their circuit. The players wintered at Norwich, then embarked on a ten-point shuttle of the eastern counties which returned them to Norwich in January in time to repair their sets and paint new scenes for the new season.

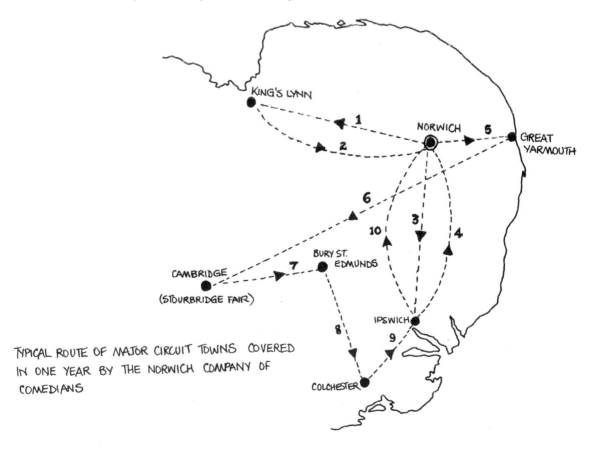

TYPICAL ROUTE OF MAJOR CIRCUIT TOWNS COVERED IN ONE YEAR BY THE NORWICH COMPANY OF COMEDIANS

The *White Swan* inn, near St Peter Mancroft Church, was the Norwich Company's permanent home from 1731-1757 and soon became known as the "White Swan Playhouse". It was fitted up with stage, pit, two galleries and an array of rough wooden benches. The first reference to the group of actors who were to form the nucleus of the Norwich circuit appears in 1726. For a decade the players were styled "The Duke of Grafton's Servants" but in 1736 assumed the cumbersome title "The Norwich Company of Comedians, Servants to His Grace, the Duke of Grafton, Lord Chamberlain to His Majesty's Household".

From the beginning, there was nothing in their repertoire to arouse condescension. Plays were performed soon after their London première as it was evidently a matter of professional self-regard in Norwich to present the most recent plays possible. "King Charles I" by William Havard appeared in the same month in London and Norwich in 1737. Fielding's "Wedding Day", a comedy which ran into serious trouble with the censor because of its "immorality", was given in Norwich in 1743, just a season after its opening in London's Drury Lane with Garrick in the leading part. "The Wedding Day" was a highly risqué piece; even in the watered-down form necessary to get it licensed, it was considered a corrupting story and was not thought suitable enough to merit a place in some of the play collections which were published at the turn of the century. It concerns the adventures of a rake called Millamour and an elderly procuress, Mrs Useful. The cast is embellished with several desirable young women, and a good deal of morally undesirable dialogue. The fact that the play was staged at all by the Norwich company demonstrates better than anything else its vigorous competitiveness, and a certain daredevil spirit.

John Gay's politically-provocative "The Beggar's Opera", new to the metropolis in January, 1728, was before Norwich audiences three months later and was soon taken to Bury St Edmunds, Colchester and Ipswich, travelling like a lit fuse to gunpowder. In his edition of popular plays in *The London Theatre* (1815), Thomas Dibdin described "The Beggar's Opera" as a piece "which has been criticised in all ways and which has begot all manner of opinions". As the popular quip put it, the "Opera" had made Rich (manager of the first Covent Garden theatre) Gay and Gay Rich. On reading the manuscript, Congreve pronounced that it would either "take greatly or be damned confoundedly". It ran for 63 consecutive nights in London and became one of the mainstays of the eighteenth century repertoire.

The Norwich manager spent handsomely on scenery and costumes. In paint alone, a year's bill amounted to £25. In 1784 an inventory of the ladies' wardrobe included silk and satin "tragedy dresses", brocades, Italian floral nightgowns, cockades and buskins and a "stuff yellow dancing Dress, Jacket, Petticoat and Lambeekeens". Country actors at this time are generally supposed to have been performing Hamlet in full-bottomed wig and fashionable coat of the day, yet the Norwich players were insistent on "proper decorations" and went to considerable expense to equip themselves aptly for their parts. Highly-skilled carpenters and decorators were taken on and the scenic artist was the best-paid member of the outfit.

"If it were not for us and the taylors," the carpenter in "An Occasional Prelude" is made to say, "you might shut up the theatre."

Sweeping improvements were carried out at the *White Swan* in 1739 and boxes were provided spacious enough to accommodate the women's voluminous skirts. The scene painter, John Devoto, whose baroque artistry enhanced several London stages, was hired to produce new sets worthy of the garnished playhouse—a legitimate occasion for price rises.

The Licensing Act of 1737 should effectively have clipped the wings of the expanding company but although trouble was certainly anticipated—the *White Swan* was ostensibly billed for concerts, and plays were advertised as gratis between the musical items—a combination of ingenuity on the one side and diplomatic blindness on the other kept the Norwich players from any disastrous confrontation with magistrates. In his *Life of an Actor* (1825) Pierce Egan quotes a poem about the approach of a strolling player seeking permission from the Mayor to perform—it explains how actors could continue not only to make a living illegally but to collect a certain amount of tacit support in doing it:

"The Mayor meantime consulted the Recorder,
Who called the Manager a vile marauder;
The actors vagabonds; a vagrant race;
And thought 'twas wrong to let him build a place;
But said, if he approved, it must be blink'd at;
The man, in short, must by the Mayor be *wink'd* at."

Far from conducting its affairs covertly, the Norwich Company boldly advertised its presence and wrote the names of its occasional visiting London actors in large type on the playbills.

Long before the *Griffin Inn* yard became Ipswich's main playhouse in the first half of the eighteenth century, actors used the Shire Hall, or Old Moot Hall, in Foundation Street.   *Suffolk Record Office, Ipswich*

The *White Swan* was smartened up in honour of Charles Macklin in 1747, then in his extended prime. Macklin was a vain and egotistical man but a giant among actors and his visit was treated by the company as though it were some supernatural manifestation. Here was the man who shook Drury Lane as Shylock, Macklin the awesome. John Bernard was one of the few young sprigs who dared to treat Macklin publicly with something less than respect. The actor was, Bernard remarked, "very seldom taken with the fit of being entertaining" and his manners were bad. "His early education had been scant and his mind had taken a long while to grow."

To the younger actor, he was a natural target for satirical banter: "He has as little appearance of dying now (1787) as when the generation around him was at nurse ... he was a broad-breasted, bald-headed, shaggy-browed, hook-nosed individual ... a gentleman considered to be about 95 years of age [there was doubt about the year of Macklin's birth but he is thought to have lived to be 100] who was more generally talked about and written about than any other member of his profession." The Norwich Company was well satisfied to have brought Mahomet to the mountain.

After a fair amount of experimentation, the Norwich circuit had by 1760 settled into a pattern of touring which served the eastern counties more or less unchanged for well over a century. The players usually wintered in Norwich, during which time stock scenes and sets could be built up and repainted ready for the start of the country tour. An artist could spend four or five weeks painting new scenes and flats—frequently local landscapes—before the waggons were due to roll. Touching up a battered drop scene or flat might be done on the spot at one of the circuit towns but all new scenes were assembled at the Norwich workshops. While King's Lynn was in the circuit (and there were few misses) the Norwich early spring season was interrupted so that the players could take advantage of the pleasure-seekers at Lynn Mart, beginning on 14th February. Ipswich was visited in June (for the races) and there would generally be a week's back-track to Norwich for the summer assizes. Yarmouth was played until about 14th September and from there the company made the 86-mile haul to Cambridge for Stirbitch (or Stourbridge) Fair. The "Great Fair" at Bury St Edmunds—an important scheduled stop—began in the second week of October and lasted for three or four weeks. By mid-November, the waggons were in Colchester; then Christmas was celebrated in Ipswich before a return to base along the difficult January roads.

From year to year, there were variations on the established route: Dereham (June) and Beccles (the May races) were both ports of call in 1749. The company went to Framlingham in 1728, Harleston in 1734, 1737 and 1748, Swaffham in 1735, Thetford in 1736, Fakenham in 1743, Saxmundham in 1743, 1745 and 1747, Sudbury and Hingham in 1744, Walsingham in 1748 and Bungay in 1754 where there was a "Great Theatrical Booth". Bungay was a popular small town venue because it was lively, appreciative and, from 1773, had its own theatre. The players stayed there three or four weeks, playing often four nights a week. Hannah More was staying in

The *White Swan* Inn, Norwich, first home of the Norwich Company of Comedians and headquarters of all their circuit activities.

Norfolk County Libraries

the town in June, 1777 and wrote to Garrick: "The dramatic furore rages terribly among the people—the more so, I suppose, from being allowed to vent itself so seldom. Everybody goes to the play every night—that is, every other night, which is as often as they perform. Visiting, drinking and even card-playing are for this happy month suspended." Dramatically, Bungay audiences were treated on a par with those in the big county towns. The June season in 1781, for instance, included "The Suspicious Husband" (John Hoadley), "Know Your Own Mind" (Arthur Murphy), "Tancred and Sigismunda" (James Thompson), "As You Like It" (Shakespeare), "The School for Scandal" (Sheridan), "The Rival Queens" (Nathaniel Lee), "A Trip to Scarborough" (Sheridan), "The Belle's Stratagem" (Mrs Cowley), "Cymbeline" (Shakespeare), "The Careless Husband" (Colley Cibber) and a new play, "The Generous Imposter" (T. L. O'Beirne).

While the company played at the *White Swan* the sequence of their tour ran (1757): Yarmouth, Aylsham, Ipswich, Walsingham, Yarmouth. But once the comedians were installed in their own theatre a different pattern developed:

1758   Dereham, Bungay, Bury, Yarmouth
1759   Walsingham, Beccles, Bury, Yarmouth
1760   Yarmouth, Dereham, Bury, Yarmouth
1761   Yarmouth, Walsingham, Ipswich, Beccles, Yarmouth
1762   Yarmouth, Dereham, Ipswich, Bungay, Bury, Colchester
1763   Walsingham, Yarmouth, Woodbridge (Town Hall), Bury, Yarmouth
1764   Yarmouth, Dereham, Bungay, Colchester, Yarmouth.

Generally it was left to other companies to cover the smaller towns of East Anglia haphazardly. Not until the arrival of the Fishers, of Dereham, working an inner circuit of their own making, were the small towns "played" systematically.

When Thomas Snagg was attached to the Lincoln circuit he described himself as travelling "in the common mode of the most respectable of the motley troop, that is, generally by three partaking of a post chaise, making one a purse-bearer, all equally sharing the expense" (it was usually 9d a mile). But his experience was fortunate rather than typical. Until well into the nineteenth-century the "common mode" of personal transport was on foot, trailing after the company's waggons. Only later were some actors allowed travelling expenses.

The Norwich caravanserai, attended by a colourful band of scruffy-looking travel-stained stage-keepers, property men, lamplighters and billstickers, comprised three to six six-ton waggons, each drawn by six horses. Its thunderous entry into the circuit towns, surrounded by excited children and noisy dogs, was triumphal, one of

Light effects: a typical piece of rudimentary equipment used in the Norwich circuit theatres at least until 1820. These 12 lamps were placed on a board at the footlights. By means of slats and a wheel they were lowered beneath the level of the stage when a dark scene was on or when the lamps needed trimming. Each oil lamp had a half-round tin shade and the oil holders of the lamps were five inches square.

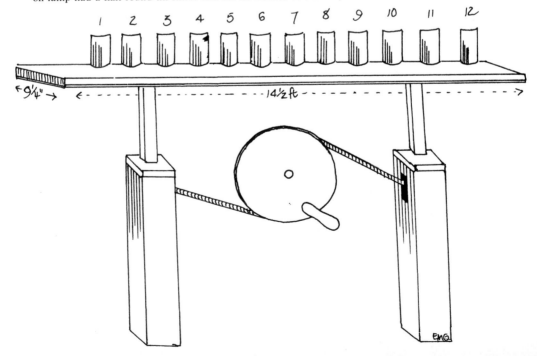

the great events of the year. Certain aspects of the arrival were, according to Tate Wilkinson, peculiar to Norwich—such as the flourish of trumpets and the method of advertising plays: "a drummer and trumpeter (not the king's) in every street |proclaimed] in an audible voice, having been assisted by his shrill notes to summons each garreteer, without which ceremony the gods would not submit to descend from their heights into the streets to inquire what play was to be acted, nor ascend into the gallery".

This was not the only Norwich custom which Wilkinson deplored. The other (which he had also encountered at Hull and York) was the expectation that performers would accompany the playbill distributor round the town, knocking humbly at every door ("honoured with or without a rapper") and stopping at every shop and stall to leave a playbill—"no matter how severe the weather, if frost, snow, rain or hail". As patentee at York, Wilkinson prided himself on having abolished this indignity.

Every clamorous entry into a new town was a minor miracle, a conquest of dangerous roads and footpad territory. The "travelling collectors of coins" were, according to John Bernard, particularly indigenous to "large uncultivated masses of land" like the East Anglian countryside. Arthur Young wrote of the turnpikes in Norfolk and Suffolk in 1770 as "vile, execrably execrable, especially those by which the water is let off by grips [small channels] which causes many an overturn". In winter, the best roads were little better than mud tracks and persistent bad weather made them totally unnegotiable. "They were ponds of liquid mud," Young elaborates, "with a scattering of loose flints, just sufficient to lame any horse that moved near them." The unwieldy long-haul waggons travelled in convoy as much for the sake of protection and mutual assistance as from any pressing need to arrive in a town at the same time.

Bernard records the nightmarish conditions of an actors' coach journey in 1784 from Bath to Bristol: "The rain came down in torrents; the road was a sea of slush; and the night was so diabolically dark that our coachman was not to be execrated if in nearing the hedge, one of the wheels mounted a prostrate mile-stone, and turned the long vehicle over into a sufficiently capacious ditch."

At the end of his Norwich season in 1763, Tate Wilkinson headed back for York. Because of the press of passengers in the Norwich-Newmarket coach he was forced to ride, seasick, in the luggage basket. "The stage coaches then were not hung on springs as they are at present, nor were the roads so good," he comments ruefully. "We arrived at Newmarket where, though I produced myself as an outside passenger, I was permitted the honour of being treated at table as an inside guest; for they all knew me and pitied my situation, but naturally preferred my suffering some torment, rather than being miserably stowed themselves by cramming the vehicle as if loaded with Norwich turkies at Christmas . . ."

Dismounting at Newmarket, he waits for the Ipswich or Bury coach. He gets as far as Cambridge, waits again, hitches a lift to Huntingdon with a farmer, proceeds to

Stamford by coach, is forced to ride in the luggage basket from Stamford to York and arrives in the city after two days' battering and exposure, feeling as if beyond recovery. "It has been known in the winter," he said, "to have been eight or ten days' journey from York to London." In 1763, according to Wilkinson, it was easier to travel to Paris from York than to get from York to London. "Fathers and mothers, then, made their wills 'ere they set forward."

Despite these hazards, the Norwich contingent seldom had more than two days to dismantle their trappings in one town and reassemble them in the next—this at a time when the 22-mile stretch from Norwich to Great Yarmouth had been known to take them five hours. Thirty shillings was allowed in each town for loading and unloading; the cost of carting itself ran to £300 a year. A rough breakdown of expenses shows how closely the company budgeted for transport: Norwich to Yarmouth (22 miles) £13; Yarmouth to Cambridge (86 miles) £15; Cambridge to Bury St Edmunds (28 miles) £14; Bury to Colchester (22 miles) £12; Colchester to Norwich (60 miles) £18; Norwich to Ipswich (43 miles) £22.

Once the touring system was tried and proved, the shire halls, inns, barns, warehouses, seemed inadequate as playhouses. The company had become in a true sense regional and one by one temporary stages were replaced by purpose-built theatres. It was at Ipswich in 1736 that one of the earliest real playhouses outside London opened its doors. Four years later Ipswich playgoers were congratulating themselves on having been the first audience to recognise the genius of David Garrick.

New Theatre, George Street, Hadleigh.

By Desire of Capt. and Mrs. GOOCH.

On TUESDAY EVENING, NOVEMBER 22, 1803,
Will be presented a New Favourite Comedy, called

LIFE;

Or, the World as it Goes.

Sir Harry Torpid, Mr. PARSONS
Primitive, Mr. PASTON—Marchmount, Mr. WIGHTMAN
Clifford, Mr. LOVEDAY—Craftly, Mr. PEROWN
Jonathan, Mr. MURRAY—Waiter, Miss WALLER
Gabriel Lackbrain, Mr. MORTIMER

Mrs. Belford, Mrs. LOVEDAY
Mrs. Decoy, Mrs. WALLER—Betty, Mrs. MURRAY
Rosa Marchmount, Mrs. MORTIMER

A SONG, by Mr. PARSONS.

To which will be added a FARCE, called

BON TON;

Or, High Life above Stairs.

Lord Minikin, Mr. PARSONS
Colonel Tivy, Mr. LOVEDAY—Davy, Mr PEROWN
Jessamy, Mr. MURRAY—Sir John Trotley, Mr. LAVEROCK

Lady Minikin, Mrs. LOVEDAY
Gymp, Mrs. PEROWN—Miss Tittup, Mrs. LAVEROCK

DOORS to be opened at 5, and begin at 6 o'Clock.

BOXES, 3s.—PIT, 2s.—GALLERY, 1s.

TICKETS to be had at the Inns, and of Mr. Laverock, at his Lodgings: where Places for the Boxes may be taken.

IPSWICH: printed by John Raw, Bookseller, &c.

The theatre in Hadleigh was occasionally visited by both the Norwich company and the Norfolk and Suffolk troupe under David Fisher, but mostly it attracted travelling companies from further afield. They offered much the same fare as the circuit actors, and at much the same prices. Tickets were sold at all the inns in Hadleigh.

Suffolk Record Office, Ipswich

CHAPTER FOUR

Ipswich and Norwich; or,
A Tale of Two Playhouses

*"Theatres in the eighteenth century, with their rococo decorations;
with the red curtains to the boxes, with their immense chandeliers,
had a glamour which put you in a comfortable state of mind to enjoy
the play. The theatres they build now are severely functional; you
can see from all parts of them what is happening on the stage; the
seats are comfortable and there are abundant exits, so that you run
small chance of being burnt to death. But they are cold."* Somerset
Maugham, in his introduction to *The Artist and the Theatre* by
Raymond Mander and Joe Mitchenson, 1955.

IN THE early days of the circuit, Ipswich was a prosperous port town with an eager,
stylish playgoing public. Several companies of actors vied for patronage at the
Griffin Inn yard in Westgate Street, near the Cornhill. It was at the hub of the town's
activity, a large, impressive booth which could put to shame the simple fitted up room
most inns offered visiting companies. Mr Dymer's Company of Comedians presented
vogue pieces such as John Vanburgh's popular comedy "The Provoked Husband; or,
The Journey to London", and assorted scratch companies from the London theatres
made Ipswich a favourite destination in their own closed season, lured by the prospect
of good audiences.

New and surprising entertainments were proffered by Signora Violante, the
famous Italian rope dancer; and in the winter of 1735 "The Beggar's Opera", which
had been blamed for a rising crime rate in London, set Ipswich by its ears. Hard on
the heels of Dymer came the Norwich Company of Comedians, squeezing in two
box-office draws, "The Miser" and "The Mock Doctor" (both by Fielding) before
Christmas.

Not all travelling players were accommodated in the *Griffin* yard. Some were
given footage in the Shire Hall, Foundation Street, others made use of a temporary
booth until it collapsed in 1729 in the middle of a performance. Moralistic tracts were
immediately circulated underlining the justice of the catastrophe: "Could you never
think that there was a rebuke of divine Providence upon those that attended these
plays, when in Ipswich, and other places, their building fell down, to the hurt of many
and the fright of many more?" The pamphleteer's warning was spiritedly ignored. In
1736 Richard Dobson, merchant of Ipswich, built the functional-looking *Tankard
Playhouse* for Henry Betts, a brewer. It was handily joined on to Betts's *Tankard Inn*
and it served Ipswich theatregoers until 1802 when it was demolished to make way for
a better.

The Griffin Inn, first regular venue the Norwich comedians had in Ipswich. Other companies also shared the inn yard. It was in Westgate Street, where Debenhams now stands. *Suffolk Record Office, Ipswich*

On 1st June, 1741, a sharing company of comedians from "the theatres in London" arrived in Ipswich. The London playhouses had just closed for the summer and William Giffard, manager of Goodman's Fields theatre, decided to strike east. Among his band was an unrecognised young man acting under the assumed name of Lyddal. It was his first stage appearance. When he took the part of the African slave Aboan in Thomas Southerne's tragedy "Oroonoko", the twenty-four-year old Lyddal confided that if he was a failure in Ipswich he would give up the pursuit of a dangerous profession. The young man was known to his friends as Davy Garrick. For someone who had only recently thrown up his interest in his uncle's wine business ("I remember Garrick living in Durham Yard with three-quarts of vinegar in the cellar, calling himself a wine merchant", the eccentric mimic and playwright, Samuel Foote, recalled irreverently) and who had not proved his acting ability on a public stage, the declaration seemed presumptuous in the extreme.

But although David Garrick appeared to be throwing himself into an arrogant or foolhardy novitiate at Ipswich, he had equipped himself for it by studying a variety of stage parts in the privacy of his rooms. For some time, according to his biographer, Thomas Davies, he had been practising "the Clown, the Fop, the Fine Gentleman, the Man of Humour, the Sot, the Valet, the Lover, the Hero, nay, the Harlequin".

Davies described Garrick's Ipswich appearance: "under the disguise of a black countenance, he hoped to escape being known, should it be his misfortune not to please. Though Aboan is not a first-rate character, yet the scenes of pathetic persuasion and affecting distress, in which the character is placed, will always command the attention of the audience when represented by a judicious actor. Our young player's applause was equal to his most sanguine desires. Under the assumed name of Lyddal, he not only acted a variety of characters in plays, particularly Chamont in 'The Orphan', Captain Brazen in 'The Recruiting Officer', and Sir Harry Wildair, but he likewise attempted the active feats of the Harlequin. In every essay he gave such delight to the audience, that they gratified him with constant and loud proofs of their approbation. The town of Ipswich will long boast of having first seen and encouraged so great a genius as Mr Garrick."

Two months later, Garrick had become, in the equivalent of an eighteenth-century blurb-writers' jargon, "the English Roscius" and Ipswich in future had to be content to watch his plays rather than the man himself: Garrick never returned. Within six years of his public debut, Garrick was joint patentee of Drury Lane and had begun to establish himself as the major civilising influence on an acting tradition which had degenerated into rant, roar and drawl. Tragedy was crippled by empty declamation and stock responses; comedy had become more akin to buffoonery:

"Theatric monarchs, in their tragic gait,
Affect to mark the solemn pace of state;
One foot put forward in position strong,
The other, like its vassal, *drugg'd* along:
So grave each motion, so exact and slow,
Like wooden monarchs at a puppetshow.
The mien delights us that has native grace,
But *affectation* ill supplies its place."

(Pierce Egan, *Life of an Actor*)

Garrick, as the exponent of a more naturalistic style of acting, set standards which were to hold for more than half a century and which, even after his death, made a return to the old manner unthinkable. As much as any professional perspicacity, it

David Garrick, whose death, said Dr Johnson, eclipsed the gaiety of nations. The portrait was circulated in 1745, four years after Garrick made his profession debut in Ipswich.
Mander and Mitchenson Theatre Collection

When players first moved out of public houses they often found themselves in severely functional-looking buildings. The theatre in Tankard Street, Ipswich, built in 1736, was such a place, but it had two claims to fame: David Garrick made his first public appearance there in 1741 and it was the first building designed specifically as a theatre in East Anglia. *Suffolk Record Office, Ipswich*

was Garrick's refined personal sensibilities which were the cornerstone of his success. John Bernard admiringly described him as "the only man I ever saw who moved, looked and spoke like a gentleman from impulse". He was on the way to becoming a cult. He made it his vocation to reform, by example, both from within and without. He insisted on appropriate costume, disciplined out-of-hand rehearsals, organised the theatre lighting and, perhaps most revolutionary of all his improvements, prevented the public from strolling about the stage during performances.

In his own first play "Lethe" he puts into the mouth of one of his characters:

> "I stand upon the stage, talk loud, and stare about—which confounds the actors, and disturbs the audience: upon which the galleries, who hate the appearance of one of us, begin to hiss, and cry 'off, off!'; while I, undaunted, stamp my foot, so—loll with my shoulder, thus—take snuff with my right hand, and smile scornfully, thus. This exasperates the savages, and they attack us with volleys of suck'd oranges and half-eaten pippins."

Establishing the principle that only players should hold the stage was uphill work. Audiences had no excessive respect for actors. They had from Elizabethan times been accustomed to placing themselves at whim at whatever vantage point they chose, often barely allowing the actors room for their entrances and exits. Groups of "tipsy

40

apprentices" would squat two and three deep on the stage. Tate Wilkinson in his theatrical memoirs, *The Wandering Patentee*, (1795), outlines the typical scene in 1753, with no apologies to Garrick:

> "The Stage was at 5s—Pit and Box all joined together at 5s. There was only one entrance on each side of the stage, which was always particularly crowded. First, they sported their own figures to gratify self consequence, and impede and interfere with the performers, who had to come on and go off stage. Affronting the audience was another darling delight—particularly offending the galleries, and thereby incurring the displeasure of the gods, who shewed their resentment by dispersing golden showers of oranges and half-eaten pippins."

He goes on to describe the final appearance of Quin, aged sixty-five, in the heavy trappings of Falstaff. Poor Quin puffed for several minutes in the wings before he could push through the crowds that hemmed him in.

Side boxes were installed on the Ipswich stage to prevent disorderly public encroachment in the 1740s—but they in themselves became an obstruction and had to be removed, despite the optimistic copywriting at the foot of playbills: "For the better reception of those Gentlemen and Ladies who please to favour us with their Company Side Boxes will be formed in a compleat Manner upon the Stage, warm and agreeable and in no ways obstructive to the Performance."

Oil lamps and candles were the only form of illumination in the Ipswich theatre—as in the rest of the circuit's booths, inns, halls and warehouses. Twelve lamps were placed on a board at the footlights and could be lowered for dark scenes or when the wicks needed trimming. Oil was a major expense: £12 for a 16-night summer season, £16 in winter. The lampman would be paid 30s a week and he took home the old oil as a perk. Six or eight lamps lit the auditorium, with three burners suspended from brackets. In the centre of the playhouse, a great candle-bearing ring glimmered over the pit.

"We can hardly realise," says Bosworth Harcourt (*The Theatre Royal, Norwich, The Chronicles of an Old Playhouse*) "that all the brilliant achievements of the local stage had been carried out, with all their boasted scenic effects, only under the dispiriting and gloomy surroundings of the tallow candles, or the scarcely more brilliant oil lamps of that day. When we see in the prompt copies of the old plays the instruction given 'lamps down' or 'lamps up' we scarcely believe that the result was gained . . . by the concerted action of many people at different points, who lowered their respective illuminants as best they could . . . the effluvia of the smouldering wick must have been at times painfully obnoxious in the house, especially in the stage boxes, which were in such unpleasant proximity to the wings and the footlights."

It was not until 1759 that the Norwich Company formally leased Ipswich playhouse—at £70 a year. (This compared favourably with the casual rent a contemporary company was expected to pay at the Jacob Wells Theatre in Bristol—anything from £37 to £58 for an 11 to 12 week season.) All the Norwich circuit theatres were from time to time rented out, sometimes to itinerant companies, when the Norwich comedians were not in residence. In 1769 Henry Betts Junior, who had received Ipswich theatre as a bequest from his father in 1762, let the building to a touring company described as "Mrs Watling's". She paid 15 guineas for the winter season. But the Norwich Company came to be regarded as the regular players with a priority claim and they began to hold certain of their stock scenes there, even a set of spindle-operated wings. The wings were operated on what was known as the "book" principle, each of them mounted on a barrel—palace, wood, cottage interior and cave or rocks. These were worked by a spindle which passed through the stage. Beneath each spindle was a large, grooved wheel; round that, a rope connected to another wheel on the prompt side of the stage. When a scene had to be changed, a man turned the wheel, changing the entire set of wings at once.

These were the years of consolidation. The players had gained in stature and professionalism; there were "bespeaks" from the upper classes, a big influx of middle-class theatregoers and a robust following in gallery and pit. Bespeaks were essentially a feature of country theatricals. The head of a local family, an organisation, a regiment, or even a young ladies' boarding school, "bespoke" plays; that is, they chose the piece to be performed and either bought a large quantity of tickets for distribution or paid a lump sum to subsidise the performance. If the licensing magistrate had been convinced by the theatre manager that the show in hand was not undesirable, he would sometimes bespeak a play himself—or his general approval could be a useful lever in attracting other influential names in the neighbourhood. Typical bespeakers at Bungay in 1781, for instance, were Sir Edmund Bacon, Mr and Mrs Bedingfield, Mr and Mrs Holland, the Ladies of Bungay, Mr and Mrs Simpson and the Gentlemen of the Book Club.

The real era of prosperity began in 1758 when the forty-nine-year-old Norwich architect, Thomas Ivory, became proprietor of the circuit. His arrival signalled a spate of theatre building in the company's major towns which was probably unequalled in any other part of England. Ipswich had led the way in 1736; in 1758 Ivory built Norwich its first theatre proper; and six years later one for Colchester. King's Lynn theatre was built in 1776; Great Yarmouth's in 1778; and in 1782 Stourbridge Fair, Cambridge, was added to the company's network.

In his will, Ivory is described as "builder and timber merchant"—a bald enough statement for the man who designed and executed at least four of Norwich's most splendid functional buildings—the Assembly House (1754), the theatre, the Octagon Chapel in Colegate Street (1754-56) and very probably the Norfolk and Norwich Hospital. The city fathers saluted his skill, vision and enterprise when they bestowed on him, at the age of thirty-six, the freedom of the city.

Norwich theatre was part of a scheme hatched by a group of leading city gentlemen for what would today be called an "entertainments complex". They had bought an estate called Chapple Field House on easy terms from the late Earl of Buckingham and, having provided the Assembly Rooms, were keen to complete their

Section from Pennington's map of Ipswich, 1778, showing the three main places of theatrical activity. Top: the *Griffin Inn* which served as a playhouse until 1736. Centre: Tacket Street, or Tankard Street, site of the 1736 and 1803 theatres. Bottom: Shire Hall, Foundation Street, where plays were performed in the seventeenth and eighteenth centuries.

43

plan with a playhouse next door. Unfortunately, they had almost run out of money. Captain William Ivory, Thomas Ivory's son, made an entry in his own hand in the Norwich Theatre Committee book of 1782 describing the theatre's genesis:

"[They] therefore encouraged Mr. Thomas Ivory to undertake this new idea Mr. Ivory being a publick spirited Man, with great activity of Mind and resolution, and great knowledge in his business as Master Builder, and employing at that time a considerable number of Workmen, and having always on his own premises, a large Assortment of Deals and Timber, being considerably employed in the profession of a Merchant in Exporting the Norwich Manufactory and other English Manufactories into the Northern Countries and Importing from thence large Quantities of Deals, Timber, Iron etc., into this Country—he was induced . . . to *oblige, the general wish and request* and with *the promise of all kinds of countenance and support*—from the principal Inhabitants, to build this Theatre . . ."

Thomas Ivory received the intended plot on a 400-year lease at a rent of £30 a year. To raise a building fund of £600, 30 Norwich worthies bought 30 shares of £20 each and arranged to pay in instalments as various stages of the building were completed. One of these shareholders was William Wilkins, who was later to figure so largely in the fortunes of the Norwich circuit.

Ivory was circumspect enough to know that he had to steer a careful course to avoid any sudden rigorous enforcement of the Licensing Act of 1737. The long brick building which shot up in ten months on the Chapel Field estate, opening in January 1758, was therefore known as The Grand Concert Hall. Its manager was Richard Hurst, a man long in theatrical experience but short in talent.

The theatre was a miniature Drury Lane. The *Norwich Mercury* of 28th January described it with characteristic immodesty: as "the most perfect and compleat Structure of its kind in this Kingdom". And although every subsequent theatre was the subject of more or less the same superlative, in 1758 the phrase still had some meaning. Every effort had been made to outshine the London patent houses and to make Norwich the gem of the shires. The scenic artist Collins was called in and several of the most fashionable pieces were brushed up for the opening season, beginning with Fielding's "Mock Doctor" and Congreve's "The Way of the World".

Unexpectedly, in the same issue as the first performance was announced, the *Norwich Mercury* carried a rumour-killing notice signed by three bricklayers and three carpenters to the effect that the structure was entirely safe and it was "impossible for any part of the building to be moved by any Weight or Number of Persons that it can possibly contain". Sabotage by rumour was a favourite trick of enemies of the theatre, and one which was employed against several of the Norwich Company's ventures. On this occasion, curiosity proved stronger than doubt: a thousand spectators, a well-behaved crowd, came to see the Norwich players in their magnificent new building, now the second most important provincial theatre in

England. To the accompaniment of soft music, the shade of Shakespeare, represented reclining on a pedestal as on his tomb in Westminster Abbey, arose, and delivered a short "Exhortation to Actors". He was a singularly dramatic choice of patron for a "concert hall".

Thomas Ivory had not only bought and worked his way into proprietorship (acquiring sets, costumes and accoutrements from the Norwich Company's circuit towns) but he also had a hand in the new theatre's running. There were some 25 players, ten doorkeepers, a morning porter, check collectors, a wardrobe staff, a carpenter and a resident haidresser; four "orange men" were paid 1s 6d a night for selling fruit there; the wardrobes were well-stocked. True, the players did not always get the audiences they could have wished for—a few Norwich simpletons were berated for interpreting "The Beaux Stratagem" as "The Boar Strangled" and mistaking "The Virgin Unmasked" for "The Virgin Mary"—but patronage was healthy throughout the social spectrum and the climate auspicious for development.

Never wholly reliant on his manager, Ivory would occasionally assume the powers of hire and fire and may even have lived to regret some of the consequences of his intervention. In 1765 he took on John ("Plausible Jack") Palmer as a recent refugee from Colchester where he had been earning 15s a week with very little acclaim. John Palmer was a brilliant talker but an erratic actor. Contemporaries saw him as one of the most inexplicable beings of the Green Room. Thomas Ivory, unperturbed by public tattle, had increased his salary by half a guinea and gave him a toehold to fame.

Palmer had not been many days in Norwich when a considerate box-keeper asked if he had any acquaintances locally—always an advantage on benefit nights. Palmer said he had not. He was speedily introduced to two single ladies at his first benefit and before the end of the season had married one of them, Miss Berroughs. Miss Berroughs's aunt, who had named her as heiress of considerable property, renounced the girl for marrying an actor and refused to be reconciled. Charles Lamb, who saw Palmer in London, said he had an air of swaggering gentility. "He was a gentleman with a slight infusion of the footman". Palmer was also posthumously distinguished as one of a suspiciously numerous band of eighteenth and nineteenth century actors reputed to have died on stage while delivering prophetic utterances. In his case, popular legend had it that while performing "The Stranger" at Liverpool he stumbled at the words "there is another and a better world", dropped down and "almost instantly expired".

Tate Wilkinson was one of Ivory's less eccentric appointments. In 1763 he was invited to join the company for a season and found Richard Hurst an attentive manager but a hard task master. "He worked me not as an horse of blood," Wilkinson wrote in his *Memoirs*, "but as an horse for burthens. I even now sink at the very thought of how I drudged and toiled in that theatrical Norwich mine." On 29th February he played Othello with distinction, and was astonished to find that Norwich audiences had an appetite for endless repeats. No fewer than 25 nights of "The

The first Norwich Theatre Royal, built by Thomas Ivory in 1758, "the most perfect and compleat Structure of its kind in this Kingdom".
Norfolk County Libraries

Padlock" were performed. "I do not believe, take it for all in all, that Norwich ever had a better company than that identical season."

On 11th April, Wilkinson's benefit night came round. He proposed to play Lear and then to treat the Norwich patrons to a short farcical piece called "Tea", consisting of a collage of his own mimic skills, in which he would take off various London actors such as Barry, Sparks, Woffington, Sheridan and Foote. His talent for impersonation was legend and his sketch had always gone down well in the metropolis. The advertisement for "Tea" was, in his own words, "seriously taken by the people in general as a contract they expected would be fulfilled; it was thought very expensive, and would be attended with much difficulty and trouble; but Mr Wilkinson was vastly genteel, but then how would he be able to find cups and saucers for such a quantity of people?" By three in the afternoon, the town was beside itself. Crowds surged in to take their places the moment the theatre opened. When the full extent of the misunderstanding was discovered, the audience broke into turmoil. No tea; and what's more the impersonations didn't mean a thing to country people. Rumour had it that Tate had to flee from Norwich in a post chaise and four, his money in a large silk handkerchief—uncounted, to escape being torn to pieces by the enraged mob.

Having put the Norwich theatre on a firm path, Thomas Ivory set about entrusting it to a multiple proprietorship. He first assigned to one of his actors, William Henry Crouse (later joint manager), a quarter of the stage wardrobe, scenery and decorations. Then in 1768 he divided and sold his interest in the Norwich and Colchester— now valued at £6,000—between 28 shareholders, retaining two shares for himself. As patentee, Ivory was also principal shareholder and his relationship to the other shareholders was rather like that of managing director of a company. His theatre manager was ultimately accountable to him.

In his ten years as sole proprietor of the circuit, Thomas Ivory had strengthened its position by changing the outfit from a sharing to a salaried company. His players were better off as a salaried group and better actors—including some from London—were attracted into the company. His other important tactical achievement was to have the theatre legitimised. In 1768, at Ivory's request, an Act of Parliament was passed empowering the Lord Chamberlain to grant a licence for "Tragedies, Plays, Operas or other Performances of the Stage" to be enacted in Norwich from the beginning of November to the end of May each year, and for three weeks in the summer (assize time). Under the new banner of Royal protection the Grand Concert Hall was translated into the Norwich Theatre Royal, the comedians were now "His Majesty's Servants", and Ivory became the patentee. The patent did not automatically devolve on Ivory's successors, however, and after his death the company continued in ignorance, without patent, licence or permit, until 1883. Norwich was legitimately a patent theatre for only eleven years.

Once the theatre had been established on its new divide-and-rule principle, a new constitution for its efficient running was drawn up and the proprietors' activities from 1768-1825 are chronicled in two bulky Committee Books now preserved in the Norfolk Record Office. They are a remarkable record of the vicissitudes of the Norwich circuit and the day-to-day business of the Norwich theatre. In her masterly analysis of the Committee Books, Dorothy H. Eshelman comments: "In the years from 1768 to 1783 (Committee Book I) there were 114 meetings held. Of these, 92 were meetings of the committees appointed to take care of the proprietors' interests; two were meetings of special committees; 20 were meetings of the proprietors. There was an unusual amount of committee activity in 1769, 1770 (10 meetings each year) and again in 1783 when the committee met 17 times and the proprietors only once." By contrast, Committee Book II (1783-1825) is a disappointingly thin record of financial and legal matters; and after 1825, notes are extremely sketchy and sporadic, sometimes written on odd scraps of paper.

The regulations and standards which the new proprietors agreed to set themselves were partly an example of learning from past mistakes and partly a determination to conduct the Theatre Royal and the satellite theatres of the circuit along the lines of a well-ordered business. No proprietor was permitted to take advantage of his position by venturing on stage or behind stage or into the dressing rooms during a performance. Free tickets were strictly forbidden. No preferential treatment was to be given to any of the mayor's officers or household servants; they were to pay at the door like everyone else. For this reason, the doorkeepers, always prey to the unscrupulous, had to be a particularly well-disciplined corps. They were swiftly dismissed at any hint of default, disorder or irregularity, and as an extra safeguard of their effectiveness, the proprietors appointed Charles Starkey to supervise them.

John ("Plausible Jack") Palmer pictured in 1776 in suitably flamboyant role as Bajazet in "Tamerlane". A slice of Palmer's early career was spent on East Anglian stages.

Mander and Mitchenson Theatre Collection

By 1766, managership of the Norwich Company of Comedians had passed from Hurst to Richard Griffith, an ingenuous but kindly man of thirty-six whose apparent naïveté was a natural target for practical jokes among the players. Integrity and experience had earned him his position as first actor-manager of the company and his good humour helped to atone for his vanity. John Bernard described him as a perfect *beau* of the old school, a Sir Philip Modelove in real life; a man who to the end of his career remained young at heart, tolerably educated and tolerably clever in the business of the stage.

One of Griffith's habits was to carry about with him at rehearsal an elegantly-bound and embellished volume of Shakespeare, heavily annotated in his own hand. The book was never out of his sight. One morning during a run-through of "Much Ado About Nothing", Griffith was called away to the committee room. He left his Shakespeare on the prompter's table. Bob Bowles, the company's practical joker had been waiting to pounce. He seized the precious volume and began reading Griffith's dense marginal notes—Benedict (Griffith's own part) "should look at least five-and-thirty, should be manly, and even elegant but not flippant"; "Claudius should be youthful and spirited, and wear a brown wig, if Pedro wore a black one"; "Dogberry should not be over-acted, nor played to the galleries". Giving a passable imitation of Griffith, Bowles chortled: "Why, Mr Garrick has never noticed Borachio," (Bowles's part). He took up a pen and scribbled in a spidery hand:

"Borachio should be a lean, long-backed fellow, with sandy hair, and red hands fond of nothing but fishing". Fishing was Griffith's passion.

Griffith possessed a strain of sterner stuff beneath a mockable exterior: he would not be bamboozled into undeserved salary increases, he finally put an end to the lingering practice of allowing playgoers on to the stage, he introduced plays swiftly after their London openings and he inspired a passionate commitment from the young woman who was to become the doyenne of literary and theatrical circles—Elizabeth Inchbald. He was a man who seemed to transcend the sum of his parts and when he retired in 1781 due to ill-health, his players were the first to acknowledge their debt. John Bernard wrote that after ten months with the company, Griffith had made an actor of him. "Under a regular and judicious system, the various bad habits and ideas I had contracted in my eight months itinerary speedily disappeared Finding me not only pliant but grateful for instruction, Mr Griffith exerted himself in that peculiar element in which he had ability, the opening to me a knowledge of the mechanism of my profession, as the means of my attaining a good style." When Bernard left Norwich for Exeter with £80 in his pocket—a sum he had hardly thought possessable by an entire company—it was Griffith he had to thank.

Although the comedians had not needed to feign concerts since the theatre gained its patent, musical content remained an important part of any theatrical performance. The long evening's programme—usually six o'clock until midnight—

James Chalmers was one of the Norwich Company's most notorious eccentrics in the second half of the eighteenth century. William Williams's portrait shows the coarse-faced comedian as Midas, one of many old men's roles at which he excelled. Chalmers was a good Harlequin and perfected his own stunt of leaping through a hogshead of flames. He and his wife were a headache for the Norwich proprietors. They were an argumentative, unorthodox couple, frequently being suspended, dressed down or dismissed. After each contretemps with the management they were usually eventually re-engaged.

British Museum

would have been unendurable unless broken up by songs and interludes, for which orchestra, musicians and soloists came into their own. In the interest of sustaining a decent musical professionalism, the Norwich Company generally employed a leading musician who would not only guide the orchestra but take on the entire company's musical education. In 1769, despite his reputation for eccentric behaviour, William Love, the thirty-eight year old leader of the band, was retained at the rate of a guinea a week on condition that he instructed the company "in all Music" and attended rehearsals diligently. Two of his colleagues were expected to write music as occasion demanded, for no extra fee. Love, an oboe player, was described in his day as "a person of great genius in his profession, of great suavity of manners and of great improvidence in conduct".

Generally, Griffith selected his players but he did not have complete control in the matter. He had to lay before the committee a list of plays and entertainments which he intended to put on in the following fortnight; sometimes, the choice had been made for him: "This Committee strongly recommend it to the Manager That he gets up some new plays against the ensuing season at Norwich and particularly Shakespear's Twelfth Night recommended by Sr Wm Wiseman." The manager was occasionally sent down to London to draw recruits or to see how a new production was being treated. The committee of proprietors might, on the other hand, nominate an actor by his reputation, instruct Griffith to engage him and then supply his travelling expenses. In February, 1769, Griffith was instructed: "immediately write to Mr Pierce [Price] and Mrs Weston and to engage them for this Theatre". He could "remit to them any sum not exceeding Six Guineas to be paid to them in London upon their giving a promissory note for the same in order to enable them to pay their expences to Norwich".

In the minutes for 1760, twenty members of the company are listed—among them a capable couple called the Hollands who were with the company for more than twenty years, Mr and Mrs Dutton, Miss Westray (who later went to the Haymarket and eventually to America), Charles and Isabella Pearson, Mrs Sarah Ibbott, a tragedienne with long experience of provincial circuits and a brief reign at Covent Garden to her name, Joseph Inchbald, talented husband of Elizabeth, the actress, novelist and dramatist, Mr and Mrs James Chalmers, and Thomas Death and his wife. These actors were all paid salaries of more than 30s a week. Less illustrious members of the company were paid according to their usefulness—William Davies, 11s 6d; his wife Elizabeth 13s 6d; Mr Price and Mrs Weston £1 6s 3d each; Robert Hitchcock 15s; his wife, a guinea.

By any standards, it was, as the public was frequently reminded, a "respectable" company. Joseph Inchbald was known in his own right as an actor and a painter but, after his marriage to Elizabeth Simpson, of Bury St Edmunds, his fame was as the husband of a brilliant, captivating woman. The Chalmers, rather a disruptive pair, both excelled in comic parts and Mrs Chalmers had performed at Covent Garden two years before joining the Norwich Company in 1856. Mr and Mrs Davies were a versatile couple but seldom rose above modest popularity or moderately good performances. The reticent Robert Hitchcock, author as well as actor, and his lovely wife Sarah laid the foundations of their spiralling careers in Norwich before moving on to join Tate Wilkinson's York circuit.

Members who refused to enter into the Norwich Company's usual three-year contract were not allowed to go on circuit, and none of them could leave the company before their articles expired without forfeiting the colossal sum of £500. In 1770 an attractive intelligent actress, Mrs Hester Brooke, who had been with the company seven years, was signed on for a further five. She was at Norwich for a total of eighteen years and the committee book entries suggest that she may well have had more than a business association with the personable Griffith: for a decade her own agreement and Griffith's contract are renewed simultaneously—and for the same number of years. Griffith left in 1780 due to ill-health. At the close of the 1781 Norwich season, Mrs Brooke also left, a sick woman herself with only a year to live.

By 1771 the 13-year-old playhouse was beginning to present maintenance problems. Open fires were kept burning both on stage and off and, since the science of ventilation was still in its infancy, the decor soon became smoke-filmed and blackened. There had always been trouble with the chimneys and it was not long before the auditorium needed repainting. One side of the roof had begun to leak, damaging several of the scenes and the carpenters had been tinkering about with some of the boxes because their occupants found them too large or too small. A

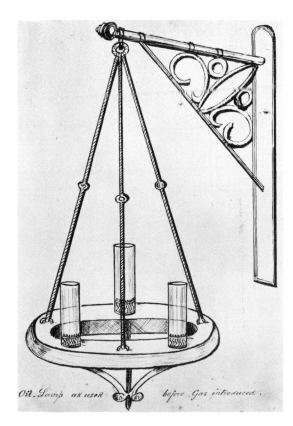

Bracketed oil lamp ring of the type used in the Norwich circuit theatres before the introduction of "The Gas". At the end of the 1817 winter season in Ipswich, Bellamy addressed the audience: "I cannot forbear congratulating you on the triumphs of science over darkness in the adoption of the gas-light in this town and I have the satisfaction of adding that such arrangements are entered into with the proprietors that this Theatre will be illuminated by that resplendent light at the next season". But it was not until the summer of 1839 that the theatre was converted to gas—for £100.

Suffolk Record Office, Ipswich

Oil Lamp as used   before Gas introduced.

complete facelift was the answer. In a frenzy of refurbishing, the interior was painted stone-colour, the scene room was retiled and William Wilkins, plasterer and future proprietor of the circuit, took on the job of creating a "compleat floated Cieling" over the gallery. Against a stone background, the ornamentation gleamed white, the pit was painted chocolate, the ironwork lacquered and the floors of the boxes were matted. While they were about it, the proprietors also authorised a complete repainting outside. All that remained was "to cure the smoaking of the Chimnies", an almost impossible task allotted to James Beevor and Thomas Ivory, and to invite James Lindoe, a scene painter from East Dereham to start painting and repairing the scenes.

The Norwich proprietors decided to begin the new year, 1772, by philanthropically setting up a fund "for the Support and Maintenance of Aged, wornout or infirm performers". Participants were invited to pay a sixpence in the pound towards the scheme for seven years and the fund would be supplemented twice a year by benefits, one in Norwich in the winter and the other during the summer circuit. It was one of the first funds of its kind in the country.

Most of the company's administrative managerial transactions were dealt with by William Crouse and Richard Griffith jointly, but both men had their own area of responsibility—Crouse for the wardrobes (in which he had a financial interest) and Griffith for productions and players. Only when Griffith was ill did Crouse step in to superintend the business. This arrangement was far from easy. Crouse attended few of the meetings and Griffith became an increasingly dominant figure in the company's affairs. Open animosity between the two men broke out in the summer of 1773 when Crouse made one of his rare appearances at a committee meeting to object to the fact that leases of Bungay and Ipswich theatres had been made to Griffith and himself jointly. The proprietors stood firm, telling Crouse that unless he agreed to the set up, the leases would be made out in Griffith's name alone.

By the following year, the two actors had something bigger to think of than petty jealousies. They and the proprietors were worried by the number of pirate companies of players who were, they maintained, "harrassing the Counties of Norfolk and Suffolk". The Norwich Company was beginning to regard itself as unassailable in the field and resented the intrusion. William Bailey was running the circuit's show at Yarmouth and the company had been used to having exclusive use of Bury, Colchester, Bungay and Aylsham "at such distances of time as have been acceptable to the inhabitants, and not burdensome . . . and in several of which places they have occupied and built regular Theatres at a great expense . . ." It was argued that the towns would be "very much exhausted and harrass'd" by having several different companies to distract them. The proprietors decided to clear the field: they petitioned for a short bill to be introduced enabling the Lord Chamberlain to licence only their own players to act in Norfolk, Suffolk and Colchester.

CHAPTER FIVE

Colchester, King's Lynn, Yarmouth; or,
New Playhouses for Old

"Patents have not only been a security for theatrical property, but have put the country actors on a more decent level, which was highly necessary . . . An actor in London is very differently respected to what he is in the country." Tate Wilkinson.

THE Norwich Company of Comedians had tasted the benefits of setting up "regular" theatres in the county towns of Ipswich and Norwich; they were now anxious to put drama on a permanent footing in some of their other principal circuit towns. A new burst of expansion, in which three major theatres in the eastern region were built in the space of fourteen years, began in March, 1764, when Thomas Ivory was granted a ninety-nine-year lease on a plot of land behind Colchester's Moot Hall.

The players had performed in the Moot Hall itself from 1728, at first visiting the town twice a year but eventually making it a winter assignment only. The procession of waggons and actors usually clattered into the garrison town towards the end of October, to take advantage of the crowds which traditionally gathered for Colchester Fair on 4th November. The audience had, by all accounts, a taste for pseudo-classical and historical plays; they liked a mixture of the domestic and the spectacular and were not at all averse to "improved" versions of Shakespearian plays. "The Beaux Stratagem", George Farquhar's last comedy and by now an established stock play in almost every theatre in the country, was chosen to celebrate the opening of the prepossessing brick-built theatre on 29th October, 1764. Important new works were judged appropriate to the new edifice and a number of plays fresh from London were tried out in Colchester. Sheridan's "The Rivals" had its première in London on 17th January, 1775; eight months later it was "got up" for the Colchester audiences and became a popular addition to the company's repertoire. The committee of Norwich proprietors enjoyed recommending new plays and as early as February they had ordered the manager, Richard Griffith, to "get up 'The Rivals' with all expedition". Despite its general London success, opinion was divided about the play's merits. The actor John Bernard, after seeing the first performance at Covent Garden, came away muttering that it was intolerably long and would never succeed. He considered Mrs Malaprop a disastrous intrusion. Earlier in the season, William Hopkins, prompter at Drury Lane, wrote to the Norwich manager suggesting John Burgoyne's "Maid of the Oaks" as a promising circuit play. The piece was immediately adopted, the actors receiving special instructions in the art of *cotillion* dancing. The novelty of introducing plays straight after their metropolitan openings proved such a box-office draw that Griffith was instructed to "get up every new Play" for the company's summer circuit.

Captain William Ivory, son of the architect of the first Norwich Theatre Royal, Thomas Ivory. He inherited his father's theatrical interests and became an intelligent and conscientious patentee of the circuit theatres. The portrait is possibly by Smart.

Ipswich Museums

By the 1770s the Norwich comedians could boast that they belonged to one of the country's top theatrical circuits. There were about 26 actors, including eight married couples (who often had a joint salary and were therefore cheaper) and no salary was less than 25 shillings a week. In 1778 the main players were John Brunton, Miller, John Follett, John Cornelys, William Dancer, Richard Griffith, Charles Murray, Giles Barrett, the Browns, the Hollands, the Bannisters, the Rosses, Mrs Simpson, Mrs Crouse, Mrs Ibbott and Mrs Brooke.

Sarah Ibbott, a spirited lady now verging on middle-age, was the company's leading tragedienne. The versifying author of *Roscius: or, A Critical Examination of all the Principal Performers belonging to Norwich Theatre for the last season* (1767) wrote of her:

> "When raging anguish, or a deep despair,
> The inmost horrors of the soul declare;
> The unparell'd graces of an Ibbot's mein,
> Enlarge the thought, and dignifies the scene."

John Bernard placed her among the four most remarkable people of the Norwich Green Room. She had, he said, "some years before accepted an engagement from Rich of Covent Garden, come up to town, made a successful debut, and would no doubt have become a favourite, but experiencing a slight neglect from the manager (one of his usual eccentricities) took the coach back to Norwich the following morning".

In the summer of 1769 Tate Wilkinson engaged the corpulent Ibbott to join his York circuit. The company was in Newcastle at the time, feeling the loss of Mrs Baker, an Edinburgh actress who had decided to return to her native city. Mrs Ibbott was a lucky replacement. "She possessed great merit," the York manager asserted, "good voice, education, and understanding—not equal in expression to Mrs Baker; her manner far from accomplished: however, if size was necessary, though Mrs Baker was not a skeleton, yet Ibbott made more than treble amends as to the quantity." She acted Queen Elizabeth better than anyone else he had seen. Wilkinson was not alone in reflecting that if Sarah Ibbott had been blessed with more alluring features her talent would have taken her quickly and permanently to London. He had watched competent actresses like Ibbott fail to make the top grade for want of a pretty face and he had seen ignorant ones dazzle audiences with a veneer of charm. "There are few instances," he lamented, "where the beauty joined to the good sense and behaviour of a Miss Farren are to be met with; or where the grateful and commanding expression of a Siddons is united to a train of good qualities."

But for all his generous opinions of her, Tate Wilkinson did not treat Mrs Ibbott quite as fairly as she deserved. He began to invite Mrs Powell—also by now acquiring a middle-aged spread useful for certain roles—to take certain parts which the Norwich actress had made her own and Ibbott in a fit of pique deserted him in favour of the Norwich theatre where, as everybody knew, her heart was. She remained in Norwich for the rest of her life, became a prominent member of the theatre committee, and retired from the stage in 1787 when a rich relative left her a fortune.

In her voluntary flight from London back to the provinces, Sarah Ibbott was the exception rather than the rule. Usually, the exchange movement was in the other direction, London being the lodestar for every ambitious actor. Many of the best

Mrs Harriet Faucit as Lady Racket. She and her husband were with the Norwich Company for many years in the early nineteenth century. Their daughter, Helen Faucit (1817-1898) was Macready's leading lady in London. Mrs Faucit left her husband to live with another actor, William Farren, a comedian whom Macready called "very ignorant".
Norfolk County Libraries

"The lovely Inchbald", at Tate Wilkinson called her. Elizabeth Inchbald, from a painting by Sir Thomas Lawrence.

Norwich players, beguiled by the promise of fame, left the provincial stage at the height of their powers. A typical piece of piracy is described with heavy irony by Tate Wilkinson: "In 1786 Mrs Brown was lured by the London manager to leave Norwich for Covent Garden, in the middle of the manager's season, and to the infinite prejudice of his Norwich campaign (Mrs B being a great favourite)—but what matters that, when the great call on the little, it must be obeyed. Nor murmur, oh, my son!—she was called to exert all her courage and combat Mrs Jordan, whose great success in London was so astonishingly rapid as unexpected."

The other outstanding woman member of the company under Griffith (who as a girl had been deeply infatuated with the Norwich manager) was a small, dark, beautiful actress called Elizabeth Simpson, later Elizabeth Inchbald. She had an expression "full of sweetness and spirit, excessively interesting" who, according to her biographer, brought men to her feet but barred them from her bed. She was born in 1753 near Bury St Edmunds, the daughter of a farmer. When she was still a child her father died and she was brought up by her mother on the farm. Much of her time was spent alone, deep in books. A speech impediment had made her shy of company but to everyone's astonishment she overcame it sufficiently to become a capable actress. In fact her slightly halting way of speaking simply increased her charm for men and audiences seemed not to mind either.

In February, 1772, impatient to start a career on the stage, she threw a few possessions into a bandbox, ran two miles across the fields and caught the stagecoach to London. She remembered Joseph Inchbald from his appearances with the Norwich company in Bury St Edmunds and resolved to contact him at Drury Lane. Since her arrival in London, the girl had been pestered and pursued. She could not go anywhere without attracting attention both by her unescorted progress through the city and by her beauty. Inchbald put her in touch with a Drury Lane performer who had recently bought a share in a country theatre but the introduction developed differently from the way either of them had intended. The actor soon demanded of the girl "other services than those required for a theatre". In reply, Elizabeth Simpson flung a basin of scalding water from the tea tray into his face and fled to Inchbald. Inchbald, scarcely expecting to be accepted, offered to protect her by marrying her. It turned out to be a love-match quite exceptional in theatrical circles and when after only a few years of marriage Joseph Inchbald died, the news was publicly treated as a tragedy. Inchbald was taken mildly ill while the couple were on tour with Tate Wilkinson's York company in Leeds, went to bed to recover, and apparently died making love to his wife. Wilkinson wrote in *The Wandering Pantentee*:

> "She [Mrs Inchbald] thought he had the cholic; he faintly answered: 'Yes' . . . however, the happy pair retired to rest, where she, a second *new-born Venus* lay—but such a vortex of perfect bliss was too rich a feast to be the lasting *lot* of mortal man. It was a banquet for the gods; and on that earthly paradise, as on a bed of roses without thorns, the poor or rather the rich, the worthy Inchbald, suddenly expired!—I say the rich, for he certainly cannot be poor who dies possessing *all he wishes.*"

Wilkinson was undisguisedly more than half in love with her himself. He called her "my dearly beloved Inchbald" and could never talk of her without betraying a swain's admiring warmth. He found, as most men did, including John Philip Kemble, that her mental qualities, her intelligence, greatly added to all her other attractions.

Tate Wilkinson, friend of country actors. As manager of the York theatre he dealt with many members of the Norwich Company—those who moved on to York from East Anglia and others who transferred from the Norwich to the York circuit. Wilkinson was a ready source of anecdotes about his own acting experiences on the Norwich circuit.

Wilkinson had seen her comedy "Such Things Are" at Covent Garden in 1787 and, going to some lengths to procure a copy, decided to have it for his Easter week benefit night in York. Meantime, Giles Linnett Barrett, who had taken over as Norwich manager in 1780, had sent a copy to one of Wilkinson's leading ladies, Mrs Belfill, who insisted on the play for her own benefit. "I persisted," says Wilkinson, "not only to the right of having it as manager, but being for my night I should be very attentive to its production, and not be niggardly as to any requisite expence to satisfy my pride, the gratification of my audience, and the merit of the fair author, for whom I in truth held then and hold now a more than common esteem and friendship". To make an end of the wrangling, Wilkinson asked Elizabeth Inchbald to "decree the prize" in his favour. To his dismay, the fair author reacted angrily, thinking that he had concocted his own version of the play and that at least Mrs Belfill's copy would be "genuine from Norwich". The author threatened to expose Wilkinson's production as a flimsy, disgraceful imposture. Later, realising his honourable, if selfish, intentions, she forgave him, but for four years he regarded the tiff as "not make-upable". Eventually, their "late friendly intercourse and chit-chat was again restored".

After her husband's death, Elizabeth Inchbald moved to London, staunchly resisting some of the most persistent and eligible suitors of the literary world. Perhaps because of her long, fascinating and unassailable widowhood, she was often looked upon as totally unapproachable. Sheridan enjoyed her company, Kemble courted her doggedly and Charles Lamb pronounced her "the only endurable clever woman" he had known. To Tate Wilkinson she remained simply "the lovely Inchbald".

Between 1800 and 1810 Colchester playhouse had fallen into disrepair. It had several times been cheaply patched up and William Wilkins, the new patentee, complained that it had become too down-at-heel to be tenable. There was only one awkward entrance to the theatre—through one of the town hall courts and part of the gaol. It had no passages along the side of the green boxes and several people had written to Wilkins, he claimed, demanding that the £12 10s annual ground rent paid to the corporation should be waived. Wilkins instead contacted Benjamin Strutt of Colchester about the possibility of a new theatre in Queen Street similar to the one he (Wilkins) had just completed at Cambridge. In January 1811, he presented plans for a substantial playhouse of brick and timber with a seating capacity of 1,200, to be leased at an annual rent of £200. A full house would be worth £150, and Strutt was to have the use of the old theatre.

Twelve years after the first Colchester theatre opened, the Norwich managers began to sound out the burghers of King's Lynn to see if they would support a "regular" playhouse. Lynn Mart began on St Valentine's day and ran for anything from six days to a fortnight. The crowds it generated was the Norwich Company's main incentive for including Lynn in its winter schedule and, later, for building there. St George's Hall, dating from 1592, had served as both guildhall and playhouse since early times. By 1750, the Norwich players were calling regularly and in 1766 they persuaded the corporation to construct a fully-equipped playhouse within the shell of the mediaeval hall. The cost was about £450. William Richards in his *History of King's Lynn* described it as "neither profusely ornamented nor disgustingly plain; and although not free from faults yet they are, it seems, what resulted from the architect having to fill up the shell of an old building which had been erected for another purpose". Its most unusual feature was a great central canopy covering the forestage—in effect, a magnificent proscenium ceiling supported on timber posts. It was an uncommon construction, reminiscent of the jutting Elizabethan stage.

As in the case of the theatres at Ipswich and Colchester, the Norwich management had no compunction about calling King's Lynn theatre the Theatre Royal. As at Ipswich and Colchester, they were mistaken in thinking that the patent granted to Thomas Ivory at Norwich was automatically transferred to the rest of the circuit playhouses. But their presumption went apparently unnoticed and drama flourished illegally but unimpeded.

Thomas Snagg went to Lynn in 1769 with Herbert's company and found the town "a good one for comedians". He described the theatre as "very pretty and belonging to the corporation. The business was tolerable and the benefits great for a country town, especially to old standards or favourites. The sharing at the mart, which generally produced full nights from the concourse of people attending, were sometimes a guinea and a half a night."

Though Lynn audiences were routinely described as "genteel" the theatre had clearly had its share of rowdyism. The editor of the *Cambridge Chronicle* noted in

Giles Linnett Barrett, manager of the Norwich Company from 1780-1788. This engraving by Scott of J. Dunthorne's portrait of Barrett shows him as Charles Surface in "The School for Scandal". *Mary Evans Picture Library*

St George's Hall, the mediaeval guildhall at King's Lynn which once housed the theatre.

February, 1774, that "the letter addressed to the proprietors of the Lynn theatres, complaining of indecency among servants, and irregular persons mixing with their superiors in the pit etc, and other improprieties, was too long and too local for insertion in this paper".

Being a fashionable seaside resort as well as an important circuit town for drama, King's Lynn attracted actors from London theatres and from a variety of travelling country troupes. As one of Whitley and Herbert's players, George Frederick Cooke, actor, printer, bankrupt and alcoholic came to Lynn in 1774 when he was about eighteen, taking a number of young lead parts. With what Walter Scott described as his "terrible visage" (a broad face and prominent hooked nose) he was well able to convey the darker passions. The Lynn audiences were mesmerised.

The Norwich Company under the new management of John Brunton drew especially good houses at Lynn in the 1790s. The *Norfolk Chronicle* announced that "the very high estimation in which the company was held, and the novelty produced by them drew crouded audiences every evening. 'The Highland Reel', 'Inkle and Yarico', 'Prisoner at Large', 'Farmer', 'Ways and Means' and (though *last* not *least*)

'The Child of Nature' were received with the greatest glee and satisfaction. The profits of this trip will, we doubt not, prove the most fortunate circumstance that has happened in Mr Brunton's management".

In 1802 a review appeared in verse describing the Norwich players who had appeared in Lynn that year. No one was spared. Bowles junior was "one of more than common worth" but his father was pulled apart:

> "Next comes with huge pomposity of air,
> and much of what's termed vacancy of stare,
> The elder Bowles—e'er heedless to excel,
> He might play middling, though he can't play well."

Philips was advised to stick to tragedy, Fitzgerald was "capable of improvement", Henley ambled impotently and Clifford should be sent from the stage to the prompter's table. Bowles junior more than justified the hopes of him; when "His Majesty's Servants, from The Theatre Royal, Norwich," opened their February/March season at Lynn he took lead parts on 23 nights.

The procedure at Lynn on performance nights was by now more or less standard practice throughout the circuit theatres. Patrons were assured that "constant fires [on the stage] have been kept in the theatre for many days past". Doors opened at 5.15 for 6.15 p.m. and no places were given without tickets. Servants were forbidden to keep seats for their employers after Act I of the main piece and no one was allowed behind the scenes. Upper boxes had now been installed at Lynn, prices following a familiar pattern—lower boxes 4s, upper boxes 3s, pit 2s, gallery 1s. At the beginning of the second week gallery audiences had become too lively for the comfort of those in the pit, whom they showered with nuts and peelings. Constables empowered to take offenders into custody were stationed both in the galley and outside the theatre to prevent traffic congestion at the door. The general drill was that carriages arriving point the horses eastward and those departing should set off in a westerly direction.

Throughout the first decade of the nineteenth century "great houses" were reported at Lynn, justifying a new playhouse in the Wilkins style. It was built in 1815 on a plot near the old Greyfriars monastery at a cost of £6,400. The first lessee, John Brunton junior, opened on 7th February with "Lover's Vows" and "Raising the Wind".

In terms of importance to the circuit, Lynn and Yarmouth were roughly on a par. At Great Yarmouth, the players had progressed from a warehouse in Middlegate to the town chamber. Their third move was in 1778 to a splendid playhouse of classical proportions designed by the Ipswich architect, Fulcher. It was constructed on a patch of sandy wasteland just inside the old town wall at a cost of £1,100. For the first season, plays were performed on Monday, Wednesday, Friday and Saturday with top seats of 3s. On the surface, there was nothing to cloud the brilliance of the opening, but certain creditors had not been paid for their building work and they were getting restless.

The first intimation of trouble arose when the Norwich proprietors began to receive bills they had not expected. Captain William Ivory, who had assumed all his late father's interests and shares in the theatres, began to suspect that the Yarmouth theatre project had been pushed through under a faulty agreement. He had not been present himself when the terms had been decided on 27th March, 1778. In fact his joint managers, Richard Griffith and William Crouse, had, he discovered, gained consent for the theatre building not from the whole body of 30 shareholders, but from no more than the five of them who were present at the meeting. Eleven Yarmouth worthies would, it was decided, finance the building to the tune of £100 each. In sealing this arrangement, Griffith and Crouse bound the Norwich proprietors to an astonishing catalogue of undertakings: to leasing the theatre from the Yarmouth subscribers for 98 years; to paying the corporation a ground rent of £5 a year; to paying £50 to the subscribers (in lieu of rent) to producing a clear yearly interest of £4 10s; to insuring and keeping the place in good repair; even to issuing the eleven subscribers with silver tickets (worth about £30 each) which would admit them into the theatre for the rest of their lives without further payment.

In effect, the Yarmouth men became owners of the playhouse and the Norwich management was left holding the bills. The extent of the Griffith-Crouse blunder was not fully apparent until three years after the theatre was built. Claims began to be

King's Lynn Theatre, built in 1815 and burned down in 1936.   *King's Lynn Public Library*

made against the Norwich proprietors for unpaid accounts and the committee ordered an inquiry, demanding copies of the agreement. Griffith had meantime retired through ill-health and Crouse, no doubt sick with anxiety at the way things were going, began to suggest that he and his wife should withdraw their financial interests in the circuit, though not without first wringing an annuity out of his fellow proprietors.

The inquest ground on through 1781. On 31st May, six Norwich proprietors, John Gay, Robert Harvey, Roger Kerrison, Jeremiah Ives, William Ivory and Edward Rigby, were deputed to meet the Yarmouth men, work out who should pay what, and report back to Norwich. On 25th January, 1782, it was decided to split the £400 outstanding debt down the middle—half to be paid by Yarmouth, half by Norwich. Special benefit nights would help to raise the money, and each of the Norwich men were to pay £6. But only 13 of the proprietors were present to ratify this settlement; Ivory was not among them.

Two months later, Captain William Ivory belatedly shouted for redress. He wrote a long account of his bitter observations about "the Yarmouth business". To apply any part of the Norwich money (deposited in a Playhouse Fund set up by his father to further his theatrical estate) to a theatre which the Norwich management could never now own was illegal, he claimed, and totally alien to the aims of the fund. How could the order to build the Yarmouth theatre in the first place be binding when five men signed instead of 30? How could the Norwich proprietors be asked to settle unpaid bills against that background?

"Can there be a doubt,—let the person,—be whonsoever it may,—that has given orders to workmen or other persons, for building this Theatre,—but that the Subscribers at Yarmouth,—the sole proprietors of this theatre,—are alone *answerable and bound to pay*,—all workmen's bills and all demands whatsoever for the building of it."

Ivory pressed his points ruthlessly:

"The Deed specifys terms of Rent to be paid for a Theatre. Persons who receive rent [ie., the Yarmouth contingent] must be owners,—or stand in the place of oweners,—The Owners must produce the free right of occupation to the Tennants [ie., the Norwich proprietors]—A Tennant cannot be liable to pay the Expence of Bills, for erecting the *Buildings*, which he *pay Rent for the use of*."

Griffith and Crouse, he said, had acted only as contractors to build a theatre for the Yarmouth subscribers, which they would rent from them, and it was up to Yarmouth's eleven good men to pay up:

"All engagements for Leases of Playhouses, out of Norwich", he laid down, "can only be made, in behalf of the Company of Comedians—as all Expences, for Rents, and Charges of all Kinds, upon the different Theatres in the Circuit, are paid by the Company of Comedians,—out of the produce of the Receipts, in each Town, on the Circuit,—and not by the Proprietors of the Norwich Theatre''.

After paying £5 to the corporation, £50 to the subscribers, £10 for rates, £6 land tax, £1 3s 6d insurance, plus travelling and other expenses, the Norwich players could not, he argued, bring the company "one single farthing for all their time and Expences". It seemed equally unreasonable, he said, that the "Inhabitants of Yarmouth, desirous of accomodating themselves,—with *an elegant playhouse* should desire, to put us,—*the Proprietors of the Norwich Theatre*—to the Expence of supporting *their Theatre*, through the term of the lease they hold from the Corporation of Yarmouth, and endeavour to bind our fund, and tax our private fortunes with securing to them a Rent for their Theatre,—which we have not, or cannot derive any possible advantage from".

Nevertheless, the Norwich side did help foot the bill. Ivory was not reconciled to the "pretended Deed of Agreement" and would never accept that it was binding on the Norwich management; but he said he would pay his share to honour the promise made when the two parties met in Yarmouth. All that came out of the wrangle was a definition the following year that 16 proprietors should constitute a general meeting.

Fortunately, the dispute did not seem to poison relations between Yarmouth and the players. Giles Barrett helped to smooth the way to concord when in 1785 he offered to give the entire receipts of the theatre one night to liberate small debtors languishing in Yarmouth prison. "The great attention which Mr Barrett has paid through his circuit to the distresses of his fellow creatures is not more laudable than it it is unparralelled", oozed the local press, knowing full well that that kind of public philanthropy, in managers, was no more than greasepaint deep. But when Barrett retired in 1788, verses were published in his honour:

> "And heaven-born Charity shall ne'er forget
> A generous donor to the hapless poor!"

Yarmouth kept a firm place in the Norwich Company's midsummer schedule and was sometimes even visited twice a year. From 1782 it became the last post before the players hauled their waggons across country to the last-forged link in the circuit's chain round the eastern region—the colourful chaos of Stourbridge Fair.

CHAPTER SIX

Stourbridge Fair; or,
The Long Road to Cambridge

"September 14, being the horse-fair day, is the day of the greatest hurry, when it is almost incredible to conceive what number of people there are, and the quantity of victuals that day consumed by them . . . Though the corporation of Cambridge has the tolls of this fair, and the government, yet the body of the university has the oversight of the weights and measures thereof and the licensing of all shew-booths, wild beasts, etc. And the proctors of the university keep a court there also, to hear complaints about weights or measures, seek out and punish lewd women, and see that the gownsmen commit no disorders." Bibliotheca, 1786.

PRE-EMINENCE in three counties might have satisfied the Norwich Company if the possibility of a fourth conquest—Cambridge—had not been so easily within reach. There was an appealing logic about capturing Cambridge as a regular circuit town. It lay within striking distance, it had proved itself capable of supporting performances from itinerant provincial and London actors and the venue—Stourbridge Fair—offered freedoms and attractions to the players which they seldom experienced in any other of their circuit towns. The world and his wife thronged Stourbridge in September. In its heyday it had been one of the greatest and most important fairs in Europe; even now, in slightly diminished circumstances, it presented a scene of boisterous industry, revelry, *comaraderie*, unrivalled anywhere in England. There were rich pickings to be had, and the Norwich manager, Giles Linnett Barrett, was not a man to let them lie.

The fair was run "like a well-governed city", a description which suited the grid-like pattern of its "streets" as much as the law-and-order measures for bringing offenders on the site to swift justice. From its frontage on the Cambridge-Newmarket road, to its outer limits by the ferry over the River Cam south of the village of Chesterton, the fair was mapped out like a modern agricultural showground into "rows" or "streets", each with its name describing the type of wares or diversions on offer. In Duddery Row as much as £100,000 worth of woollen stuff was reputed to be sold in a week in the mid-eighteenth century. One booth in the duddery consisted of six apartments which alone harboured goods worth £20,000 belonging to a dealer in Norwich stuffs. Clothiers also came from Yorkshire and Lancashire, hop-men from Kent, cheese-makers from Cheshire, Wiltshire and Gloucester. The Cam was navigable from Cambridge to Ely and bulky goods from Yorkshire would be seaborne to King's Lynn and then transferred to barges from the Ouse to the Cam.

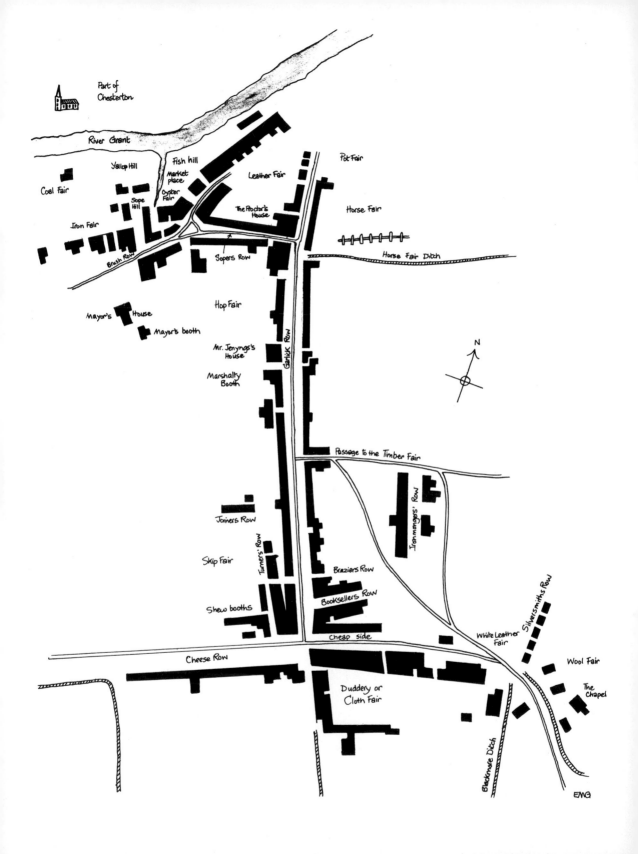

A London merchant, writing in 1827, related his colourful impressions of sixty-years' experience of the fair:

"Like all other fairs," he said, "your ears inform you, before your eyes, that you are on your way to it. After passing Barnwell, the numerous booths and long range of standings burst on the sight, and the clamour of trumpets, deep-sounding drums, screaming of toy-trumpets and din of a thousand discordant voices assailed the ear and confused the thoughts."

The first booths on the north side of the road were occupied by customary shows of wild beasts and still wilder men, by conjurers, tumblers and rope-dancers. The merchant names two of the occupants of the "shew booths"—Mr Bailey's Norwich comedians and Mrs Baker's popular company of comedians with the famous well-born clown, Lewy Owen, in tow. His eccentric wit and amusing grimaces accounted for a good deal of the company's popularity. "Other show booths occupied by giants and dwarfs, savage beasts and other savages, extended with stunning din along the noisy line." In front of them stood the fruit and gingerbread stalls. Walnuts had just been harvested and vendors patrolled the fair bawling "Twenty-a-penny walnuts! Walnuts! Twenty-a-penny! Crack 'em away—crack 'em away here!"

Close to the entrance to Stourbridge fairground stood a small, early twelfth century chapel called the Chapel of St Mary Magdalene, or the Leper Chapel, where some of the fair people would not think it amiss to store their wood and canvas trappings. In 1783 it was offered for sale with an interesting inducement to potential buyers:

"To be sold, a freehold building known as the Chapel of Sturbitchfair. The tenant draws between seven and eight barrels of beer during the fair. It is also convenient for laying up the buildings materials for the fair."

In 1819, when J. S. Cotman, the East Anglian watercolourist, produced a book of etchings of the Leper Chapel he noted: "Of late years the chapel has served as a stable, and very recently was threatened with complete destruction."

Most of the tradespeople hired a plot (about 25 feet for £2 10s) and built open-fronted booths of wood and canvas, with pitched roofs covered with hair cloth to keep out the rain. Heavy rain would frequently soak through, and autumn storms brought ruin to the least well-equipped traders and theatre companies. In 1741 gales blew down many of the booths altogether. Most booth-holders would construct a rough sleeping apparatus from two or three boards nailed to four posts about a foot from the ground. Four boards were fixed cot-like around the sides to prevent them from falling out. They were said to have "laid almost neck and heels together".

Thomas Snagg detested this sort of accommodation. "Temporary booths," he said, "scarcely ever answer. Even in summer they are cold and damp, the rain will penetrate." And actors faced special problems in trying to get someone to build them such a booth. "The charge and delay of tradesmen working for players are as bad as church work. Everyone thinks he has a right to make the most of money easily earned—

The layout of Stourbridge Fair, Cambridge, as it appeared in 1725. Lack of shops in rural towns and villages meant that people for miles around used the fair to stock up for the year. Everything from horses to bobbins was sold. The plot marked "shew booths" near the bottom of the plan was where puppeteers, showmen and actors traditionally entertained the crowds. Copied from a plan in the Cambridge Record Office.

tho' that does not hold good with the actor who for fear of their demands they are mostly paid in advance, and even that will scarcely ensure diligence and common honesty, so much is the players' profession preyed upon."

The London fair-going manager, Richardson, offers a lively account of a typical scene at Bartholomew Fair which could apply almost equally well to the cheek-by-jowl entertainers at Stourbridge in the second half of the eighteenth century:

> ". . . in those days the exhibitions were generally up the inn yards, or in the upstairs of public houses; but by way of explanation the following list will suffice, Old *Jobson*, the great puppetshow man, in one yard; *Jones* and *Penley* in the George Yard; the celebrated Mrs Baker at the Greyhound, in a room up one pair of stairs; O'Brian, the Irish Giant, in the King's Head, also in a one pair of stairs room; and myself with my company."

But competition between companies at Stourbridge Fair was an acceptable fact of life compared with the harrassment from Cambridge University. There was constant antagonism between town and gown—mainly because of the university's attempts to prevent players from setting up within a ten-mile radius of the colleges. Taverns and theatres were top of the list of diversions liable to corrupt students. The poem of 1708 entitled *The Long Vacation, a Satyr address'd to all disconsolate traders* still had a dangerous relevance:

> "The Actors, too, must take the pleasant air,
> To Oxford some, to Sturbridge some repair,
> And quite debauch the hopeful Students there."

Joseph Kettle, in the early part of the eighteenth century, first built his playhouse in the town precincts and then applied for permission to use it for plays and interludes during the fair. The authorities were not impressed by his tactics; they refused, banned him from the area and pulled the building down.

But the Mayor and corporation of Cambridge, fattening on the charges they imposed on traders for the right to sell, at the fair, took a more lenient line. In 1701 they put themselves deliberately at loggerheads with the university by giving Doggett permission to perform at Stourbridge without the Vice Chancellor's sanction. This stung the university to retaliate. The Senate decided that the privileges of the university should be defended and vindicated at the public's expense. Meantime, to prevent a breach of discipline, the Senate conferred the authority of Proctors during the fair on 62 masters of arts. It was decreed that players who disobeyed them should be expelled. Soon after, Doggett was thrown into gaol and his booth demolished.

By 1748, despite the prohibitive Licensing Act and local bans drama was alive and well at Stourbridge. The *Cambridge Journal* of that year reported that a company of players from "the theatres in London" (clearly taking advantage of their vacation months) performed a new pantomime called "Harlequin's Frolics; or, Jack Spaniard Caught in a Trap" in Hussey's Great Theatrical Booth at the upper end of Garlic Row. Puppet shows had never been the subject of dispute and neither apparently had other entertainments such as tumbling. Elizabeth Rayner, a rope-dancer, was the principal attraction of a company from Sadler's Wells who visited the fair in 1745. Between 1765 and 1782 provinical companies began to infiltrate and competition became intense. Thomas Snagg, smarting after his abortive King's Lynn venture, dropped by in 1772 and built "the compleatest temporary theatre than can be imagined". A fortnight's use cost him £200. His receipts totalled £351 and his actors received 6 guineas each. The *Cambridge Chronicle* of 11th September, 1773, announced that two large booths were to be put up. One was in the Cheese Fair for William Bailey's Norwich company, which was to be joined by performers from "Richmond and other theatres"; in the other booth, Mrs Ann Wakelin was billed to "exhibit the favourite diversions of Sadler's Wells [rope dancing and tumbling], with occasional interludes and other dramatic performances".

Bailey, a portly, good-looking gentlemanly character, and Wakelin had a third rival. He was James Whitley, notorious manager of a Midland circuit and proprietor of the theatres at Nottingham, Derby, Shrewsbury and Stamford. "Jemmy" Whitley was a name to conjure with. John Bernard wrote of him: "The name and fame of this person pervaded the three kingdoms, and a hundred recollections of his personal and managerial peculiarities are now thronging my head; but most of which, as their effect depends upon a certain dramatic illustration, I regret are untransferable to paper". Wherever he went, Whitley meant business. In 1775 his company of comedians installed themselves in a new and much bigger booth in Garlic Row. Bailey retreated to the Grand Music Booth in Cheese Fair, playing safe, and other competition seemed to melt away.

A typical booth of wood and canvas used by the traders at Stourbridge Fair in the eighteenth century. The "show booths" where players performed did not have these pointed roofs but looked like large square tents with a high platform at the front for a stage. *Cambridge Collection*

Giles Linnett Barrett's first attempt to annex Stourbridge to the Norwich circuit, in September 1781, failed. He made a dignified exit from Cambridge, telling the public, "As Mr. Glassington [head of a motley company of 'disengaged' actors from several counties] is determined to oppose, and as the sentiments of the gentlemen of Cambridge are against an opposition, Mr. Barrett, ready to convince them of his respect and determination of obliging them, postpones his visit to Stirbitch this season". On 18th May of the following year, Barrett announced well in advance that he had engaged "the theatre" and intended to perform "most of the new pieces from London".

Stourbridge was the high point of the circuit tour in East Anglia—socially, if not professionally or financially. For six autumnal weeks, the company had an almost captive audience, a city on the fringe of a city, a nexus of trade and entertainment of mediaeval vigour. They had permission to perform there every night of the fair. Some onlookers took a jaundiced view of the proceedings but the report of a visitor in 1773 was by no means a general complaint:

> ". . . all the Eating Houses swarm with Jockeys, who, like locusts devour all their Provisions. For these 20 years past Stourbridge Fair has been upon the Decline. A heavy Load of Taxes entailed upon the People ever since the last War, the exorbitant Price of Provisions, the easy communication with all commercial cities and manufacturing towns, the great Increase of Land Carriages, the navigable canals lately cut and the Number of Riders from the Capital and other trading places who take Orders for all kinds of Merchandise all over the Kingdom, have ruined all the Fairs."

To Barrett and his players, the picture was altogether more sanguine. They saw the market stall of England set out with enticing splendour—shops, multifarious provisions, livestock auctions, festivity and barter, all compressed into a large cornfield off the main road from Cambridge to Newmarket. (If the corn was not cut by 24th August the fairkeepers could move in and flatten the crops. Similarly, if fair-people outstayed their term, to Michaelmas Day, ploughmen could overthrow the booths.) True, the event had contracted in scope since the days when regional trade centres were few, but it still presented an industrious, profitable spectacle, neither too engrossingly trade-oriented nor, as both Stourbridge and Bury St Edmunds fairs were to become in their decline, too frivolous.

At the time Barrett secured a stand for the Norwich Company in 1782 the character of Stourbridge Fair was changing. It was becoming less single-minded in its business and more inclined to attract the fun-seekers. From being a vast national market it was developing a bias towards southern or regional patronage. A passage in Walter's *Gazetteer* of 1801 indicates how far and fast the transition had gone:

> "Sometimes 50 Hackney coaches from London ply morning and night to and from Cambridge as well as all the towns around and the very barns and stables are turned into inns for the accommodation of the meaner sort of people. After

Giles Linnett Barrett (1744-1795), manager of the Norwich Company. He was a competent though not brilliant actor, but he had no hesitation in casting himself in major roles opposite visiting London stars. He brought off his most spectacular coup in the final year of his managership when Mrs Siddons played in Norwich for nine nights. Here Samuel de Wilde has depicted him in the characteristic pose and garb of Pumpkin in "All the World's a Stage". *Norfolk County Libraries*

the wholesale business is over, the countrie gentry generally flock in, laying out their money in stage-plays, taverns, music-houses, toys, puppet-shows etc. and the whole concludes with a day for the sale of horses."

By the time the Norwich Company moved in, the traditional first-day pomp and revelry had become a slightly attenuated scene of jollification. The procession of Mayor and entire corporation of Cambridge had been discontinued and so, it seems, had the custom of boys competing on horseback. But the Mayor, town clerk and a small band of bailiffs proclaimed the fair and processed about the field, fortifying themselves with mulled wine and malmsey in the morning. Ritual oyster-eating and ale or porter followed in the afternoon and the theatre opened at 6.30 in the evening, attended by the official party. Henry Gunning, of Cambridge University, notes that the people's wine was "execrable" and that the university got itself into further bad odour with fairgoers by ordering that beer should be served in undersized mugs.

Barrett decided to open on 14th September, 1782, with Mrs Cowley's popular comedy "The Belle's Stratagem" which had appeared at Covent Garden two years earlier with a very successful run. For the first time, places for boxes were bookable in the morning before a performance. The company was rewarded for its comprehensive advertising (and possibly for its curiosity value) by huge audiences and each successive year seemed to establish the players in greater popularity. In 1784 receipts topped all previous records and the season was extended by a month. They were attracting good bespeaks. The *Cambridge Chronicle* regretted that such excellent performances should be taking place outside the city. "The only thing we regret is the *distance* of the theatre from the town, why it should be continued at Stirbidge we cannot conceive." Barrett ingratiated himself with the authorities in the 1784 season by announcing that the opening night's takings were to be given for the release of debtors in Cambridge Castle. In the following year six men were released for a sum of £12 14s 8d, house receipts that night having been £20 5s 0d. The "theatrical booth" had become a "theatre".

Competition was, of course, the natural penalty of success. In 1786 Mr W. Palmer of the Theatre Royal, Covent Garden, opened at another booth with "The Suspicious Husband" by John Hoadley. The *Cambridge Chronicle* reported primly: "We have received several remarks on the performers of both Theatres; but as they would afford no entertainment to our readers at a distance, and might be prejudicial to individuals we omit them." Patrick Cotter, the Irish Giant was exhibited to the delight of a freak-hungry public. He had toured most of the great fairs in England. At 8' 4" tall, he could light his pipe from the street lamps and when he appeared at Sadler's Wells was able to shake hands with the audience in the upper boxes.

In 1787 the Norwich Company was taking front page advertisements headed "Theatre, Stirbitch Fair" and its season there was now three weeks. The following year, when theatrically there were few clouds in the sky—between £60 and £70 a night was being collected at Stourbridge—Barrett left the company. The *Chronicle* reported at the end of the season: "We hear that Mr Barrett has the offer of many respectable engagements on his quitting managership of the Norwich Company".

Barrett was succeeded by a Norwich-born fellow actor of the previous decade, John Brunton, a man of talent and tact. In the 1790s, Brunton and Richardson found themselves in tandem at the fair. Richardson had arrived from Stepney with his splendidly decked-out booth and rich trappings. It was said that the whole magnificently-draped edifice could be erected within a few hours. In quality of props and wardrobe Richardson far outshone anything the Norwich Company could muster; the front of his theatre alone was reputed to cost £600. It was all the more galling, therefore, when Stourbridge proved the London manager's undoing. He refused to pay his ground tax, was taken into custody by the site police and would have been committed but for the kindly intervention of the Norwich manager, "old Mr Brunton".

> "This veteran of the stage had also a company at Stourbridge fair at the same time. I found out that the magistrates could not commit me, without also sending to prison Mr Brunton and his actors. The university law is not to suffer any theatre to be opened within a specified number of miles of Cambridge; therefore the university was liable to lose a part of their privileges by suffering either of us to perform. Our audiences were so trifling in number that I was completely

ruined; and old Mr Brunton, witnessing our distress, generously made me a present of five guineas: which feeling disposition I shall always remember with the highest sense of gratitude."

All except three of Richardson's horses were drowned in an ensuing flood and Brunton's five guineas was all he had between himself, his actors and destitution. His problem was how to get back to London. He decided to leave two of his waggons in the yard of a Cambridge public house and to busk his way. The landlord of the pub held such a low opinion of players that instead of advancing Richardson a shilling or two on the waggons left in his possession, he demanded payment for every week they stood in his yard. There was no alternative but to pay up. Without a penny in their pockets, Richardson and his company left Cambridge, singing, playing and passing the hat round in every pub on the road. As fast as the money came in, it was spent—on "tea, sugar and other necessaries" and corn for the horses. Eventually, Richardson was back in business broadcasting his gratitude to Brunton. The gesture was no more than typical of the Norwich manager: it was his generosity as much as his professional expertise which made him one of the most honoured figures of early nineteenth century provincial theatre.

Ancient Leper Chapel, Cambridge, the sole relic of Stourbridge Fair days which would be recognisable to a Norwich player today. It stands close to the noisy A45 Cambridge-Newmarket road, near Barnwell Junction in the Parish of Fen Ditton.　　　　　　　　　　　　　　　　　　　　　　　　*Author's collection*

John Brunton (1741-1822), a prince among theatre managers. As actor, administrator, leader of men, he was unrivalled in the country circuits. Under him, the Norwich Company had the most successful decade of its existence. The portrait of Brunton was painted in about 1780, apparently by an artist of the Reynolds school. It hangs in Norwich Theatre Royal.

Norwich Theatre Royal

CHAPTER SEVEN

John Brunton and William Wilkins; or,
An Inheritance of Theatres

"The City of Norwich has many charms to be gathered by the man of gallantry; nor are the ladies over fastidious in their morals and favours, but seem sensible their beauties were not bestowed to be churlishly selfish, and they are pleased in communicating that happiness nature has been so bountiful and lavish in reposing in them." Thomas Snagg, 1771.

JOHN Brunton was born in Norwich in 1741. One of the few things about his provenance which seems to be generally known is the prosaic fact that he was the son of a soap-boiler. After brief schooling, he was directed into an apprenticeship as a wholesale grocer—but not in Norwich; in London, and significantly, in Drury Lane, with all the lure of the theatre on his doorstep. "The Drama had long floated in his imagination superior to the produce of the East and West Indies," according to the anonymous author of the *Green Room Book*. Brunton threw over the grocery trade while still in his twenties and by the age of thirty-three was playing Hamlet at Covent Garden. A year later, in 1775, he had returned to his roots in Norwich. He could hardly fail to commend himself to the management of the Norwich Company for his credentials were impeccable: he had the twin advantages of being Norwich-born and of having distinguished himself in the metropolis.

For five years, John Brunton was one of Richard Griffith's leading actors—sensitive, versatile, reliable and a popular man with his fellow actors. By no other combination of personal characteristics could he have walked into the great romantic and tragic Shakespearean roles at Norwich—Hamlet, Romeo, Macbeth, Richard III—without incurring the resentment of his colleagues. John Bernard called him "our leading tragedian and one of the best Shylocks I have ever seen".

In 1780, about the time that persistent ill-health forced Griffith to retire from the Norwich managership, Brunton, with his wife and young daughter, Anne, set out for Bath, one of the most profitable provincial circuits in England. Of Brunton's three actress daughters—Anne, Elizabeth and Louisa—none was so rapturously received as Anne, the eldest. While the family were in Bath she made her debut at the age of fifteen in 1785, playing Euphrasia in Arthur Murphy's tragedy "The Grecian Daughter". Brunton applied himself to the education of all his daughters, rehearsing them in their lines and their movements tirelessly. Anne's instruction gave him particular delight. She was a pliant, eager girl totally unlike the sluttish, indolent creature which some of her jealous contemporaries in the theatre labelled her. Anne Brunton's great misfortune was her too-rapid popularity; she had presumed to soar early to the heights of

Elizabeth Yates, pictured in her mid-twenties soon after her marriage to the actor Frederick Yates. She made her professional debut when she was sixteen, on the stage of the King's Lynn Theatre where her father, John Brunton Junior, was manager. On 15th March, 1815, she played Desdemona to Charles Kemble's Othello at Lynn. Later, she went to Covent Garden.   *Norfolk County Libraries*

tragedy at her first attempt when everybody expected that she would be humbled. In a short time she was being talked of in Bath and Bristol as "a phenomenon in the theatrical hemisphere". John Brunton angled publicity for her in the London press where she was puffed as a rival to Sarah Siddons—more with a view to bringing Siddons down than from any serious conviction that she could match the great tragedienne. Anne Brunton, a slighter, unsophisticated and altogether less mature girl, could not hope to live up to the extravagant prophesies of stardom. She was not a prima donna.

Her first season at Covent Garden, later in 1785 was well-received but, although a fine actress in her own right, she had suffered by comparison with Mrs Siddons and a volatile public soon tempered its fervour. According to a contemporary account:

"Her person and countenance are by no means formed for Tragedy; she is short, lusty and her features are neither delicate nor expressive, but her voice is sonorous, flexible and sweetly melodious; her deportment is graceful, and her action nicely and judiciously adapted to the situation; her enunciation is animated—she catches the fire of her Author, and is guided by a feeling heart."

In other words, she was a sensitive, capable and rather dumpy country girl who had assimilated her tuition admirably but who remained essentially lacking in the charisma, the experience and the *savoir faire* necessary to a prominent London actress. All that the verdict proved was that these were early days. Both father and daughter had to wait for warmer recognition.

The family returned to Norwich in time for the Norwich Company's Assize Week engagement. Brunton, his wife, and Anne all had parts in the stock pieces of the season. In August, they made their first appearance in Ipswich. Father and daughter played Evander and Euphrasia ("The Grecian Daughter") and Lear and Cordelia to a

"The amiable Mrs Merry" they called her. She was Elizabeth, one of the talented daughters of the Norwich manager, John Brunton. De Wilde painted her playing Calista in Nicholas Rowe's tragedy "The Fair Penitent". This engraving, taken from de Wilde, appeared in Bell's British Theatre in 1782. It was used to illustrate the passage:

"And you, ye glittering heavenly host of Stars
Hide your fair heads in clouds or I shall blast you."

Norfolk County Libraries

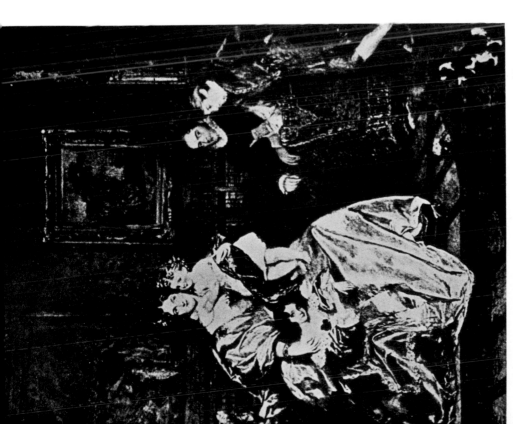

William Wilkins, architect of the second Norwich Theatre Royal, of Bury St Edmunds Theatre Royal and of the National Gallery, peers with uncharacteristic wariness from the shadows. A. E. Chalcon's portrait shows Wilkins and his family in theatrical costume of various periods.

Norfolk County Libraries

particularly large and "brilliant" audience. The *Ipswich Journal* was in no doubt that "Miss Brunton was the object that attracted them . . . To describe the beauties of her attitudes, action, declamation, would far exceed the limits of a newspaper". The following year Anne was engaged for another four performances at Norwich at "the greatest fee ever paid by the theatre"—but the amount went unrecorded. By now, her impact was striking wherever she went. At the age of seventeen on a visit to Cork she was praised for her "rare sweetness of modulation, expressive face and elegant taste in dress". The *Ipswich Journal*, always prone to commit its sentiments to verse in praise of Anne Brunton, offered a short acrostic in her honour on 13th May, 1786:

> B orn to brave the critics' rage,
> R ichly to adorn the stage!
> U ncommon powers, spirit, ease,
> N ature ever sure to please,
> T hou art truly blest with these:
> O nward tread thy graceful path,
> N am'd the Brilliant Star of Bath.

Before long, she transferred to Covent Garden again, occasionally returning to Norfolk and Suffolk as a "star". John Brunton from now on had the doubtful privilege of being described as "father of the celebrated actress of the *Theatre Royal*, Covent Garden"—or as "father to the amiable Mrs Merry" (John Bernard— *Retrospections*).

By 1789, Anne's sister, Elizabeth, was appearing with the Norwich players, admired chiefly for her comic powers. One critic who had witnessed her as Beatrice, Belvidera, Juliet and Polly Honeycombe, however, claimed the audience was "at a loss which most to admire, her Tragedy or her Comedy". The third sister, Louisa, was renowned for her beauty but had her brief Covent Garden career (1803-1807) cut short when she was swept into marriage to the Earl of Craven. They were married at his home in Berkeley Square and John Brunton gave his daughter away. The earl was thirty-seven, Louisa twenty-five. She died, almost forgotten, in 1860.

The fourth famous Brunton girl was John Brunton's granddaughter, Elizabeth, known as Eliza to distinguish her from her aunt. She was the daughter of John Brunton Junior, born in 1799, the final triumphant year of her grandfather's term as manager of the Norwich Company. At sixteen she made her first stage appearance at the new King's Lynn theatre, under her father's management. On 15th March, 1815, she was Desdemona to Charles Kemble's Othello there. Eliza went on to play at Drury Lane, Covent Garden, the Adelphi and the Lyceum in London. In his journal of 1818, Henry Crabb Robinson noted her performance in "She Stoops to Conquer" at Covent Garden: "I was charmed by the beauty of Miss Brunton, though her acting is not very excellent". The London theatre was harshly competitive for any young actor; for a girl of nineteen it was both tough and rough. Managers were forced to tighten up on the female entourage around their theatres after complaints that "ladies of a certain

Norwich Theatre Royal in 1805 as used to illustrate James Winston's survey of provincial theatres, *The Theatric Tourist.*
Norfolk County Libraries

description" had intruded. "It is most respectfully announced," said one manager unrealistically, "that no female will in future be permitted to enter the theatre whose chastity is not attested by two respectable housekeepers—N.B. Ladies under 10, and above fifty years of age will be considered exempt from this regulation." Repeated attempts to pass forged banknotes and counterfeit coins at the pay offices prompted more alarmist managers to equip their money-takers with blunderbusses and to issue the warning that anyone who presented even a bad sixpence would be instantly shot dead and his body delivered for medical dissection.

Eliza Brunton never completely espoused the bitter, brilliant London theatre circle, but she married one of its players, Frederick Henry Yates. The wedding was in Bath in 1823. Their son was the famous nineteenth century actor Edmund Yates.

At the peak of his own and his family's success, John Brunton took over the Norwich Company of Comedians, leading it through its most stable, profitable and adventurous years. His predecessor, Giles Barrett (who had taken on the lease from the Norwich proprietors for seven years from 1786) approached the proprietors in 1788 asking that the remaining five years of the lease be transferred to Brunton. The formal hand-over of Norwich, Colchester, Ipswich, Bury St Edmunds and Yarmouth theatres took place on 1st November, when the players were on the road from Colchester to Ipswich. Terrific applause broke out after Brunton's address opening his first Norwich season as manager on New Year's Day, 1789. His reign had officially begun in Colchester but the coronation had to wait for Norwich, marking the beginning of the most confident decade in the history of East Anglian theatre. There was a time under Richard Griffith when the company felt threatened by rival groups of players who were "harrassing the counties of Norfolk and Suffolk"; it was now strong enough not to mind rivals. Brunton's personal standing was high, his actors were of good calibre and he demonstrated that he had their interests at heart. In pioneering spirit, he instituted the Norwich Theatrical Fund (1791) "for the relief of sick and decayed actors who have been members of the Norwich Company", and gave them an annual benefit. According to James Winston (*The Theatric Tourist*), there was only one other fund of its kind in the country, outside London.

An almost complete set of playbills exists for the year 1799 which indicates the range of plays in a typical year's repertoire. As well as up-to-date pieces such as "Lover's Vows", "Wives as They Were", "The Stranger" and "Pizarro", were mingled Shakespearean plays and gothic novelties such as "The Castle Spectre" by Monk Lewis. The opera "The Duenna" was introduced at Stourbridge, and at Yarmouth additions to the nucleus of plays were "The Mountaineers", "The Battle of Hexham" (both by George Colman the Younger) and, a particular favourite, "Jane Shore" (Nicholas Rowe). Brunton's company at this time included Joseph Inchbald, Sophie Goddard, Blanchard, Bennett, Beachem, Dwyer, Wordsworth, Taylor, Lindoe, and Seymour. The year 1799 was a prosperous one—benefits totalled £1,300. Brunton took £100, his wife £84, Miss Goddard £95, Mr and Mrs Chesnut £86 and Dwyer £46 6s—it was also Brunton's last year as manager: he decided not to renew his lease.

A newspaper paragraph spelled out the change neatly emphasising the inflationary side of the transaction: "The management of the Norwich theatre is to pass to Mr. Wilkins, plaisterer of that city, on the expiration of the lease of Mr. Brunton. About 18 years since, this theatre was let to Mr. Barrett for £180 p.a.; at the expiration of his lease, Mr. Brunton took it at £300; and now Mr. Wilkins has agreed to pay for it £750 p.a.". In an indenture of 3rd October, 1789, William Wilkins then described as a "surveyor of Norwich" had a share in the Norwich and Colchester theatres assigned to him. On 30th July, 1790, now dubbed "architect", he acquired another share; and on 28th January, 1792, a third. Each step represented a growing power-base in theatrical management which helped to make him a plausible candidate as successor to John Brunton. In 1793, Wilkins and a Norwich stationer and printer called Richard Bacon added another share in "Norwich, Colchester and certain other theatres in Norfolk, Suffolk and Essex". Wilkins had moved to

Cambridge in 1780 but he prudently kept his Norwich business and contacts until at least 1795. The following year he became a Fellow of the Society of Antiquaries.

What finally clinched his acceptance as patentee was the minutely constructive blue print he submitted for giving Norwich Theatre Royal a facelift. He brought an architect's eye to bear on the problems; he was unsparing in his criticism of the inconveniences of the building; and his plans for overhaul were so thoroughgoing that he was in effect without a rival in the field. The ruder he was about the state of the place, it appeared, the better the proprietors liked it. Here was a man who would shoulder burdens, get things done. The behaviour of unruly audiences and the general abuse of theatre property swelled repair bills to an extent hardly credible today. In addition, there was the ever-accumulating grime from smoking chimneys and tallow candles. The convenience of having an architect—with friends in the building trade—as proprietor appealed to the Norwich shareholders.

In what amounted to his manifesto, headed *The Proposals of William Wilkins, for hiring on Lease, the Norwich Theatre Royal with other Theatres belonging to the Circuit* Wilkins paraded his knowledge of the theatre as an artistic centre. He trotted out the names of several revered actors to support his definition of Norwich in former years as "the first Nursery of Actors in the Kingdom" and regretted that since Thomas Ivory built the new theatre few actors had moved on to London. (He was on shaky ground here, as he probably realised.) Wilkins insinuated in a gentlemanly sort of way that the managers were to blame for this state of affairs. "It is not the fault of the public," he asserted, "for they have even in the hardest times evinced their fondness for Theatrical exhibitions." Wilkins then moved on to the area of his real concern—the building. Here he was better qualified to play the critic, and he refused to sugar his pill.

Mrs Bramwell as Edmond in "The Blind Boy" published as "a grand melodrama in two acts, as it is performed at the Theatres Royal, Covent Garden and Norwich".   *Suffolk Record Office, Ipswich*

William Blanchard, a leading light of the Norwich Company who achieved metropolitan fame. As "Mr Blanchard of the Theatre Royal, Covent Garden", he returned to star with his old provincial company during the summer season of 1818. *Suffolk Record Office, Ipswich*

Mr Beachem and Miss Binfield as the Wood Daemon and Leolyn in a performance at Ipswich. Beachem was a stalwart of the Norwich Company in the late eighteenth century; Miss Binfield became organist of St Mary-le-Tower Church, Ipswich. *Suffolk Record Office, Ipswich*

According to his survey, the building was labouring under so many handicaps that patrons had to be addicted to drama to think of approaching it. Boxes had been opened out with no consideration for design and the only alteration or improvements had been merely to cram as many fee-payers in as possible. The entrances were so badly placed that only one person could approach the lobby at a time and "a Lady must be seperated [sic] from the Arm of her protector" both coming in and going out. It offended William Wilkins's notions of a place for everyone and everyone in his place that the various social stratifications of the audience were huddled together waiting to get to the exit one by one "where they are obliged to run the Gauntlet thro' Coachmen, Footmen and Porters and if a carriage is not in readiness at the Door it is almost impossible to return 'till the house is nearly emptied". To avoid the crush, audiences understandably deserted the theatre before the end of performances—usually missing part of the farce, or afterpiece. This was the only way, Wilkins argued, that fashionably-dressed women could reach their carriages without spoiling their dresses or if they were to avoid the indignity of being squeezed between doorkeepers, porters and prostitutes who were crowding in. There was similar congestion in the gallery—plus the extra hazard of fire which kept many away. Wilkins's insistence of fire precautions was not misplaced. Candles, open fires and, later, fearsome gas appliances had made a pile of ashes out of many theatres—and several on the Norwich circuit were to go the same way in the next one hundred and fifty years. It would only take a fire *alarm* (and there were several prankish false alerts), said Wilkins, for the gallery's one outlet to be choked in a few minutes "and the destruction of numbers would be the consequence".

Attempts to improve the orchestra's quarters had been unhelpful: the area had at the best of times been cramped; now it was intolerable. There was so little room for the fiddlers that some of them could only gain the necessary bowing room by being raised up, obstructing sight-lines for the pit. The object of the squeeze had been to create extra seats in the pit, but as they were all on the same level as the seats behind, the result was merely aggravating to musicians and caused scuffles among the audience. Wilkins had three other complaints (his disgust at the inconvenient jostle of prostitutes was briefly alluded to): the box and pit seats were not sufficiently raked; there was not enough leg-room ("the want of room for the Knees") and the darkness of the auditorium had made it a popular resort for any self-respecting pickpocket. For all these deficiences, Wilkins naturally had a remedy. As candidate for the lease he made out a splendid case: he would tackle the theatre inside and out. Glass chandeliers would ensure that "company in the back seats of the Boxes shall appear equally splendid with those on the front Seats" and the exterior would "yield up its Barn like appearance and shall assume that of a public building". New scenes and wings would be introduced—some were now reputed to be not worth the canvas they were painted on—and Wilkins, outraged that scene-painting should have so degenerated as to be "valued by the Yard Square", resolved to employ artists equal to the eminent early practitioners—Collins, Williams, Hodgings and Luppino.

Wilkins estimated that his master plan would cost £1,000. He would give the Norwich proprietors a clear rental of £600 a year (equal to £20 a year on each share) and continue paying an annuity of £50 to the widow of the former manager of the company, Giles Barrett. In 1799, William Wilkins, now practising chiefly as an architect in Cambridge, secured the lease of Norwich, Colchester, Bury and Yarmouth Theatres by 16 votes to 11.

After summer renovation, the theatre opened in the autumn of 1801 under the auspices of its new patentee and a new manager—John Clayton Hindes. The *Norwich Mercury* reported: "The House had undergone an entire change; except the walk scarcely any part of the old building remains". Nor did it. There were two complete rows of boxes and what were formerly the slips had been converted into upper boxes at the same price as the other tiers. Doorways had been widened and a bar provided. The auditorium had become horseshoe-shaped, the boxes were lined with painted canvas, each was supported by a gilt pilaster, its panels lavishly ornamented. Four private boxes, trellised with gold, stood on the stage. Chandeliers "after the eastern manner" were, ironically, the only disappointment: they refused to burn steadily during performances without the cumbersome intervention of a lamplighter. Arms bearing the motto *Conabimur* (we will endeavour) hung above the stage. The stage itself was new and the scenes "worked on an improved principle, by which all the wings are moved at once. Within the first entrance are inward wings which hide the actors from the view of the spectators in their boxes till they make their appearance on the stage". Dixon was the artist responsible for most of the new house design and he was to remain with the company for many years.

Wilkins had been as good as his word; Norwich was declared one of the handsomest theatres in the provinces. It was now up to Hindes and his players (Bennett, Beachem, Bowles, Blanchard and Fitzgerald were still with the company). Misfortune struck soon after the *eclat* of the opening, however. One of his leading actresses, Sophie Goddard, died at the age of twenty-six. She was buried at the Norwich actors' church, St Peter Mancroft, on 20th March with Hindes and all his principals at her graveside. The *Norfolk Chronicle* commented: "She supported with great fortitude and resignation a long and painful illness, brought on by exertions that her constitution was unequal to."

The ensuing years unrolled more or less evenly, but against a menacing background of a threatened Napoleonic invasion. The men in the company enrolled themselves in a class to learn how to use arms; Mrs Bennett gave birth to triplets; Miss Aickin, "an actress of superior talents and personal attractions" made her first appearance as Widow Cheerly in Cherry's play "The Soldier's Daughter" (she was also a female Hamlet). The following year Henry Bowles, junior, a stalwart of the company, married her. Mr and Mrs Bowles abruptly ended their theatrical careers in 1810, announcing that they were going into the "scholastic line", and netting a farewell benefit in Norwich of £160 15s 6d. Soon after, Bowles advertised that he was conducting, single-handed, an "academy" in Queen Street, Great Yarmouth; he went on to qualify as a dissenting minister.

Interior of the second Theatre Royal by William Burgess who was the scene painter in 1882. Apart from details of decoration, the theatre had not been altered since it was built in 1802. *Suffolk Record Office, Ipswich*

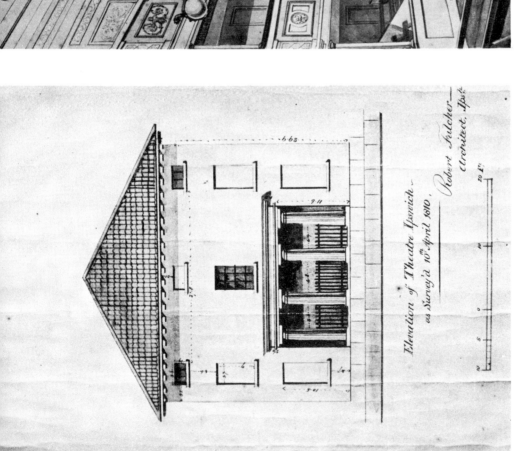

Elevation of Theatre Ipswich –
as Survey'd 10th April 1810.
Robert Fulcher –
Architect. Ips

Ipswich's second Theatre Royal was built on the same site as the first in Tankard Street in 1802/3. As Robert Fulcher's plan shows, it was a little more imaginative than the building it replaced.
Suffolk Record Office, Ipswich

The Bonaparte threat was countered with patriotic songs on the stage and a sudden increase in historical plays. Lady Mary Jerningham of Costessey in Norfolk wrote in 1803 to her daughter, Lady Bedingfield: "Bonaparte's Invasion must, I am afraid, take Place; and what a Scene of Danger! I do not fear for my own personal Security, nor for Sir William's: but for the *younger* people who may find it necessary to defend themselves". And notice went up in the Ipswich Green Room advertising a meeting "for the purpose of learning the manual exercise", to prepare all able-bodied men to defend their religion, liberties and laws against threatened invasion.

It was in this year that the actor James Winston (calling himself as "a Theatric Amateur") began an exhaustive survey of country theatres for *The Theatric Tourist*, a book he described as "a genuine collection of correct views with brief and authentic historical accounts of all the Principal Provincial theatres in the United Kingdom". He wrote to (and often visited) most theatres in England, compiling his report from the great bank of material he gathered. The Norwich circuit managers were generous in their supply of words, drawings and "views" but in the end, only Norwich featured (the final entry in the book) in the *Tourist* with a potted history and fine coloured engraving of the colonnaded brick-built theatre.

> "The value of this theatre," Winston wrote, "has encreased more rapidly than perhaps any of its contemporaries . . . Hindes is the Manager; but is by no means equal to the task of catering for the Norwich apetites; the salaries are very fair, for if they have none exceeding fifty shilling, they have none (which is more essential) under five and twenty, and very few so low; this is a very profitable circuit, and deserves a freer-spirited proprietor than it enjoys at present. The year is made out thus: first, Yarmouth, then Ipswich, a distance of fifty three miles; forty-three more to Norwich (for the Assizes); back to Yarmouth, twenty-two; then to Stirbitch, eighty-six; to Bury, twenty-eight; Colchester, twenty-two; to Ipswich again, eighteen; to Norwich, forty-three; Lynn, forty-four; back again to Norwich, forty-four; and again to Yarmouth, twenty-two; making in the whole a very pretty twelvemonth tour."

By now William Wilkins's son William, an architect like his father, had begun to take an interest in the circuit theatres though it was never more than a useful sideline to his considerable professional pursuits. Wilkins the younger was a man of ambition. He was educated at Norwich Grammar School and became a Scholar and Sixth Wrangler of Caius College, Cambridge. He was appointed a Royal Academician in 1826 and in 1837 took on the duties of Professor of Architecture at the Royal Academy after Sir John Soane. He retained his Cambridge connections throughout his professional life—benefiting in at least one major respect from his allegiance when he had his plans for the university's Downing College accepted. Wilkins was an imposing figure, mentally and physically. As architect, classical scholar and man of the theatre, he circulated in some of the best professional, academic and cultural circles of the day. His tall, muscular, frame was matched by a strong, vigorous mind and his obituarists were unanimous in praising his "exceedingly high, correct and polished taste". Though he failed to have his designs accepted for several architectural competitions (the Waterloo Monument, the Duke of York's memorial, the Houses of Parliament), he did receive the commission for the National Gallery, enhancing his reputation as a talented exponent of the Greek Revivalist style in England.

Before entering into more grandiose national undertakings, he had been practising his skills nearer home. He was responsible for restoring and adapting Norwich Castle as the city gaol in 1792-93 and extensively repaired the Cathedral in 1806. Between these two achievements, he built the new Ipswich theatre—on the same site as the old one in Tankard (now Tacket) Street. The money for it was raised in 1803 by subscription of 14 shares of £100 each. Much of the former structure was incorporated into the new building but Wilkins set his own stamp on the facade by adding heavy imposing colonnade along the street front; to a classical man, that touch was irresistible. The playhouse was spacious, attractive, elegant, encouraging the *Ipswich Journal* to voice a pious hope that "the spirited exertions of the proprietor" would meet with due reward.

Wilkins father and son were now deep in theatrical affairs and, so far, it suited them. But at Cambridge in 1802 they experienced for the first time the darker side of a patentee's responsibilities. Rowdyism was not a new problem at Stourbridge fair and Hindes's initiation into the Cambridge season was troublesome. He was forced to issue a warning: "Insults having been given by persons from the Gallery to Ladies and Gentlemen in the Boxes, *Notice is now given* that if they are repeated the Proprietor is determined to prosecute". The same high-spirited element in the audience next cried fire during the 1802 season and in the ensuing rush to get out of the booth, four people, three young girls and a young man were trampled to death. It was a ghastly prefiguring of "The Sadler's Wells Accident" when the London theatre was under Charles Dibdin's management in 1807. After a similar false alarm 19 people died in the stampede. In 1806 it was maliciously rumoured that Stourbridge theatre was unsafe. The company stayed away and Wilkins decided to demolish it to make way for a purpose-built playhouse at Barnwell nearby. In September, 1807, workmen pulling the theatre down had found it perfectly solid and capable of standing very much longer. Bowles in his opening address tried to make the best of the costly error by emphasising the previous theatre's inferiority:

"Too long our shapeless Theatre of wood,
A just reproach to taste and judgment stood."

Wilkins's neo-classical mark was stamped on Barnwell theatre as conspicuously as on Norwich, Ipswich and, later, Bury St Edmunds theatres. The *Cambridge Chronicle* noted: "The fronts of the boxes are painted in *Arabesque,* and the proscenium, which is supported by four *Giallo Antiquo* marble pilasters, is really simple and magnificent. The frieze is ornamented with figures in *rehaussée d'or,*

Representing Apollo and Minerva visiting the Muses . . . This theatre is the best provincial Theatre in the Kingdom".

Two years before his death, Wilkins secured a new thirty-year lease for the circuit theatres at £600 a year. Norwich was to be insured at £1,000; its machinery at £600, wardrobes at £400. By 1808, Wilkins junior had taken over Bury St Edmunds theatre and it was natural that when his father died at Newnham, Cambridge, in 1815, William II should inherit the circuit. His sisters, Willett, Emma and Harriett Wilkins, shared the legacy—"the Theatre Royal Norwich, the theatres of Ipswich and Barnwell, and all his rights in the Theatres Royal of Norwich, Yarmouth, Colchester, Bury St Edmunds or any other circuit theatre". Control of the entire circuit, a small empire, was now concentrated in the hands of one man.

Second Theatre Royal, Tacket Street, Ipswich. Though this plan was not drawn until 1876, it shows the theatre almost unchanged since it was built in 1802/3. Some of the material from the theatre it replaced was incorporated, the stage was greatly enlarged and an imposing colonnade was built along the street front. "Nothing omitted in the ornamental department that could conduce to its elegance", said the *Ipswich Journal.* Copied from a plan in the Suffolk Record Office, Ipswich.

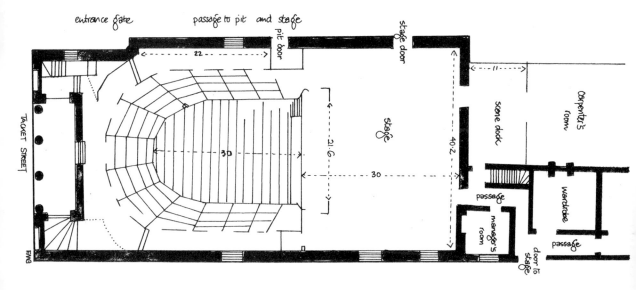

CHAPTER EIGHT

The Fisher Dynasty; or,
Life on the Inner Circuit

"The Fisher theatres were supported by all classes. Plays used to be 'bespoke', or, as it was understood, 'bespeak nights' took place, when the names of Lord Rendelsham, Berners, Suffield, Heniker, Sir Edward Kemson, Coke of Holkham, Villebois etc. would be found at the head of the bills; and the family of the patrons also in the theatre, with large parties from the mansions of the family. In fact the families of the counties from the very highest estate were the constant patrons of the theatre and I have recollections as a boy of dress-circles filled on occasions by persons of the highest distinction."
David Fisher III (1816-1887).

WHILE William Wilkins and his son steadily gathered a monopoly of the major theatres in the Norwich circuit, a one-time member of the company, David Fisher was developing his own group of actors, circuit and theatres in an undertaking which, in its way, outmatched anything the Norwich Company's proprietors had achieved. Most counties in England with an established circuit were also visited by groups of itinerant actors, though the "resident" company seldom tolerated simultaneous performances and often invoked the law to prohibit rivals. Norfolk and Suffolk had their share of assorted travelling entertainers. Occasionally, conflict broke out but most of the time the passing showmen secured their necessary licences—or unobtrusively got away with it—and rubbed along well enough with the "home" company, either by simply keeping out of their path or by offering very different fare. The public was considered by its magistrates as "harassed" only when the strollers trespassed too far and too often. They were treated by the resident company with a mixture of annoyance or wariness, their main threat lying in their potential for diverting audiences from "legitimate drama".

David Fisher's company, touring the smaller towns of Suffolk and Norfolk which had been dropped from the Norwich Company's schedule, soon placed itself on a different footing from the other minor companies such as Hounslow's, Coppins's, Atkin's or Eldred's which had all at some time sought regular or fleeting patronage in the eastern counties but were usually content to come and go. Fisher's was never from the outset operated as a strolling company. It was rooted in East Anglia. Like the Norwich Company, it was a permanent feature of social life, accumulating enormous respect, a tight-knit band of actors and a fixed route of towns. Most remarkable of all, Fisher built his own theatres. The inner circuit, as it was known, was run on ideally complementary lines to the main circuit, one dovetailing with the other in a

Miniature of Mary Fisher (1730-1819), mother of David Fisher I. The portrait, now owned by a direct descendant of the family, was probably painted by one of her actor grandsons. *Norfolk County Libraries*

David Fisher I (1760-1832), founding father of the Fisher theatrical dynasty, indefatigable theatre builder, head of the Norfolk and Suffolk Company of Comedians. *Norfolk County Libraries*

manner unique among country theatres. If it were not for the total independence of the Fisher contingent, East Anglian theatre at this time could have been described as served by a circuit within a circuit. The interlocking of the two concerns was so tight that it is impossible to follow the Norwich circuit without also running into Fisher's complementary activities.

David Fisher, a young Norwich carpenter,* began to attract attention in musical circles in the 1780s. He had a startlingly good voice which he exercised to greatest effect in patriotic sea songs. He was induced to join the Norwich Company as a singer and one of his first appearances on a playbill was in 1786 when he was mentioned as singing interludes. The theatrical milieu suited him. Giles Barrett, then the Norwich manager, offered him, as an amateur, the part of Lubin in "The Quaker". It was common practice to give aspiring members of the public an occasional chance to perform with the company. Most of the volunteers wer never heard of again. One or two were discovered. Barrett was so impressed with Fisher's performance that he urged him to take up acting as a profession. Two years earlier, in 1784, the new theatre at Beccles had been opened "by a Company of Comedians from the Theatres of London, Dublin, York and Edinburgh". This was the troupe led by William Scraggs, and David Fisher lost no time in joining them, believing it his most realistic opening to the stage. Scraggs was well-known in the locality: for 20 years he and his actors covered the

*The Fisher family tree is on page 119.

smaller towns in East Anglia. Except for the factual entries on playbills, little is recorded of his life, but a long, impressive torchlight procession followed his body to the graveside in Beccles churchyard in 1808.

By 1792 David Fisher had taken over the management of the company. Two years later, the new theatre at Bungay was opened "by Fisher and Company's Comedians" with the opera "The Duenna; or, the Double Elopement".

That same season, David Fisher excelled as "Don Juan"; among his stage colleagues were Paston, Glasington, Pratt, Stackwood, Miss Howard, Miss Jessup, Humphries, Worthington and Courtney. The company well knew the value of publicity but handbills were not always properly distributed and it was sometimes necessary to put these responsible on their mettle. A Bungay theatre playbill of 1811 headed "Fisher and Scraggs Co." contains the notice: "If Bills be not left at the Houses of the principal inhabitants of the adjacent villages, or within *six miles* of Bungay, Fisher and Scraggs (as they employ Persons for that purpose) would esteem it a favour to be made acquainted with such omissions".

After Scraggs's death, his son Robert Beeston Scraggs assumed partnership in the Fisher/Scraggs company, now known as "The Norfolk and Suffolk Company of Comedians". But in March, 1812, the *Norfolk Chronicle* reported: "The partnership between Messrs Fisher and Scraggs having expired, the theatre at Thetford was opened for the season commencing with the Assize week under the direction of Mr. Fisher only, with that success which diligence and long-established integrity merit". Shortly after this, it becomes clear that Robert Scraggs had gone independent. On 25th July, 1812, he is reported as having just ended a season at Holt. "There is ground to hope that the patronage which was so liberally conferred by the county on the late Mr. Scraggs, will be continued to his son and family." Scraggs rather pointedly

David Fisher II (1788-1858), actor, scene painter, musician, eldest son of David Fisher the theatre builder. The engraving was published in 1818 when David II was playing in London.

Norfolk County Libraries

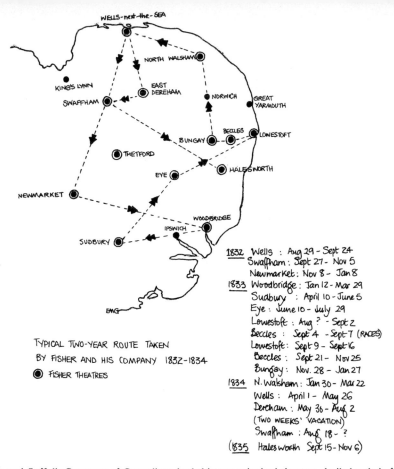

WELLS-next-the-SEA

NORTH WALSHAM

KING'S LYNN

EAST DEREHAM

SWAFFHAM

NORWICH

GREAT YARMOUTH

BECCLES LOWESTOFT

BUNGAY

THETFORD

HALESWORTH

EYE

NEWMARKET

WOODBRIDGE

IPSWICH

SUDBURY

EMG

TYPICAL TWO-YEAR ROUTE TAKEN
BY FISHER AND HIS COMPANY 1832-1834
⦿ FISHER THEATRES

1832   Wells   :   Aug 29 - Sept 24
      Swaffham : Sept 27 - Nov 5
      Newmarket : Nov 8 - Jan 8
1833   Woodbridge : Jan 12 - Mar 29
      Sudbury   :   April 10 - June 5
      Eye : June 10 - July 29
      Lowestoft : Aug ? - Sept 2
      Beccles : Sept 4 - Sept 7 (RACES)
      Lowestoft : Sept 9 - Sept 16
      Beccles : Sept 21 - Nov 25
      Bungay : Nov. 28 - Jan 27
1834   N. Walsham : Jan 30 - Mar 22
      Wells : April 1 - May 26
      Dereham : May 30 - Aug 2
      (TWO WEEKS' VACATION)
      Swaffham : Aug 18 - ?
(1835   Halesworth Sept 15 - Nov 6)

The Norfolk and Suffolk Company of Comedians had thirteen principal theatres, built by their founder David Fisher. In the course of two years they visited them all. The map shows their route from 1832-1834. Only Thetford had had to be abandoned, because the assizes had been transferred to Norwich in the early 1830s and without the influx of people the assizes brought theatricals were rather poorly supported.

advertised his company as "The Original Norfolk and Suffolk Company". The parting of the ways between the two men had perhaps been marked by only the stiff nod of civility.

David Fisher was called one of "nature's gentlemen". It was as easy for him to mingle with the nobility and gentry of the counties as to garner the respect and affection of poorer people. Generous patronage for his productions came from families like the Hennikers, the Berners, the Stradbrokes and the Huntingfields— people who gave not only their names and their occasional attendance, but who delightedly welcomed Fisher into their homes. He enjoyed their hospitality and their bespeaks; they took a genuine interest in his personal and professional pursuits. "As a manager he was highly esteemed," said the *Norfolk Chronicle* when he died, "as an actor he displayed much talent; in the strictest sense he was an honest, just and upright man."

Waggonloads of people from villages, hamlets and isolated farmsteads flocked into the inner circuit towns, their vehicles decorated with flowers. For the duration of Fisher and company's visit, towns were *en fete.*

David Fisher III, actor-grandson of the founding Fisher, wrote from his retirement in 1880: "The families of the counties from the very highest estate were the constant patrons of the theatre, and I have recollections as a boy of dress-circles filled on occasions by persons of the highest distinction. To look at the towns now, it could not be believed that families remained longer in the country then; *high prices* ruled up to the end of the war, and it was some time before the reaction set in and destroyed the little circuit; but the six or eight weeks of the visit of the company was a *gala* time. They played but four nights a week—Tuesdays and Fridays being devoted to *parties,* musical and otherwise."

Fisher's method of encouraging a taste for drama in the country was to send a pioneer or advance company to perform in any available building—a barn, inn room or yard. For a season or two he would return to the same place until he had been able to gauge public demand and test the temperature of his support. Then he would build a theatre, negotiating a central site where he was sure of being prominent in the town's social life. In this simple and methodical manner David Fisher studded East Anglia with twelve new theatres in the space of sixteen years (1812-1828) and established not so much a family as a dynasty of talented actors and theatre men who enriched the social life of the two counties in a more intimate and thorough going way than would ever have been possible if they had relied for dramatic entertainment on the Norwich Company alone.

Typically, the Fisher theatres were moderate-sized buildings with a steep sloping roof. Hard backless benches covered with green baize furnished gallery, boxes and pit alike. There were two "doors of entrance" facing the audience. A green baize curtain hung upstage of the doors, leaving a deep fore-stage.

Stage properties, scenery, costumes and other impedimenta were conveyed from town to town in three large waggons, each bearing six tons of goods and drawn by a team of six horses. At first Fisher's company acted in fitted-up places or existing theatres but as the circuit became more profitable Fisher began to design, build and, in many cases, equip his own theatres. His son, David II, was a clever scene-painter. He had studied the art in detail and had acquired, too, an excellent grasp of architectural principles and linear perspective. Fisher's third son, George decided to go into the printing business as a compositor with the express aim of producing the company's playbills. Almost every member of the family acted.

One of the many outstanding aspects of the company was their attention to detail in costume: there was a complete wardrobe for everything and everybody. But the real excellence of the Fisher wardrobe was its comedy period dress. "Old David" received costly presents of eighteenth century dresses from his upper class patrons and in addition bought old swords, quantities of wigs and expensive dresses from gentlemen's servants.

The high prices mentioned by David Fisher III were no deterrent to playgoers in the days when country people were prepared to stint themselves to afford "theatricals" perhaps once a year. Boxes were 4s, upper boxes 3s, pit 2s and gallery 1s. At these prices, the theatres held anything from £50-£70, depending on their size. Only during the few last struggling years were prices lowered—but never below 3s, 2s, 1s and 6d respectively.

The Fishers were a theatrical family to the core but they were conscious of a need to widen their interests beyond the stage. David Fisher I had always thought ahead of his contemporaries, particularly in education. He insisted on sending his four sons, David, Charles, Henry and George to a "classical school" near Cambridge. Their inherited natural gifts for acting he could work on himself but he decided to entrust to others the job of bringing his sons up to the mark academically. He hoped they might also acquire the social advantages lacking in a homespun environment. The Fisher boys were tutored in French and their inherited musical gifts brought to flower at an early age. Fisher proved at least as exacting a master in stagecraft. Almost from infancy his sons and daughter were schooled, both at their home in Dereham and on circuit throughout Norfolk and Suffolk, in singing, dancing, fencing, music and drama. Later on, their wives and their own children were to join the Fisher-weighted castlists. Among playbills for Halesworth Theatre in 1825 three generations of Fishers are listed in "The Celebrated and Grand Historical Play of 'William Tell'". During the winter season at Bungay in 1823, eight Fishers acted in "Othello". The following year "The Merchant of Venice" was another prodigious family affair. David Fisher II was Shylock; his father, Lorenzo; George Fisher, the Duke of Venice; Charles Fisher, Bassanio; Portia, Mrs Charles Fisher; Nerissa, Mrs George Fisher; and Jessica, Mrs J. Fisher (probably Sarah, the wife of David Fisher I's brother, John). The playbill came from the presses of George Fisher. Perhaps the most extravagant example of family involvement was on 20th December, 1823, when no fewer than nine Fishers appeared in "Ivanhoe".

Although most of the family participated, and the enterprise therefore tended to be monopolistic, the inner circuit was treated as a training ground for aspiring actors and many of the Fisher troupe who began playing modest roles to find their stagelegs moved on to more prestigious circuits, such as the Norwich-centred one, which offered an apprenticeship nearer to "the London boards". The Fisher family's corporate musical ability was almost as famed as its acting — David I was a fine singer; David II a violinist of repute, his younger brother Charles (1792-1869) a brilliant organist, cellist and singer. What is more, they proved extraordinarily interchangeable. During interludes at the theatre, as soon as the curtains came together Fisher actors transformed themselves (top-coats flung over their stage costumes) into Fisher musicians, went into the orchestra pit and supplied the *entr'acte* music—often minuets and trios from Haydn or Mozart symphonies. The four sons played the violin and before the death of Henry in early manhood they joined in quartets, changing the instruments round, two of them playing right-handed and two left-handed. In the very earliest Norwich music festivals, the names of the Fishers appear time and time again. During the 1839 Norfolk and Norwich Musical Festival six Fishers played in the orchestra for Handel's "Messiah". David III gave a hornpipe when he made his first stage appearance, at Bungay, aged eight.

The second child of David Fisher I and his wife Elizabeth was a daughter, also named Elizabeth. She made her debut on her father's stage, a beautiful, sensitive girl of great promise. When she died suddenly at eighteen, lavish poems were published in the local press enshrining her qualities:

> "Though now a lonely tenant of the tomb,
> Fairer than opening roses was thy bloom.
> Ah, who can paint the beauties of thine eye,
> Who on a parent's stage thy place supply?"

One of the few theatres David Fisher and his family visited regularly but which he did not build was at Halesworth in Suffolk. The townspeople had always responded exuberantly to drama, and usually of the sort provided by William Scraggs. He stayed for a ten-week season in October-December, 1784, playing on Tuesdays, Thursdays and Saturdays. Untroubled by opposition, Fisher and Scraggs visited the town in the days of their partnership but in 1808 an exceedingly

Fisher's Dereham Theatre, photographed in an advanced stage of neglect shortly before it was substantially rebuilt in 1935.   *Norfolk County Libraries*

Sudbury Theatre, copied in 1889 from an old un-
attributed sketch. The drawing is probably the early
theatre which David Fisher adapted for his Norfolk
and Suffolk Company of Comedians in 1814.

Suffolk Record Office, Ipswich

acrimonious controversy sprang up, led by a theatre-hating Methodist Minister, John
Dennant. The battle opened when Dennant delivered a sermon against the theatre
and announced from the pulpit that on Fisher's next visit to Halesworth he would
preach a sermon "On Theatrical Amusements and the impropriety of Professors of
Religion attending them". A pamphlet war began—the sheets printed and distributed
by two rival printers in the town—W. Harper, for the anti-theatre faction and
Thomas Tippell for the defence of plays and players. Dennant condemned plays for
their "love intrigues, blasphemous passions, profane discourses, lewd descriptions
and filthy jests", and considered the theatre "the resort of the most worthless
characters in existence". He was clearly condemning in ignorance; typical of the Fisher
company's inoffensive productions in 1808 was Thomas Holcroft's "The Road to
Ruin", the pantomimes "Harlequin" and "Mother Goose", "Town and Country", a
"melodrame" "Ella Rosenberg", "The Child of Nature" (Elizabeth Inchbald), "The
Blind Boy" (J. Kenney) and "Laugh When You Can" (Frederick Reynolds).
Dennant's opening salvo produced a defensive pamphlet *Audi Alteram Partem*
(Tippell) from Dr Morgan, a physician in the town. In reply came *Five Minutes
Intrusion on your time before you go to the Play*, written anonymously by Dennant.
Six days later, on 22nd September, Dennant again weighed in with *A Letter to the
Writer of an anonymous pamphlet in defence of plays*. Dr Morgan rose to the bait,
and Dennant again went into print on 8th October. At this point a new contender
entered the arena—Mr P. Jermyn, an attorney, published *The Halesworth Review
from 14th September to 14th October 1808*. It came from the Tippell presses and
purported to review the first four pamphlets but with a Tippell and pro-stage bias.
The *Review* was in fact a passionate denunciation of "these geese of the temple of

96

Puritanism", who "hear not a playbill move but they cackle the alarm; their preachers froth in the rage of declamation and roar in the agonies of zeal". If prostitutes ("the daughter of Venus") were driven from the theatre, he suggested, they would go into the streets—even to the doors of Mr Dennant "and, perhaps (oh! thou conscious moon forbid it!) triumph over even his chastity". This absurdly partial personal attack was circulated with relish in both camps.

A Mrs Douglas offered the first verse contribution with *Stanzas Objurgatory and Interrogatory*, printed by Tippell and quickly followed by the poet John Hugman's *The Halesworth Dunciad* from the same printer. David Fisher, whose innocent amusements had ignited this incredible blaze of prejudice, characteristically produced a song on the pamphlets already published. It was printed as a broadside by Tippell and, naturally, sung on stage. The company discovered they had a useful advocate in the Reverend Mr Scot, a Catholic priest at Thorington Hall who submitted a letter in verse, again from Tippell's establishment.

They were heated weeks, generating more bitterness than enlightenment. *The Halesworth Dunciad Anatomized* was next thrust upon a bemused public, and a farmer called Thornby from Wenhaston (a member of Dennant's congregation) offered *Gentle Strictures on the Halesworth Review*; both were printed by Harper. Hugman slipped in two more pamphlets in verse and Jermyn brought out the second and last issue of *The Halesworth Review, 14th October to 14th November, 1808*. Dennant it appears, had the final shot with *A Poem . . . or a satire on vanity dogmatism and malice*, dated 28th November, 1808. In reality, the victory was Fisher's—when the hubbub had died down he returned. Perhaps significantly, Halesworth was one of the few inner circuit towns never to have a Fisher-built theatre. Halesworth theatre was used until 1846 for plays. It later became a rifle hall and was finally put to use for concerts and lectures.

Fisher's spate of theatre construction began in 1812 with the successful little playhouse at Wells-next-the-Sea in Norfolk. For a small coastal fishing village, Wells had an unusually big dramatic following. The *Golden Fleece Inn*, long established as a venue for players, managed to draw other companies of actors even after the Fisher theatre was built; and there is evidence that Twiddy and his troupe used the Fisher building when the family players were working other parts of the circuit.

Many bespeak performances at Wells went under the banner of the Coke family, the Earl and Countess of Leicester, of Holkham Hall. In some of the Holkham Hall cash books payments are recorded to the Fisher family—£10 for a bespeak on 7th August, 1838; £5 for the tenants and servants to attend on 27th July, 1840; a donation of £20 on 17th May, 1844.

After the Fisher company was disbanded in 1844 (Wells was one of the last theatres the comedians played in) the steep-roofed theatre was eventually converted into three cottages. Nothing now remains of them. The site is a car park and the only vestige of theatrical connection, as in so many "Fisher towns" today, is the name plate "Theatre Street".

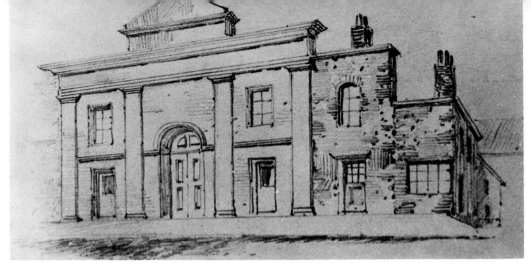

Bungay Theatre, built by Fisher in 1828.   *Suffolk Record Office, Ipswich*

Fisher straddled both Norfolk and Suffolk. He saw excellent potential in Woodbridge, Suffolk, and selected in 1814 a plot near the barracks, one time part of the premises of the *Angel* inn. There was no impressive frontage in Bridewell Street and an entrance to the theatre was constructed down a long passage—which can be seen in Theatre Street today.

Woodbridge's fancifully-gabled shire hall had in the early days doubled as a theatre and this is where Scraggs's company performed in the latter part of the eighteenth century. It also served for the Norwich Company while they were still covering minor towns.

David Fisher spared no cost on Woodbridge Theatre: it was one of his more elaborate projects. He drew up his own plans for a deep stage, fitted with traps and proscenium doors, flanked by two tiers of boxes, a large pit and elegant gallery. David II was naturally commandeered to paint the scenery. For a capital outlay of £2,000 (£70 to £80 could be taken a night with capacity audiences) it was indeed grander than most of the Fisher theatres but became a basic model for all of them.

5th February, 1814, was appallingly inhospitable for an opening night. A cold thaw had started, making the place dismally damp. The audience was consequently thin. A report of the event remarked: "the House is lighted with Liverpool lamps, illuminators which, as is obvious at the Ipswich Theatre, require more attention, to give them their full effect". Fortunately, the setback was brief. Within weeks there were accounts of excellent bespeaks from "some of the first families in the neighbourhood". In 1829 an proscenium was added with imitation marble pillars, full-length statues, a drop curtain and new front scenery designed by a Drury Lane artist. More care was lavished on Woodbridge than any other theatre save perhaps the one at Dereham. In both towns the Fishers had homes. David Fisher's wife, Elizabeth, died at Woodbridge in 1814, just after the theatre was opened, and her son David II lived and died there. Woodbridge also attained a legendary significance in local theatrical circles as the place from which Charles Gill set off on a sensational elopement with the actress Miss Vining. The poet Edward Fitzgerald wrote to William Bodham Donne from Woodbridge in March 1846: "We have actors now at Woodbridge. A Mr. Gill, who was low comedian in the Norwich, now manages a troop of his own here. His wife was a Miss Vining; she is a pretty woman and a lively pleasant actress, not vulgar. I have been to see some of the old comedies with great pleasure, and last night I sat in a pigeon hole with David Fisher and 'revolved many Memories' of old days and old plays". The occasion would have been understandably nostalgic for by this time the circuit had broken up, the theatre had been empty for a year, and Gill was trying to keep drama alight, against heavy odds. A decade later, the theatre was in real decline and Ipswich Elocution Society moved in. It became a warehouse in 1861, later a school and finally an auction room.

A town as consistently patronised as Eye was another obvious asset for the inner circuit and on 19th June, 1815, a Fisher theatre was opened there "with great éclat". "The convenience, comfort and general appearance of the house which was built from a design of Mr. D. Fisher and under his immediate direction are much approved. And the machinery and decorations executed by that gentleman himself are of superior order. The company are highly respectable". David Fisher II, "who is allowed to possess very superior qualifications for the stage in general". had been applauded at Eye as Richard III. People wrote to the local paper about his talents. "I prophecy," said one correspondent extravagantly, "with no inconsiderable share of reason, this young man will ere long reap the harvest of his merit, and the need of his high, histrionic genius, beneath the eye of a *Metropolitan* audience, amidst the simultaneous and electrifying thunder of spontaneous approbation." Eye theatre struggled on as a playhouse until 1850—but was afterwards let for meetings, exhibitions and concerts. There was a brief return to drama in 1870 but the building afterwards became a

Bungay Theatre under new management. Despite its various changes of use, the building has kept its Fisher facade almost unchanged.

Author's collection

furniture store. It still stands in Magdalen Street, a neat, red-brick edifice, now a motor spares shop adjoining a garage.

Although Thetford in Norfolk was a popular circuit town for the Norfolk and Suffolk comedians, David Fisher appears to have been content to adapt the existing theatre in White Hart Lane. But whatever was incorporated of the old building, the theatre facade as it stands today certainly bears something of the Fisher imprint. A typical Fisher-Scraggs playbill, headed "Theatre, Thetford", is preserved at the Ancient House Museum (opposite the theatre) and shows that although the two men were still in partnership, the Fisher family contingent was beginning to dominate the cast lists:

Fisher and Scraggs' Company
on Tuesday, March 21st, 1809
will be presented a Comedy, called

The Marriage Promise

Merton, Mr REYMES
Sidney, Mr MOLESWORTH—Consols, Mr PASTEN
Tandem, Mr FISHER
George Howard, Mr C FISHER—Policy, Mr SCRAGGS
Farmer Woodland Mr J. FISHER
Jeffries Mr HIGH—Bailiff Mr J. SCRAGGS
Thomas, Mr POINTER
Mrs Howard, Miss NEWMAN—Mrs Hervey, Mrs HIGH
Emma Mrs SCRAGGS
Mary Woodland, Mrs G. FISHER

To which will be added a MELO DRAME, in three Acts, called
ELLA ROSENBERG
[this cast list included 3 male Fishers and Mrs Fisher, who
played Ella Rosenberg, as well as Mr and Mrs Scraggs]

to begin at 7 o'clock
Tickets to be had at the Inns, of Mr Fisher,
Mrs Scraggs and Mr Mills.
Boxes 3s, Upper Boxes 2s 6d, Pit 2s, Gallery 1s,
second prices boxes 2s [?—figure damaged]
pit 1s. Children under ten years boxes 2s, pit 1s 6d.
Gallery 1s.

J. Fisher, Printer

It is possible that Henry Crabb Robinson, the Suffolk-born lawyer and man of letters, may have been referring impatiently to the Fisher company (though if he is he inaccurately calls them "strollers") when he wrote from Thetford on 29th March, 1827:

Former Fisher theatre in White Hart Lane, Thetford, with typical steep Fisher roof. The cheek-by-jowl door and window arrangement is referred to as "the old ticket office". *Author's collection*

"A set of strollers acted *Othello* and a very ridiculous and even comical exhibition it was—An amateur of celebrity enacted Iago egregiously—Othello a ranter in worst taste, but who now and then stumbled on the right feeling and expression—the Iago not once—I could not sit out the farce, though one or two of the low parts were decently played—Comic talent is a drug compared with tragic capabilities."

He was, after all, fed almost exclusively on a diet of Drury Lane.

Drama in Thetford was curtailed far sooner than in the other country towns for in 1833 the crowd-pulling assizes were transferred to Norwich and after this the Fishers found it unworthwhile to call.

Six or eight Italian marble busts are said to have decorated the parapet of the theatre in Fisher's day. The originals were brought from Italy by the Earl of Arlington in the seventeenth century, together with a marble staircase. These figures (or copies of them) later passed into the hands of "a private gentleman" and were eventually transferred to embellish the theatre. After Thetford theatre closed, they were acquired as an interior decorative feature of a house in Wells Street, Thetford, and later still became the property of a stone and marble mason in the town, W. Sharpe. By 1870 four of the busts were in the possession of a land agent, Thomas Fisher Salter of Attleborough. Now only two of the figures exist in Thetford—Tiberius and Othone—at the Ancient House Museum.

A. Leigh Hunt wrote in *The Capital of East Anglia* (1870): "Six of these [busts] were, until recently, in the town and two are still remaining. One is believed to be the bust of the Emperor Nero, and the other of Roscius, the great Roman actor, to whom Shakespeare alludes in the tragedy of *Hamlet* in the lines beginning: 'When Roscius was an actor at Rome'. The figures are exceedingly well sculptured in Italian marble, evidently by an accomplished sculptor . . .". Though old, Tiberius and Othone do not

Remnants of the Fisher theatre in Theatre Street, Swaffham. The original walls still stand but the corrugated roof was fitted after a serious fire in 1928.
Author's collection

appear to be products of the seventeenth century and it is possible that Fisher had the Earl of Arlington's figures copied for the frontage of his theatre.

On 16th July, 1816, the *Norfolk Chronicle* announced that a new theatre had been completed at East Dereham for the Norfolk and Suffolk Company. "It is fitted up in a style of neatness and elegance scarcely to be met with in any Country Town. The painting and decorating of the interior were executed by Mr D Fisher, Jnr., to whose known taste they do ample credit." Dereham was the Fishers' home town and became the headquarters of the company. Next to the theatre, Fisher built a spacious house capable of accommodating most of his large family of actors and musicians when they were in town. They could walk more or less from their drawing room straight onto the Dereham stage.

When a group of actors and Fisher descendants gathered to put up a new headstone at David Fisher's Dereham grave in 1933, they also made a pilgrimage to his theatre. They found it "derelict and forlorn". Two nostalgic special performances by David Fisher III and David IV had been given long after the company had disbanded, but the place was beyond revival. Although Dereham theatre was used for drama longer than any other playhouses of the inner circuit, it was gradually falling into disrepair. In 1912 it became a drill hall. In 1935 it was extensively rebuilt and made almost unrecognisable as anything other than a functional public hall. All the scenes and trappings were removed, its walls were rendered, giving it a blank, characterless appearance and it lost all its Fisher features. The last useful years of the theatre had been spent as a junior school but when the children were transferred to another school it stood neglected. In April, 1977, the building was demolished to make way for surgeries. As workmen stripped it down to its foundations, they uncovered Fisher's raked auditorium floor and the curved footings where the boxes stood.

The next strategic mid-Suffolk town Fisher aimed for was Sudbury. Fisher and Scraggs when in partnership had enjoyed good takings there in the 1790s. In the seventeenth century the upper room of the Moot Hall doubled as a theatre and council chamber, as well as being, on occasion, parish room and Sessions Court. So much damage was done by players and audiences there that plays were eventually banned altogether. "Muche ruyn and decaye by means of divers disordered and unrulie persons resortinge thither to playes of interludes and other playes" had driven away patronage and players took refuge in a barn. In 1814, a new theatre was built in Friars Street by T. Jones. Three years later it was put up for auction, described as "spacious, substantial, and commodious . . . partly brick-built, with stage, dressing and reading rooms capable for a trifling expence to be fitted up in a handsome manner". The theatre was sold to David Fisher who had for a good many years been its principal tenant. More than likely Fisher began to remodel it to suit his own tastes; certainly David Fisher III has no hesitation in listing Sudbury as one of the theatres *built* by his grandfather. It was finally refused a licence in 1847, the equipment was sold and the theatre was pulled down in 1848.

The annual races at Beccles had made the town a natural resort for players from at least the early eighteenth century. The Norwich Company are recorded as having enjoyed a splendid August season there in 1761, performing at the town hall.

The corporation had taken a liberal attitude to the stage and recognised that a playhouse would "conduce to the benefit, advantage and prosperity of the town". Their enlightenment was repaid by the diligent attention Beccles received from several groups of players—Hounslow's, Scraggs's, Fisher-Scraggs's and, in 1819, from David Fisher, who built a new theatre in Sheepgate Street, behind Queen's Square and returned to it for two or three months every two years. Beccles at this time had a population of some 3,000 and an entertainment-loving public. In 1814 Fisher had converted the £18 proceeds from "The West Indian" into 3d loaves which were distributed by churchwardens for the relief of 1,300 poor people of Beccles "during a very inclement season". It was a typical gesture.

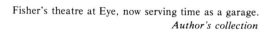

Fisher's theatre at Eye, now serving time as a garage.
Author's collection

Members of the Fisher family were born at various towns all over Norfolk and Suffolk, according to where the company happened to be performing. It was while his parents were on circuit in Beccles that Charles Fisher II, who was later to become a prominent actor in New York, made his first appearance, as they said, on the stage of life. The Fisher theatre at Beccles was disposed of in 1844 and was converted into a corn exchange. Later it was substantially rebuilt. Part of it is incorporated into the present Lloyds Bank, but none of the exterior remains.

Wherever Fisher could acquire an existing theatre he did so, usually converting it to conform to the pattern he found successful elsewhere. Swaffham suited his needs admirably and he bought the playhouse there in 1822 and virtually rebuilt it for £800. The town had become the centre of a coterie of rural aristocracy, a fashionable provincial society, self-sufficient and assured. Its stage pedigree, too, was excellent.

A leading spirit was the Reverend William Yonge, not a man to let his calling interfere with pleasure-seeking. Plays were one of his pleasures. A box flanking the stage in the pre-Fisher theatre at Swaffham was reserved as the Vicarage Box for Yonge and his family, in much the same manner as the Fisher family might have had a box pew reserved for them in Swaffham church. James Hooper wrote: "The theatre was run regularly for a few weeks each summer, and there was a very fair company. Pleasure-loving clergy of neighbouring parishes preferred to live in gay Swaffham". Swaffham Theatre was probably the last place to house the Fisher company: there is a playbill for as late as 20th November, 1844, the year the circuit folded.

Not only is there still a Theatre Street in Swaffham, but the remnants of the Fisher theatre, now heavily disguised as a garage. After its heyday, it sank to the role of building store. In 1911 it was extended to form a Roman Catholic Church. Eventually, like Eye theatre, it was converted into a garage. Although badly damaged in a fire in 1928, the shell and upper facade of the old building is still recognisable. When new petrol tanks were installed under the floor some years ago, the stage traps came to light and, alongside them, trenches filled with hundreds of oyster shells.

It was probably after building at Swaffham that David Fisher turned his attention to Newmarket. His grandson wrote emphatically that Newmarket was a Fisher theatre, but no date can be assigned to it. Gardner's *Directory of 1851* describes "a small Theatre in the High-street, seldom used for theatrical purposes; this was formerly The Royal Cockpit". There is evidence that in 1823 plays were still being performed in a cockpit in Newmarket but the Fisher theatre, whether an adaptation of that cockpit or a new design, may have been built soon after.

Three more theatres followed rapidly—Lowestoft, about which little is known, in 1827, and North Walsham and Bungay in 1828. Bungay had traditionally put drama high on its scale of social priorities. Its "Great Theatrical Booth" was used by the Norwich Company of Comedians during the fair and races, was taken over by Scraggs and was eventually played almost solely by the Fishers. In 1773 the Norwich Company arranged with a local speculator, Nathanial Godbold, to rent the new red-brick four-storey theatre he had built in Castle Yard and they opened there in June with

Lloyds Bank, Beccles, is the site of the old Fisher theatre. The theatre was disposed of in 1844, the year the company broke up. Fisher's theatrical partner, William Scraggs, is buried at Beccles.

Author's collection

"Who's the Dupe?" One of the playbills which has been preserved in the little museum at Bungay reads: "The manager, in soliciting the attendance of the Public, begs to inform them that no pains have been spared to render the Theatre fit for their reception. The Ladies need not be under any apprehension of injuring their dresses or of suffocation, as the Spiders have had legal notice to quit, and the Theatre is in an excellent state of Ventillation.

No potato Cans or Smoking allowed in the Pit. Peace officers in attendance.

Boxes 4s, Upper boxes 2s 9d, Pit 2s 3d, Gallery 1s".

Fisher's theatre at Bungay was built near the Cornhill and the first night in February, 1828, was a brilliant, crowded occasion, reputedly as thick with gentry as with labourers. The building was converted into a corn exchange in 1843, then became a cinema. It did long service as a laundry and is now occupied by Bungay Textiles. The original facade is unmistakably a Fisher design.

As Fisher theatres went, North Walsham's was an expensive project. It cost £1,800 and probably represented the smallest return on investment of any. Less than twenty years later, in 1845, it was sold for £400. On the grand opening night, 6th May, 1828, Charles Fisher gave a recital in which he recalled the draughty old premises the players had been used to in North Walsham:

"When two years since on the same spot we met
In cold clay walls, with roof of thatch ye sat".

It was common belief that David Fisher had made his own and his family's fortune by building theatres in the eastern counties. People supposed that he had grown fat on these enterprises, that rich patrons made for rich managers and that having a company conspicuously overloaded with his own kith and kin gave him the excuse to economise on salaries. Fisher certainly possessed a head for business but he was not ruled by it. It was of no use to him beyond the practicalities of choosing where and how to build, of expanding his company, fixing routes and selecting plays that were going to attract good houses.

As his capital grew, he ploughed it back into more theatres, more improvements, more repairs, better salaries. He was incapable of amassing wealth, even if he had wanted to; profits were for spending. He left nothing. When he died in 1832—and he held on as manager right to the end, with all the theatres under his name—he had a grand funeral in Dereham—not grand because of any extravagance on the part of his family, but by virtue of the scores of carriages from appreciative patrons in the neighbourhood. They formed a procession a quarter of a mile long.

The survivors: Otho and Tiberius, two of the six Roman emperors whose busts are reputed to have decorated the Fisher theatre at Thetford. Mossy and unregarded, they now lodge in a garden plot attached to The Ancient House Museum at Thetford, opposite the scene of their former glory. They are to be cleaned up and given a place inside the museum. *Author's collection*

CHAPTER NINE

Second Generation; or,
Men of Many Parts

"Our theatre now began to be less flourishing, in common with all Theatres; and this state of declension had gradually increased from the commencement of the general Peace, which was proclaimed in London on June 20, 1814. Indeed, as far as my experience goes, Theatres prosper most during war . . . There is a tide in the affairs of Theatres, as well as in those of Men—and our tide had turned . . . We dropped the Curtain, on the last night chopfallen; we had not been used to such reverses, and their novelty made them all the more irksome." Charles Dibdin the Younger , of Sadler's Wells.

THERE was little to distinguish the type of plays put on by the Fisher circuit and the sort of fare the Norwich Company of Comedians were offering in the early nineteenth century. David Fisher had always held Garrick as his model, he had a sincere reverence for Shakespeare and he enjoyed staging Restoration drama which made dazzling use of his exceptionally fine wardrobes. The popular taste for melodrama could not be ignored and nor could an equally strong prediliction for sentimental pieces. Nothing would be easier than to take a dismissive view of the dramatic pabulum of Fisher's day, of Barrett's or of Brunton's. Their companies' style of acting, although it had made some few concessions to naturalism since the old declamatory ranting, would undoubtedly seem artificial or "ham" to modern audiences. A theatre-goer who saw the Fishers on stage in his boyhood wrote in 1880: "I thought then that they played superbly, although to modern tastes the performances might nowadays appear mediocre". There are a few such first-hand accounts, the impatient judgement of Henry Crabb Robinson at provincial efforts; the frustrations of Macready when on tour in the country; and the success of certain "country" actors (David Fisher II included) on the London stage is well documented. But the problem remains of discovering any kind of adequate yardstick by which to measure standards of performance. Audience reaction was often exaggerated since newspaper reports were seldom totally disinterested. The most that can be said with certainty of the Fishers is that their public was with them. They were popular entertainers with professional skills—they claimed no more and no less for themselves. At the beginning of this century there were still people alive who knew David Fisher II in his prime. A Harleston theatre-goer (who was taught dancing and the violin by the actor) recalled: "I used to go to the Theatre at Bungay, where I saw him as Macbeth, as Massarene in 'The Brigands', and as William in 'Black-Eyed Susan', and no

Charles Fisher II as Falstaff in "The Merry Wives of Windsor", one of his favourite roles. He was photographed in the part in New York in 1872.

Norfolk County Libraries

Actor in the old style: Charles Fisher II (1816-1891). After the family circuit collapsed, Charles joined the Norwich Company. He went to America in 1852 and joined Daly's company there in 1872. His stage manner was described as "that of elaborate and diversified artifice".

Norfolk County Libraries

performances I have ever seen call up such vivid recollections of enjoyment—it all seemed so real to a boy. He came to see my father at the *Tuns Inn* after the performance, and I still remember with what feelings of awe I beheld that he still had under his overcoat the same dress that he wore when Macduff gave him his quietus".

Most of the well-known Shakespeare plays were in their repertory, as were those of Massinger and Beaumont and Fletcher. Their stock pieces included comedies such as "The Way to Keep Him" (Arthur Murphy), "The Rivals", "The School for Scandal", "The Road to Ruin" (Thomas Holcroft) and other plays which were being seen in London theatres. Popular farces were gaining ground, and melodramas such as "The Floating Beacon" by Fitzball drew big audiences. A contributor to *The Theatre*, 1st April, 1880, recounts: "I have seen David Fisher II play Hamlet, Richard III, Macbeth, Sir Giles Overreach in 'A New Way to Pay Old Debts', and the chief character in 'Rule a Wife and Have a Wife' as well as Jaffier in Otway's 'Venice Preserved', and 'The Stranger', he being supported by his brother Charles in the leading walking gentleman's parts in each, as Laertes, Richmond, Macduff, Wellborn, the Copper Captain, and Pierre. I have seen the two brothers alternate Othello and Iago, and the one play Romeo to the other's Mercutio. In comedy the elder took the heavier and the younger the lighter parts; the former, in Sheridan's creations, being Falkland and Joseph Surface; and the latter Charles Surface and Captain Absolute". At North Walsham on 5th January, 1818, it was announced: "positively the last night, Shakespeare's celebrated tragedy of 'Richard the 3rd'". Nine of the family were in the cast and at the end of the performance they invited the audience to a "farewell and parting glass". One can only ask, as James Carver did in his excellent paper on the Fishers read at the Norwich Science Gossip Club in 1909: "Is it not extraordinary that these performances could be made to pay in a town like North Walsham even for a month?"

The David Fisher enumerated in so many prominent roles was the second David, born in 1788, a marvellously gifted man—as artist, musician and actor. In his early days with his father's company he played the fiddle in the overture and then appeared in every act of Hamlet—probably *as* Hamlet—finally taking the part of Dr O'Toole in Butler's farce "The Irish Tutor". In provincial circles, his talents were so outstanding that friends encouraged him to try his luck in London. As the *Norfolk Chronicle* of 3rd October, 1818, reported: "On Thursday se'nnight Mr David Fisher commenced his engagement at *Drury Lane Theatre* and made his first appearance for the season as Jaffer [sic] in 'Venice Preserved'. We have received a letter from a gentleman who was present in which he says that the applause Mr Fisher received was general and even vehement. The play was loudly called for again and it was repeated on the Saturday following". One of the morning papers pronounced him the best Jaffier that ever appeared there. He was put through other substantial parts and was not only compared favourably to Edmund Kean (it was natural that he should be, for Kean was ill at the time and Fisher was filling the gap) but was put forward by the press and theatre pundits as a serious rival to the great actor. The *Ladies Monthly*

Museum of 1817 was less eulogistic about Fisher's performances: "Mr David Fisher performed the character of Richard III in a respectable manner; he is not without requisites for the stage; but has not sufficient discrimination to portray the craft, duplicity, ambition and courage of the relentless tyrant . . . However, if he is not likely to become a first-rate actor, he may be made a useful one". The *Norfolk Chronicle*, in the familiar language of local-boy-makes-good, mentioned David II several times that year, imparting the news that Fisher had performed so excellently in the title parts of Hamlet, Macbeth and Richard III, that the Drury Lane managers were engaging him "at a liberal salary" for a further season. Naturally he became sought-after on his home ground like any other London star and was soon secured by the Norwich Company to appear as Hamlet.

Suddenly, mid-way through his second London season Fisher broke contract and returned to Norfolk. The reasons were undoubtedly more pressing and complex than has ever been recorded. The day after Christmas, 1818, his wife had died at their London home. She was only twenty-nine, and they had been married little more than three years. David was not equal to coping with his two young children, David and Elizabeth, as well as a demanding career. His family successfully entreated him to return: his talents were being missed and all was not well on the circuit. Six years later, on 15th December, 1824, Fisher married again. His wife was Sarah Howard of Dereham.

Before either of his marriages he had a love affair with an aristocratic local girl, Mary Wilson, daughter of the fourth Baron Berners. David Fisher was a personable young man, greatly attractive to and attracted by women. F. C. Burton, of Norwich, last survivor of the Norfolk and Suffolk Company of Comedians, wrote of David II in 1907: "I saw him about the year 1844. He was then a very handsome man, curly hair, blue eyes, florid complexion and a jovial temperament . . . The little I know of the love affair between him and the Hon. Miss Wilson was obtained second-hand from old members of the company. It was stated, and I have no reason to doubt it, that she remained single all her life and took care of her old lover till he died. David was almost forced to marry a person he did not like in order prevent any future trouble with Miss Wilson. There was no doubt a sincere though romantic attachment to the handsome young actor, and it even went so far that an elopement was contemplated and nearly carried out, but both fathers interfered and the young couple were separated, but the lady remained true to the last." She looked after him in his old age after the death of his second wife, outliving him by sixteen years. Their graves are side by side at Woodbridge, where both died.

It was from Woodbridge that David Fisher, just married for the second time and firmly back on the family circuit, wrote to his uncle, Thomas Sadler, to ask him to assist in ensuring that his costume box reached King's Lynn in time for his appearance there. Part of any respectable actor's stock in trade was his own set of costumes, particularly for his favourite roles. Even actors dependent on the often shabby wardrobes of provincial theatres would carry with them certain wigs, hats,

Backstage at Daly's: Augustin Daly reads a new play to his company. Charles Fisher II, a prominent member of the company in America, is on the left of the lamp. This is one of very few early photographs in which the subjects are not staring straight at the camera.

rings, daggers or other accoutrements. Transport of the bulkier items was always a particular headache. Although everyday enough in itself, Fisher's letter has a three-fold interest. It has been preserved and is now in the possession of Mrs Kitty Shaw, David Fisher II's great-great-granddaughter; it illustrates the winning, humorous and spontaneous nature of Fisher himself, and it demonstrates the kind of obstacle race actors faced in getting their stage chattels transported from place to place. The letter is dated Woodbridge, 23rd February, 1825, and was despatched to Norwich where Sadler had a grocer's shop near St Giles's Church.

"Dear Uncle,

You know very well you never behold my beautiful handwriting but when I want to Bother you about something or other—The present is no exception to the above Rule—But I am in a hurry therefore to Business—I am going to exhibit my sweet person on the *Lynn Boards next Monday*—It will be necessary that I should have the wherewithal to decorate, etc etc. I have therefore sent of a large Box this morning per carrier to Norwich—he puts up at the Pope's Head, St. Peter's—at least so they tell me—Now they also tell me there is a waggon from the aforesaid Pope's Head to Lynn on the Saturday Afternoon—Now my request to you is that you would be so kind as to see that the said Box is safely deposited in the aforesaid Lynn Waggon, provided it can be conveyed to Lynn and arrive there to a certainty on the Monday by two or three o'clock—that is to say, in time for me to get my dress out and air it in time for the Evening Performance. Unless the Waggoner can faithfully promise that he always arrives at Lynn at the said time I know not what to do!

I must have my box there—that is a *sine qua non!* It must be there—This is the most inconvenient place in the whole circuit for conveyances, but I must have my Box—Therefore if the said Waggoner does not arrive at Lynn in time will you form some bargain with him to send a man and cart (with a horse in it) on to Lynn from some (the nearest place he can to Lynn) place where it stops? I know of no other plan. I *must* have my Box, and so I must not mind a guinea or two if it must be so, for I must have my Box. I have no doubt but you understand my meaning though it is rather strangely as well as hastily expressed. You understand and know the carriers etc. etc. Therefore I will leave the Business to your superior judgement.

I am sorry to give you the trouble, but I have no other means of at all ensuring the arrival of my goods and Chattels in time for the Market. Adieu. All well. Love to all. Yours ever obliged and all that and everything in the world and so forth,

D. Fisher, Junr."

It was to Thomas Sadler, together with William Weatherby of Newmarket, that David Fisher senior willed "all and every my Theatres". The management of the theatres naturally remained with his sons. However, it was not David II who took the reins. The assumption among members of the company that there had been a feud between David and Charles (because Fisher was supposed to have settled the larger share of the management on the elder brother) was discredited in 1880 when David III gave his version of events: "The supposed quarrel between the brothers David and Charles never took place. There could be no such arrangement of the management. The brothers both received a salary and good benefit terms. My father left the stage entirely in 1831, and my grandfather dying the following year, the management devolved on Charles; my father, in fact, although the eldest son, never having been the manager." David Fisher II became a music master at Great Yarmouth and retired to Woodbridge in 1838, aged fifty.

Even before his succession, Charles Fisher had been used to checking the company's takings and later he was in charge of salaries. In his record book he frequently accompanied an unusual night's turn out—good or bad—with a few notes explaining the cause. Charles was also, as sole manager in the months between his brother's voluntary change of career and his father's death, responsible for hiring, firing and acquiring new plays. On 4th May, 1832, he writes from North Walsham to Kennett of Covent Garden, who had offered him a piece called "May Queen": "If this delay has prevented or retarded your disposal of the 'May Queen'," he tells Kennett, "I will take it, but if otherwise I would rather decline it for the present, having several pieces as yet unproduced—If my memory does not deceive me I ordered the piece on

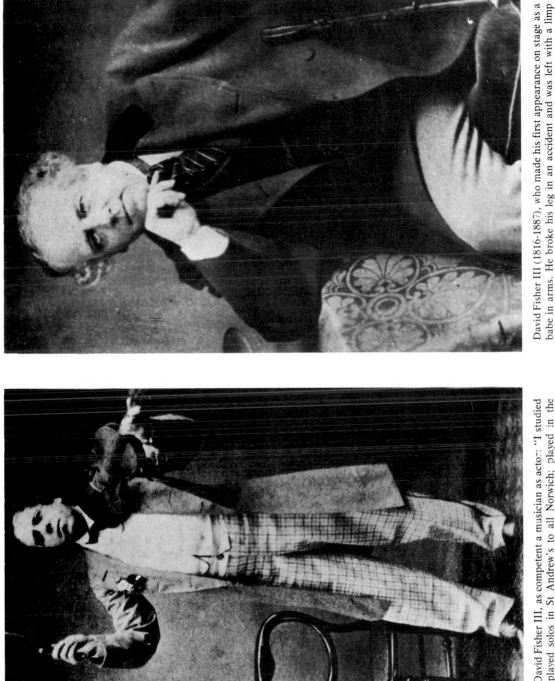

The young David Fisher III, as competent a musician as actor: "I studied the violin; played solos in St Andrew's to all Norwich; played in the orchestra under Benedict and Spohr."

David Fisher III (1816-1887), who made his first appearance on stage as a babe in arms. He broke his leg in an accident and was left with a limp which seemed as though it would finish his stage career, but he recovered to pursue as active a theatrical life as his father and grandfather—first in Norwich, then in Glasgow and London.

the supposition of its being a published one—I shall bear it in mind, and when the stock of pieces I have now on hand are disposed of by representation, shall most probably order it in Ms if not published by that time." Kennett also inquired whether the Fishers had a vacancy for a young actor. Charles replied that he had someone similar to the description of the applicant already and graciously declined.

By now the third David, David Nunn Fisher, was appearing as a promising and musically gifted boy with the Norfolk and Suffolk Company. In later years he offered his own synopsis of his career: "When my father left the stage in 1831, I, a boy, went with him to teach music. I studied the violin; played solos in St. Andrew's to all Norwich; played in the orchestra under Benedict, Spohr, etc. An accident, by which I broke my leg, seemed to banish me from the stage, but on recovery I joined Glover at Glasgow at the *Prince's Theatre*. I obtained for my uncle Charles [Charles I] the engagement with Glover, where he remained for 20 years, dying at his post. From Glasgow I came to town in 1853." Behind these laconic details lies a career at least as remarkable as that of his father, grandfather or uncles. In 1833 he appeared at Norwich Corn Exchange in selections from the Oratorios of "The Creation" and "Samson". The local press hailed his violin concerto as the high point of the evening. "With the exception of Paganini, Kieswelter, and Mori, no such violin-playing has been heard within our walls." His four years in Glasgow enabled him to progress with distinction to the Princess's Theatre, in London, then under the management of Charles Kean. It was chiefly as a musician, however, that David Fisher III benefited the family circuit in the difficult 1830s.

His uncle, Charles I, proved himself in these precarious years a competent and practical manager if not a brilliant one. His first love was not drama but music and if the theatre into which he was born had offered less scope for singing, playing and composition, he would almost certainly had chosen a musical career. At one point, he thought hard about leaving the stage altogether and toyed with the idea of becoming organist of a cathedral or large parish church where a particularly high degree of accomplishment was demanded. With this in mind, he approached the pupil of the organist of Norwich Cathedral, Dr John Beckwith, a musician of tremendous range and ability. Beckwith naturally regarded the "poor player" with some scepticism and set Fisher a gruelling test of skill. From the cathedral library he extracted several of the most difficult service scores and anthems he could lay his hands on—Orlando Gibbon's eight-part anthem "Hosanna, to the Son of David", "Child in D" ("the most cramped and crude Te Deum that was ever put on paper"), Croft's "God is Gone Up" and Greene's "God is our Hope". The anthem was not printed, in the manner of later church music, in the treble clef with an organ part, but as an arrangement of various clefs handed down "from the ancients". Fisher executed them all with an amazing facility. Beckwith was so astonished by Fisher's technical mastery that he argued passionately about how the actor might sufficiently overcome popular prejudice to abandon the stage for the church. In the end, Charles Fisher chose to stay with the theatre.

His nephew, David Fisher III, has left a vivid portrait of this complex and many-talented man which underlines not only his versatility, his broadly encompassing, artistic temperament, but also his grasshopper eccentricity.

"From youth he was a violinist and violincellist. But he took it into his head on one occasion to learn the double bass. As was usual with him, the one thing absorbed him morning, noon and night. For about a year he was at the double bass, and it is a fact, when he played the same on orchestra with Paganini, the latter said to the Rev. Robert Elwin (who managed the festivals), he was glad there was one man besides Dragonetti who could play the double bass in England. Sometimes, however, he ran mad on pictures, and had a small gallery. Then it was conchology. However, music was the ruling passion. During his latter years, for recreation he scored all Haydn's and Beethoven's quartets; then made an arrangement for his own use of Beethoven's quartets for pianoforte."

In this respect, he was the antithesis of his clever but plodding younger brother, George. George Fisher, the third son, made neither the stage nor music his life. He was a competent actor, inheriting a feeling for drama which, under his father's tutelage, developed into a more than ordinarily competent performing skill. But his inclinations were scholarly; they were those of a self-tutored academic—a fine student of Greek, Latin and mathematics who had narrowly missed a university education.

It is entirely in character that this erudite and meticulous man should have kept a record of takings at the joint benefit nights he and his wife Marianne had throughout the circuit from 1823, the year of their marriage, to 1827 and again from 1837-39. In many cases he gave staccato comments on the figures, generally to explain why they were lower than usual. In Woodbridge on 4th March, 1823, they collect £11 6s. In Eye on 23rd July, 1823 "incessant rain" is the explanation for a low receipt of £1 2s 6d. At North Walsham in November of the same year they netted £10 12s for themselves from a £26 4s house. In 1824 they did rather better, with a total of £34 8s from their benefit nights at Bungay, Beccles, Halesworth, Wells, Dereham, Swaffham and, unusually, Downham Market. In 1929 the Fishers actually declined to make Downham a regular part of their circuit. Their benefits looked even healthier from the 1825 tour—£47 9s. Yet it was an unlucky sequence of nights for the most part. On 21st January, 1825 at Newmarket, rain and two local balls on the same night reduced the potential for theatre-going and £6 3s was all the couple took home. The Saturday before Passion Week at Woodbridge they drew £12 1s but had two severe disappointments later in the year—"great rain and tempest" resulted in a paltry £3 12s 6d on 6th August, and rain at Lowestoft that autumn was blamed for their £2 2s profits. "Rain and late market" at North Walsham on 27th April, 1826 are the enemies of a better benefit than £9 16s and at Dereham on 11th August (£14 5s 9d) George Fisher comments: "Rain incessant—many in without paying!—rascally." Their 1826 total benefits were £60 16s from six theatres; three theatres brought them

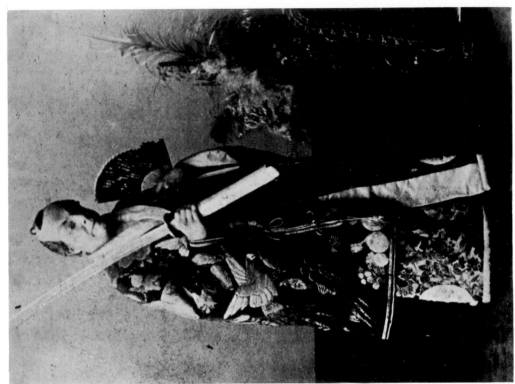

David Fisher IV joined the D'Oyley Carte Company. He is pictured here elaborately garbed as Koko in one of the company's Hamburg productions of "The Mikado" in 1888.

David Fisher IV in mufti. He was the last of the Fishers to make acting a full time profession. He died in 1889 at the age of forty-four, two years after his father.

jointly £28 14s 3d in 1827 and during the rest of the circuit three more nights brought George alone £16 16s.

In about 1827 he left the company and became Master of the Academy at Swaffham where he lived with his wife. Here he wrote a work of monumental tenacity and detail, *The Companion and Key to the History of England*, now an extremely rare book. He researched for this massive tome for 12 years, labouring under the almost incredible disadvantage of having to conduct his studies eighty miles away from the great libraries of England. It is said that he sometimes had to wait weeks before some knotty point of genealogy could be cleared up by correspondence. The history was published in 1832, attracted a few favourable reviews and was then swallowed up in financial failure. The following year, George's name ("Mr George") was back regularly in cast lists. It also appears in small type at the foot of the playbills. As "G. Fisher, Printer", he was registered as owner of a printing press and produced handbills (programmes were not to come until late in the century) and posters for the theatres in North Walsham, Wells, Dereham, Swaffham, Thetford, Newmarket, Sudbury, Woodbridge, Eye, Halesworth, Lowestoft, Beccles and Bungay.

George's return to the Norfolk and Suffolk Company was brief. In 1834 he took a school in Calvert Street, Swaffham, and ran it apparently successfully for two years. By 1837, the company was under serious stress and he rejoined Charles to keep the enterprise afloat. County theatres throughout England were enfeebled by declining patronage and the Fishers, because of the relative smallness of their concern, were among the first of the managers to feel the strain. A leader from *The Times* of 3rd October, 1826, had even then been able to discern a darkening and a contracting of stage horizons:

> "Theatrical performances seem to be losing speculations not only in this country, but even in France . . . The state of theatrical property in England is wretched beyond description. Many of the large towns which supported a theatre three or four months in the year do not now encourage even a week's acting, and in many of the places where theatres are open, the performers are almost starving."

Country theatres did not feel the chill so quickly, but by the mid 30s it was clear that a change in public taste was in the wind. Among the family papers of the descendants of the Fisher family, there is a little salaries book kept by Charles Fisher from 1832 to 1839. It is a unique record of the typically valiant struggle of provincial managers in the mid-nineteenth century to keep their companies alive, amounting, towards the end, to an account of a pathetic terminal illness. James Carver rightly described Charles Fisher's meticulous documentation of his company's hard times as eloquent testimony not only to the fight for survival but to the honourable way in which earnings were distributed. "Over and over again," he wrote, "we find that the salaries had to be reduced, but as soon as there is a stroke of better luck, pay is raised."

At the beginning of the book, salaries at Dereham, 1832, are given as "C. Fisher—£2; C. Fisher, Jun—15s; G. Fisher, snr—£1 8s; J. Fisher—£1." Some of the non-family members of the company of 18 were receiving £1 6s. and a typical weekly wage bill would be around £21. The tour for 1832-34 was *Dereham* (August), Wells (September), Swaffham (October), Newmarket (November), Woodbridge (January-March, with a break for Passion Week), Sudbury (April-May), Eye (June-July), Lowestoft (August), Beccles Races (4th-7th September), Lowestoft (9th-16th September). The Company returned to Norwich for the musical festival (17th-20th September) and then resumed at Beccles until 25th November. Bungay (December-January, 1834), North Walsham (February-March), Wells (April-May), *Dereham* (beginning 30th May).

The route looked profitable enough and had proved so in the past, but there was trouble springing up from within and without. On 14th September, Brooks was discharged for "intoxication and neglect"; receipts were falling. By midsummer 1834, George Fisher was offering to take a drop in salary of 4s. Three shillings was accepted instead, and his brother's terse comment reads: "June 7—G. Fisher reduced from 28s to 25s at his own suggestion, in generous consideration of the badness of the business." Nichols was sacked in April, 1835 for the same failing as Brooks and by 1838 half salaries were being paid to everybody. Members of the family were always the first to feel the cuts. Beccles produced good audiences that year and the company were all able to be advanced 1s but the steady loss of ground more than outweighed the occasional fillips. David Fisher came out of retirement to try to help the failing business in 1841, accepting a modest weekly salary of 30s. "He came to assist your grandfather George," the former Fisher actor F. C. Burton told Ruth Carver, "but it was too late. Things had altered. The old patrons had died out and railways had completely altered the state of things in our profession." The following year Charles and his wife left the company (they had recently been earning 31s and 25s respectively), presumably feeling themselves freed by David's return, and the management devolved solely on George—but not without some bad blood. Charles, in a gesture which posterity is bound to judge harshly, joined the Norwich Company as leader of the band. His son Charles was already leading actor on the circuit.

In 1843, Woodbridge theatre reported "little support in comparison with former times" and a much more dramatic falling away was evident in the smaller Fisher theatres. In 1844, after more than fifty years, the company was dissolved, the victim of a changing social pattern. Leases were terminated, theatres were sold one by one, some of them lingering purposelessly on for another ten years but most of them disposed of within the decade. An advertisement appeared in July, 1844 under a Halesworth heading: "Lot 7: The Theatre: a spacious brick-built and tiled building, dimensions about 66 feet by 40, with boxes, stage, gallery, dressing-rooms and fittings and a small Garden adjoining, now let to Messrs. Fisher on lease which expires at Michaelmas 1849 at the low rent of £16 per annum copyhold. Landtax redeemed." It was an ignominious but common epilogue. From a falling off in theatre-going it was a short step to the demise of provincial companies and the end of the circuits. The Norwich Company was not immune and its own collapse, though more prolonged, exactly mirrored that of the Fishers.

FISHER FAMILY TREE

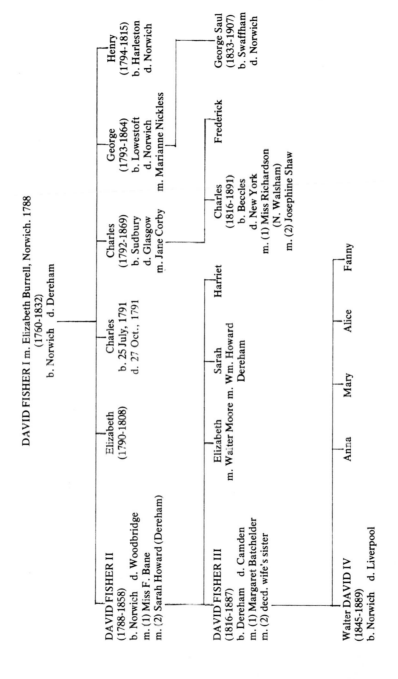

DAVID FISHER I m. Elizabeth Burrell, Norwich. 1788
(1760-1832)
b. Norwich d. Dereham

DAVID FISHER II
(1788-1858)
b. Norwich d. Woodbridge
m. (1) Miss F. Bane
m. (2) Sarah Howard (Dereham)

Elizabeth
(1790-1808)

Charles
b. 25 July, 1791
d. 27 Oct., 1791

Charles
(1792-1869)
b. Sudbury
d. Glasgow
m. Jane Corby

George
(1793-1864)
b. Lowestoft
d. Norwich
m. Marianne Nickless

Henry
(1794-1815)
b. Harleston
d. Norwich

DAVID FISHER III
(1816-1887)
b. Dereham d. Camden
m. (1) Margaret Batchelder
m. (2) decd. wife's sister

Elizabeth
m. Walter Moore

Sarah
m. Wm. Howard
Dereham

Harriet

Charles
(1816-1891)
b. Beccles
d. New York
m. (1) Miss Richardson
(N. Walsham)
m. (2) Josephine Shaw

Frederick

George Saul
(1833-1907)
b. Swaffham
d. Norwich

Walter DAVID IV
(1845-1889)
b. Norwich d. Liverpool

Anna

Mary

Alice

Fanny

CHAPTER TEN

Rebellion; or,
Players Versus Critics

"For my own poor part, I hold it villainous and cowardly to publish a censure of any man's actions Anonymously. It is a kind of Literary Assassinship, a sort of Stabbing in the Dark". Benjamin Plim Bellamy, 1813.

"Nothing on earth can stop the mouth of an actor." Alfred Bunn, 1840.

APART from occasional insulting references to actors or managers in the correspondence columns of the local newspapers, East Anglian theatres had been used to receiving the press they wanted, the press they in some cases paid for. Opening nights were diligently puffed, and the manager's florid thanks at close of season were printed almost verbatim. If there were drama "critics" at all, they were generally in the pocket of the manager, careful not to obtrude themselves on the public unless they had something laudatory to say. When, therefore, the *Suffolk Chronicle* offered its columns to a reviewer of scorching outspokenness, the theatrical scene was thrown into turmoil.

The anonymous writer, a kind of self-appointed watchdog of literary standards and dramatic professionalism, set about demolishing complacency among actors and audiences with a vigour as sudden as it was devastating. Within the space of a few brutally frank reviews, he had become the scourge of actors and the bogey of managers. Even playwrights, pandering to soft-centred audiences with execrable farces, were cut down to size.

The Norwich Company seems to have first felt the impact of a new, corrosive pen during its summer season in Ipswich in 1810. "She Stoops to Conquer" had been ostensibly well-received on 2nd July. It was a creditable addition to the repertoire with Frederick Vining as one of the protagonists. Five days later the *Suffolk Chronicle* delivered a crushing review. "The performance," it reported, "possessed all the worst defects of a provincial exhibition and the few occasional touches of excellence which appeared were insufficient to dispel that langour which the prevailing dullness was so calculated to produce." The popular Fred Vining was rapped for his "schoolboy recitation" and the managers were accused of having dredged up "a miserable orchestra". Nothing like it had been printed before.

Worse was to come. The *Chronicle* sent its unpopular reviewer to every other play that week, trailing clouds of opprobrium. The opera, "The Seige of Belgrade" (J. Cobb) "performed under the grandeur of three violins and a horn", he found defective in its dialogue; "The Foundling of the Forest" (William Dimond) was

Frederick Vining's benefit night at Norwich Theatre in 1812. It was the first time he had played Hamlet—a part he repeated time and time again throughout the circuit and later at Covent Garden. The Faucits, also destined for the London stage, are in the same cast, and the Ghost of Hamlet's father was played by the man who was to become Norwich manager James Smith.
Norfolk County Libraries

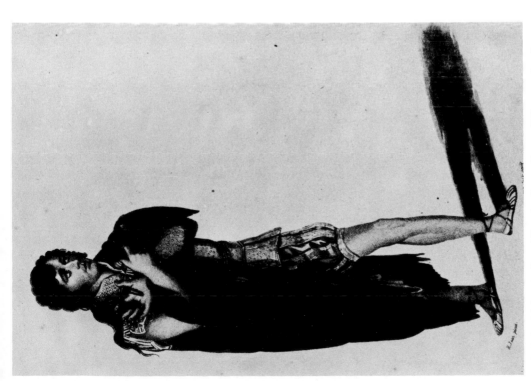

R. Jean, pinx.

Frederick Vining, darling of East Anglian audiences. This engraving, from a portrait of the actor as Octavian by R. Jean, was published in Ipswich in 1814 when Vining was the company's leading player and a sort of Byronic hero to female theatregoers.
Norfolk County Libraries

dismissed as "one of those monstrous compositions of the present day"; "Budget of Blunders" (Greffulhe's farce) was just that. Only Benjamin Plim Bellamy, on this occasion (in "The Clandestine Marriage", by Garrick and the elder Colman), emerged with any credit.

As if suddenly unmuzzled, the critic bit deep into the over-delicate sensibilities of the company and drew blood. With reckless attention to duty he compiled a league table of actors, with Bellamy, Bennett and Fitzgerald as the top three. Vining ("his acting never goes beyond the tuition of a dancing master") featured, and so, to his chagrin, did Smith ("humble mediocrity"). Those absent from the list could not fail to be relieved.

The man on whose head most of the dishonour fell was John Clayton Hindes, manager of the Norwich Company. The *Suffolk Chronicle* had not been the first journal to canvass his ineptitude. A Norwich contributor to the *Monthly Mirror* of 16th January, 1805, remarked when Hindes took over that Norwich people had no reason to rejoice at the change. He harked back nostalgically to the days of John Brunton whose

> "management of the theatre, if not conducted on the most liberal scale, was always respectable. His performers were uniformly well-chosen, and there were few of them who did not remain with him many years. He was respected by all who knew him . . . Mr. Hindes, on the contrary, is universally disliked by his performers and by the town in general. In his short but inglorious reign he has discharged four of the most favourite actors, seemingly for no other reason but because the audience liked them. In the management of the theatre, he is niggardly to the greatest degree. He has reduced the band, which in Mr. Brunton's time used to be very respectable, to five regular performers; and in every other department of the theatre, his whole aim seems to be how 6d. may be saved."

More reprehensible still was Hindes's practice of packing the house with non-paying spectators on his benefit nights to suggest what a popular fellow he was. Quite whether all this mud-slinging was warranted is questionable. Hindes was still capable, by whatever cajolery, of drawing impressive receipts. His benefit night on 6th April, 1811, at the Theatre Royal, Norwich, netted £177 15s. And he kept the company's reputation before the attention of London managers. Vining was snapped up for a season by Covent Garden. Mrs Harriet Faucit left in the same year and both of them were soon being ostentatiously billed.

A July performance of "Hamlet" in Ipswich in 1813 was the signal for new hostilities between critic and actors. Ben Bellamy, a spirited young man and promising actor, had been playing Polonius to Vining's Hamlet. Vining, a Byronic-looking figure who had gained something of a reputation as darling of the Ipswich audiences, was commended but Bellamy claimed he had been grossly slandered by the *Suffolk Chronicle's* representative. "We never saw a viler Polonius than

...very rebuke: he had
...iscast. Bellamy had
...have his reputation
...ith a tract headed "A
...P. Bellamy, of the

...t of being "a hireling,
...he sale of Mr. King's
...nicle] . . . the Job you
...the public estimation
...is accused of "vending
...which practice has so
...not yet learned to live
...y. One theatre review in
...n so far extended, that
...fourth act. A few brief
...we can offer". But he
...t three.

...ocative pose:

...om the *Theatre Royal*,
...town of Ipswich with a
...have found it a serious
...ntageously, and far more
...nd shot upon crows, we
...shall not lose sight of the
...e us, it is our intention, in
...nature of the histrionic
...es of theatrical criticism;
...Company of Performers."

...rd. Instead of belabouring
...icism of the type of plays

...ls, upon families and even upon nations, by the encourage... es as 'The Stranger', and 'Lovers' Vows'—the former a disgusting apology for adultery, the latter, a mitigation of the crime of seduction, with the additional mischief of eulogising the factitious virtues of the poor, at the expence of the rich and noble of the land . . . That actors possess and equal aptitude for blundering, every day's experience both in London and in the Country affords abundant conviction. The object of theatrical criticism therefore is improvement . . . It is our wish to raise, not debase."

123

SPECIAL EVENTS

Admission: £3 (£2.50 Concs.)

'Second Southampton Comedy Film Festival'. This screening forms part of the 106 minutes. Running time is Eric also appear. Cantona brothers Joel and footballer Michel and Sabine Azema. Oh, and ubiquitous Michel Serrault, Eddy Almodovar regular Carmen Maura, the Major players include erstwhile Return Of Martin Guerre'! a good old 'Carry On' film with 'The comedy of manners which seems to cross idea of what to expect from this 'Condom'. This should give us a good features French towns 'Dole' and

Admission: £3 (£2.50 Concs.)

at 8pm Straw Dogs (X)

Sam Peckinpah's violent 1971 chiller stars Dustin Hoffman and Susan George. Still a shocker.

broadcaster ... British Board of Film Censors member Ken Penry, and Richard Falcon. Do come along and air your views too. The bar will be available, and . . .

He claimed that it was a far more rewarding occupation to point out beauties than expose defects but justified his attacks on the Norwich Company by declaring that everyone of taste and education in Ipswich would agree that "by our critical attentions we have effected an astonishing improvement in the Norwich Company". So longwinded had his apologia become that the main examination of the performers had to be postponed for yet another week. It was on 4th September that the promised analysis was delivered. Fitzgerald was declared "wholly incompetent to sustain the first cast of characters" and had a harsh manner and grating voice. Vining, young and heady, was too slight a person for tragedy. "In his voice there is an unfortunate crack which we are fearful it will never be completely in the power of time to solder." His deportment was rather brisk and careless and "altogether his tragic exertions are deficient in weight and energy". Bellamy had, on the whole, "little to apprehend from criticism".

As an emollient to the bruised actors and to energise a flagging public, Norwich Theatre Royal was given a facelift and reopened on 10th January, 1814. The *Ipswich Journal* commented sourly: "The example of the Norwich Theatre we trust will not be lost upon that of Ipswich, which is as dingy and gloomy as a prision."

Norwich Theatre Royal had been smartened up on both sides of the curtain. The backs of the boxes had been lined with scarlet camlet, imparting a badly-needed aura of warmth and richness. "The ornaments in front of the boxes are gold, upon a veined marble ground, which, with the other decorations, copied from the antique, produce a light and brilliant effect" ran a local report of the refurbishing. Correspondingly, it was a good season for new pieces and new sets.

The truce with the critic was, however, fragile. During the 1814 summer season at Ipswich, Frederick Vining was playing at Covent Garden and the critic remarked that his place had been "more than supplied by the accession of Bromley". Bromley's face fitted. "It is highly gratifying to see an Actor upon the stage who understands his profession." Fred Vining's brother, Henry, was still with the Company, however, and seemed to be heir to abuse. He was called "that miserable stick" who would "disgrace the lowest booth at a Country Fair", the ultimate insult.

Before the season was over, the notices had led to blows. The *Suffolk Chronicle* man referred on 13th August, 1814, to "a brutal violation of the peace" by the players and declared that Henry Vining was at the bottom of it all. Hostility had been in the wind right from the start. Henry Vining was ringleader of a group of players who harboured a grievance at not being spoken of in quite the same terms as Kemble or Young. They decided to make their protest in print. For several days, the Ipswich presses turned out vehement anti-critic propaganda. Playbills and advertisements ended with scornful references which the *Chronicle's* man in turn described as: "pathetic and supplicatory lines calculated to elicit the pity, the compassion and the protection of the public against a being, who, for a week, they had been labouring to prove, was too feeble and contemptible for notice". Matters were being forced to a head.

At the close of the second act of Bickerstaffe's "The Maid of the Mill" the critic assumed his usual seat in the lower circle. Vining, who had been diverting attention with mimickry in the adjoining box stationed himself, with his hat on, by the side of the critic, ready for a confrontation. Seeing the actor on the wrong side of the footlights, the audience rose indignantly, but the players applauded Vining's mimickry. Bedlam broke out in the house. Struggling from the backstage, the manager hauled Vining out of the usurped box.

Though the show patently could not go on, Hewett, who had been billed to offer a ditty, appeared dressed as a ballad-singer and refused to be done out of his turn. It was his professional duty, he insisted, to sing the song announced. No one else seemed to agree and there was renewed uproar. Hewett with dogged tenacity protested that he was the victim of a plot to prevent his act and pointed to a culprit in the pit.

The accused figure fled from pit to boxes and from boxes into the street, losing his hat in the escape. The *Chronicle*, with no intention of showing itself a sudden convert to reticence, named names: Wallack and Bromley were, after Vining, the chief troublemakers, and Page ("one of the underlings of the theatre"), distinguished himself throughout the evening "by an animated display of blackguardism". A character from the pit joined the unfortunate Hewett on stage and began a ludicrous imitation. Bellamy and his fellow actors Bennett and Wilkinson also muscled in, beginning a song which was totally drowned in the pandemonium.

Bennett had, the *Chronicle* reminded its readers, smudged his reputation during the previous year's upheavals when in the course of generally insulting conduct, he "threatened to pull a gentleman's nose". This time he was reported as having blown his nose at the audience. Bennett was no more than a tolerably useful member of the company. He was described by a contemporary as a person who had been accustomed to the stage from infancy but had derived little advantage from the opportunity. He had a stiff manner and harsh voice but his one above-average talent was singing, and in less turbulent circumstances he would have deserved to be heard.

Once a measure of calm had been re-established, the Company attempted its afterpiece. But the actor Richard Jones, with a speech comparing the *Chronicle's* critic to "canker worm insects" upset the volatile crowd again. In the next issue of the *Chronicle* it was reported: "The grossest personal abuse, and the most insulting and threatening gestures, were employed by the ruffians in the pit against the critic, who amidst this hurly-burly kept his seat."

As the house thinned slowly, the intrepid reviewer heard that a "band of desperadoes", supporters of the actors, had planted themselves outside the theatre to intercept him. He enlisted the protection of a few sympathetic members of the audience and retreated under cover. But Vining was lying in wait in Tankard Street shouting "Let him come out! Let him come out!" The critic took some bad knocks, had his coat ripped from his back and narrowly escaped a ducking. An inglorious season was at an end and the Company returned to Norwich with as much dignity as it could salvage.

The LAST NIGHT but ONE.

BY DESIRE OF

MRS. HENRY BERNERS,

THEATRE, IPSWICH.

By his Majesty's Servants, from the Theatre-Royal, Norwich.

On FRIDAY, August 13, 1813, will be presented,

A Tragedy, called

HAMLET,

PRINCE of DENMARK.

Claudius, Mr. POWELL
Hamlet, Mr. VINING
The Ghost, Mr. SMITH
Polonius, Mr. BELLAMY—Horatio, Mr. HEWETT
Laertes, Mr. FAUCIT
Rosencraus, Mr. BEACHEM
Guildenstern, Mr. MORELAND—Ostrick, Mr. HAMMOND
Marcellus, Mr. H. VINING
Player-King, Mr. CLIFFORD—Lucianus, Mr. WILKINSON
Grave-digger, Mr. BENNETT—Sailor, Mr. GUYTON.

The Queen, Mrs. FAUCIT
Ophelia, Miss KING
Player-Queen, Mrs. FITZGERALD.

To which will be added, a Farce, called

TURN OUT.

Restive, Mr. BELLAMY
Dr. Truckle, Mr. BEACHEM
Gregory, Mr. BENNETT
Somerville, Mr. MORELAND
Forge, Mr. HEWETT—Cook, Mr. H. VINING
Gardner, Mr. GUYTON—Boy, Master JONES.

Mrs. Ramsay, Mrs. CLIFFORD
Marian Ramsay, Mrs. W. CLIFFORD
Peggy, Miss JONES.

BY PERMISSION,

The Band of the 1st Hussars of King's German Legion,
Will attend the Theatre this Evening.

Benjamin Plim Bellamy as Dr Pangloss at Ipswich in 1814. Bellamy was one of the most popular Norwich comedians. He went on to become lessee of the Upper Assembly Rooms at Bath. *Norfolk County Libraries*

Playbill from the troublesome Ipswich season when a fierce disagreement between actors and critic ended in blows. The offending performance was *Hamlet*, with the Norwich favourite, Fred Vining, in the title role and Ben Bellamy as Polonius. Vining's brother, Henry, was playing minor parts in the cast. *Suffolk Record Office, Ipswich*

On 20th December, 1814, the players were once more wintering in Ipswich, not without misgivings. Bellamy and Bennett were so applauded on their return that their first performance was held up for several minutes. Relations seemed to be on the mend. Traditional drama, laced with farce, song and burlesque had begun to pall, however, and the Company was soon trying to remedy its lean houses by introducing equestrian shows and tightrope antics. It was a cue the *Chronicle's* critic appeared to have been waiting for. He was in coruscating form:

"When we heard that the rights of the Menageries and Riding Schools have been infringed by the introduction of living elephants and troops of cavalry at the winter Theatres of London, we considered that absurdity had attained its acme; but alas! we had not contemplated the probability of witnessing the condemnation of eight unfortunate horses to kick and prance and curvet and display all their 'wonderful evolutions' on a stage of 10ft × 12ft."

The night was cold, the house empty and comfortless and the exertions of the actors "seemed perfectly to harmonise with the dreary prospective".

An "Observer" writing to the *Ipswich Journal* on 31st December, denounced these observations as mean and petulant, not to say snobbish. Why the outrage, the alarm? People knew what they liked; if instead of tedious afterpieces, spectacles with horses were substituted which audiences enjoyed, where was the harm?

"I yield to no one in admiration of the muse of Shakespeare", the writer went on, "but I have observed with regret that the most favoured plays of that great author have not attracted such crowded benches as have successively followed melo-dramatic performances. If so great a revolution in the public sentiment has taken place, how can the manager help it?" It was an argument which had more than a suspicion of Hindes about it, especially the final parry: "I am aware that the Ipswich theatre is very ill-calculated and too much confined to give effect to the manoeuvres of the horses . . . but . . . great applauses constantly attend the representation, and from numerous and highly respectable audiences."

A few days later, shortly after the company had returned to Norwich, the critic was stung into abandoning his anonymity. He was T. Harral, of Ipswich, and he now rose in self defence. He retaliated in an open letter to King, printer and proprietor of the *Chronicle,* upholding his worthy motives, his undeviating pursuit of the fair, honest and liberal viewpoint. He justified his criticism of candlesnuffers masquerading as actors and explained his attempts to drill players in the art of proper pronounciation. For Hindes, he had no soft words; the manager had, he asserted, a mendicant spirit.

Harral's "unqualified contempt" for most performances was by no means totally unjustifiable. He genuinely felt that since the summer of 1813 the Norwich Company had greatly degenerated. The impoverishment showed in playbills, in sets, in the morale of the players. Only the *Ipswich Journal* kept up a furiously pro-theatre patter, whatever the signs (even Bellamy's Polonius was "most correct").

Vining aired his grievances publicly. On 18th May, 1815, he told theatregoers of the "injustice and cruelty" which had been heaped upon him, and left the Norwich Company for Covent Garden for a season of 100 nights. In his absence, Richard Jones took Vining's usual parts but on Vining's return, Jones received notice. The incident created mayhem for two or three weeks and the affair reached Quarter Sessions but was eventually settled out of court.

Bellamy, too, had had enough of a generally ungrateful press. On 5th August the "favourite" comedian of the Norwich Company was engaged at Covent Garden "at a liberal salary". On 26th July, the last night of the season, he thanked the Ipswich people for their support and announced his departure. "Not to have accepted," he told them, "would have been the extreme of folly." The *Cambridge Chronicle* did not agree, and when Bellamy arrived at Barnwell on 11th October, 1816, the paper regretted his preference for "the London boards, occupied as they are by veteran performers in the same line". Ironically, long before he had made his mark, the London papers were criticising his "provincial twang" and dubbing his performance as Polonius as "somewhat outlandish". Three years later, he too was back in East Anglia—as actor-manager in Norwich under James Smith, successor to the inept Hindes.

In 1814 Mr Fitzgerald, another of the company's favourites, had also delivered a farewell address; he was leaving the circuit to become patentee at Hull and York. The years of dissent had brought unease and undermined loyalties. The Norwich Company badly needed new blood and a new impetus. Two developments gave it a temporary transfusion—the appointment of James Smith as manager, and a deliberate policy of engaging a leaven of London actors.

Smith, however, did not move into Hindes's seat without a familiar figure at his elbow: Bellamy had returned from a lightning experience in London and was eager for work. Smith was therefore deputed to take care of the company's administration while Bellamy assumed the role of acting-manager. In a letter to Elizabeth Cobbold Robert Rushbrooke wrote from Bury St Edmunds: "I hear a new arrangement is to take place in the Norwich Concern—that Bellamy is to be acting [manager] and Smith to be Chancellor of its Exchequer. I fear the temper of the former will scarcely allow this appointment to be advantageous—but with regard to the latter—it could not be in better hands. He is quite supersaturated as a performer—and will take on him this new and lucrative office with great benefit to himself and the Establishment." That office was to have every drop of its lucrative potential exploited by bringing national actors into the Norwich orbit as a regular feature.

Sarah Siddons as Euphrasia in "The Grecian Daughter", a role she played while visiting Norwich in September, 1788, at the height of her London fame.

British Museum

CHAPTER ELEVEN

Great Personages; or,
All the Stars Came Down

"Great theatrical personages, who formerly used to look upon a city or town as a bore, now, on the contrary, in the summer grant they are commodious, respectable, and even alluring; and with great good manners, compliance, and condescension, will consent to trifle away a few nights at such insignificant places." Tate Wilkinson, 1790

UNTIL the turn of the nineteenth century the Norwich troupe had, with a few exceptions, been content to rely on their own resources on the stage. Any movement between London and the provinces had been confined to local actors "making good"—or not—by landing engagements in the metropolis. Otherwise, although playgoers may have had the satisfaction of recognising the talent of a young Garrick, for instance, and giving him a first foothold to fame, it was relatively rare before 1800 for provincial audiences to glimpse a famous actor in full prime outside the capital.

The Norwich Company of Comedians were, in the space of fifty years, hosts to most of the great actors of the era—Charles Macklin, Samuel Foote, Sarah Siddons, Edmund Kean, John Kemble, his brother Charles, William Charles Macready and many others. They had established themselves as a company of distinction who could be relied upon, most of the time, to provide a decent standard of acting which would not be a source of embarrassment to the guest star. Some of the provincial companies could be a severe test of patience. Macready, at Bristol in 1835, complained that in the only passable scene of the lot, the prompter kept shouting "the word" to him when he paused for effect. "I was cut up right and left, root and branch, and—as usual—I grieve and shame to say it—was very angry," he complained.

The increasing appearance of "names" for one, two, three or four night stands in any of the Norwich circuit towns is explained in two ways: they were a box-office draw at a time of doldrums and insecurity and they helped the men and women of the London stages to stay in business during the close seasons at Covent Garden or Drury Lane. Provincial visits could, in addition, prove a tonic for the morale. Tate Wilkinson said that "even the Jordan [Dorothy Jordan, the famous London actress and mistress of the future William IV] herself, who at present reigns as our modern Thalia, has deigned to visit Cheltenham, Reading, Margate, Richmond, and Harrowgate, which places yielded great profits, silver medals, and subscriptions falling at her feet in plentiful showers".

For the resident company, star nights were rather like first nights—loved and feared. Local actors felt privileged to be seen on the same stage as a Kean or a

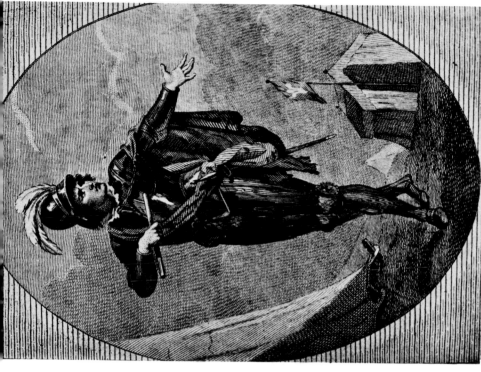

Norwich Theatre Royal

At the peak of her popularity Sarah Siddons (1755-1831) played nine nights at Norwich. On the sixth night she took the part of Isabella with the Norwich manager, Barrett, as Biron. "I should be afraid to say how many times Isabella was successfully repeated with still encreasing favour", she said. In this part she was acknowledged as the leading tragedienne of the day. She took £423 from her Norwich visit.

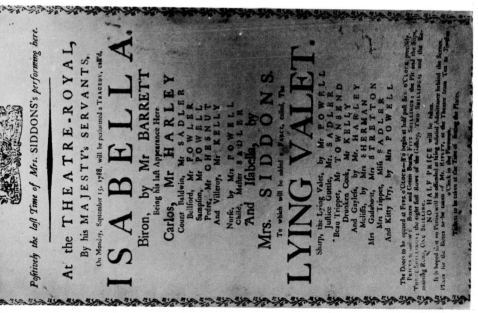

Suffolk Record Office, Ipswich

John Philip Kemble (1757-1823), brother of Sarah Siddons, was in the forefront of the procession of visiting stars to East Anglia. Audiences paid highly to see England's greatest tragedian as The Black Prince. But star nights were eventually the ruin of the company. G. R. Clarke of Ipswich saw the trend as early as 1830: "Before provincial managers adopted the custom of bringing down the London stars, to enlighten their rural hemisphere, the Norwich company was excellent, and the theatre in Ipswich well attended; but now, unless some celebrated London actor condescends to favour us with his performance, for half the receipts of the house, there is nothing but 'a beggarly account of empty boxes'".

Macready, but many of them, far from collecting any reflected glory, found themselves eclipsed with startling suddenness. In the playbills, the newspaper advertisements, the taverns and the market places, they were outshone; and when the visitor had fretted and strutted his hour they were left unsettled, their natural jealousies magnified, their own standing diminished in the public eye.

One of the earliest triumphs was the queen-like visitation of Sarah Siddons in Norwich in September 1788. Giles Linnett Barrett, nearing the end of a short and unremarkable managership of the Norwich Company, was trying to inject some zest into the season. Siddons was thirty-three and at the height of her popularity; it took Barrett a whole month's preparation to secure her. The *Norwich Mercury* built up expectations with a pen portrait:

> "Her person is well-proportioned, inclining to the *en bon point;* her features are strong and flexible, without coarseness or vulgarity . . . a large and penetrating eye . . . No words can convey an idea of the pleasure she communicates."

She stayed in Norwich for nine nights acting in eight different plays, and receipts totalled £852, of which £423 went to Siddons herself.

In a sense, Mrs Siddons owed a special debt to provincial audiences: they had acclaimed when others despised her. Her debut at Drury Lane had been a failure and she and her husband toured the provinces, on and off, for six years before London was ready for her. She seemed conscious of that debt and seldom stinted her appearances in the counties, even when she was the leading actress of the day.

Tate Wilkinson worked harder than most to establish the regions as centres of drama worthy to be considered. He maintained that "tho' London improves and matures, and is the most enviable theatrical situation, yet genius will be found in every rank, soil and station". Apropos of Mrs Siddons, he reminded the readers of his memoirs that if country people had taken any notice of London's trend-setting, the whole theatrical world would have lost the finest actress of her day. His own softness for her was well known. "I do not mean to insinuate Mrs. Siddons has not foibles or faults," he said in *Memoirs of His Own Life* (1790)—"I can only say, if she has, I am not acquainted with them."

On 1st September she captivated her well-primed Norwich audience as Jane in "Jane Shore". Her other roles were Belvidera in "Venice Preserved", Mrs Beverly in "The Gamester", Lady Randolph in "Douglas" (Home), Calista in "The Fair Penitent", the title role in "Isabella" (Southerne/Garrick), Euphrasia in "The Grecian Daughter" (Murphy), Rosalind in "As You Like It". She ended with a repeat of Isabella. To Barrett, there was only one man suitable to take the male leads opposite her—himself.

The other great female attraction of Georgian stage was the reputedly beautiful Eliza O'Neill, a short-lived phenomenon whose rumoured talents probably far exceeded her actual capabilities as a tragedienne. The Irish actress sent audiences mad. She was twenty-seven when she was engaged to play in Norwich for five nights in

EDMUND KEAN as RICHARD THE THIRD.

Pub. by M.& M.SKELT H.Street, 6.º Minorie London.

N.º 3

Edmund Kean as Richard III. An Ipswich playgoer, Thomas Green, saw Kean's performance at the Tankard Street theatre and noted: "Full house . . . Bits of his acting beautiful, particularly the whisper to Bolingbroke 'I wish the bastard dead', but oftener failing . . . his gesticulations extravagant and monstrous."

Suffolk Record Office, Ipswich

It is hard to see what, in this rather matronly face, made audiences mad for Eliza O'Neill. She is pictured here as Belvidera in "Venice Preserved", a part she played in Cambridge, at the Barnwell Theatre, on 16th September, 1818. "There is a dove-like softness in her blue eyes and a melody in her 'honied accents'," wrote the *Cambridge Chronicle's* reviewer. We must take his word for it. At any rate, her five nights were worth £700 and in the fight to get a seat "no law prevailed but that of the strongest".

Mander and Mitchenson Theatre Collection

September, 1818, and the city was beside itself. The box office was beseiged every morning and a contemporary remarked with not too much regret that "the spirit of politeness and gallantry maintained only a very feeble influence over the conduct of the assembled multitude". Nor could the *Norfolk Chronicle* hide its enthusiasm at the opportunity to provide some colourful reportage: "No law prevailed but that of the strongest. There were shrieks, reproaches, lamentations; bonnets were cramped up, hats squeezed flat, gowns torn . . . the motley mob were in the highest state of exasperation, fermentation and desperation. The house was crowded in every part . . . families of the highest respectability were in inconvenient situations." The public invaded the orchestra for a closer look at this captivating girl. She had a lively, expectant face, with wide-set eyes and the nose of a Roman matron. It was her voice which seemed the most alluring of all her qualities. The *Cambridge Chronicle* was bowled over on both counts . . . "there is a dove-like softness in her blue eyes and a melody in her 'honied accents'." She was compared to Mrs Siddons. She was exquisite; her Belvidera was extolled to the length of more than a column while the rest of the cast were disposed of in a total ten lines. Every man appeared to cast himself as Romeo to her Juliet (she was reported to be "exquisitely and playfully impassioned" in the balcony scene).

Takings were, on average, £200 a night and Eliza O'Neill left Norwich £700 better off. She had burst on London in 1814; but her career was short. Eliza married William Becher, M.P., a few months after her Christmas appearance at Ipswich in 1818. Up to her final performance she had been acclaimed. "The O'Neill is as perfect as ever," wrote Robert Rushbrooke from Bury St Edmunds, "the Public Favour has not intoxicated her. She plays from and to the Heart as when she first appeared."

Singers of national repute—at a time when musical interludes were still dragging performances out from 6 pm to midnight—were also attracted to the Norwich circuit. Charles Incledon was perhaps the most curious. Incledon, who acquired the title The Wandering Melodist, was a man more at home in song than in acting. In his day he was as popular as Kemble or Kean but the mistake of his career was to prolong it years beyond the suitable point for retirement. In old age, he became a laughing-stock.

As a young man he had sung several summers at Vauxhall before turning his expectations towards Covent Garden. The manager was indifferent to his talents but allowed him a debut in the 1788-89 season. The result was, in the words of a fellow actor, "the greatest dramatic triumph of my observation". Music always came to his aid when he fluffed his lines so that audiences tended to ask themselves whether he was singing the music or recollecting the words.

Henry Crabb Robinson met Incledon "the Singer" in the London coach. "I found him," he wrote, "just the man I should have expected, seven rings on his fingers, five seals on his watch ribbon and a gold snuffbox at once betrayed the old beau. His first conversation at once showed him to be a vain and frivolous being." Incledon was clearly a boaster, but there was more to him than that he had a grandiose notion for nationalising the English stage so that actors would not have their genius traded on by unscrupulous managers and he supported Crabb Robinson's belief that "nothing but smaller theatres and more of them could save the Drama from ruin."

Incledon made several trips to East Anglia, was generally generously billed and almost always well received. One of his houses at Ipswich in 1804 amounted to £118. He sang at the Theatre Royal, Norwich in 1805 and was back again the following year singing in "Hospitality, or the Harvest Home"—somewhat unseasonally in June. In 1816 the verdict was much less favourable. Thomas Green the Younger, of Ipswich, noted in *The Diary of a Lover of Literature* that Incledon was old and broken, his voice shattered and his bad style in full force. His falsetto (his natural voice was tenor) had become an absurd scream, lisping and inarticulate. It was his last performance in Ipswich to Green's relief. It remained only for the worn out actor to make a similar spectacle of himself in 1817 in Norwich before he left for, as he hoped, more deserving audiences in America.

A few months later, during the Norwich Company's brief return to base for the races, the celebrated Edmund Kean joined them for several nights, and then went on to Yarmouth with the players during their September week. By Christmas, Ipswich theatregoers were paying inflated prices to see him. Complimentary tickets were suspended. The Ipswich diarist Thomas Green ransacked his very considerable vocabulary in praise of Kean as Sir Giles Overreach, as Othello, as Shylock, finally and superhumanly as Hamlet. "The finest acting, unquestionably and beyond all comparison I ever beheld. How his mind and frame endure such dreadful convulsions is wonderful." Kean was barely thirty. Less than four years earlier he had been a tramp. Green's view of him was not unanimous; another contemporary accused him of coarse vulgarity (certainly not a new complaint in Kean's ears) and, more puzzlingly, of displaying an awkward swing of the shoulders and "Methodist tones". Green had the advantage of attending a dinner party to meet Kean. He was surprised to find him bland, gentlemanly and without any theatrical strut. "Mr Kean is a small man," he wrote, "neatly made, with delicate but marked expressive features, dark sultry eye . . ." The London actress, Helen Faucit, found him pale and haunting: "A stray lock of very dark hair crossed his forehead under which shone eyes which looked dark, and yet as bright as lamps."

Elizabeth Cobbold's literary correspondents were similarly impressed. Capel Lofft wrote to her in 1818: "I have seen Mr Kean, as you are aware, in three characters, Richard III, Sir Edward Mortimer and Hamlet and certainly with progressive admiration. I know not when I shall have collected my ideas sufficiently to present to you anything like an analysis of this wonderful actor. But I can say that since Garrick I have seen nothing which resembles or approaches one . . . His Richard gave me a picture of concentrated energy . . . his Hamlet filled in one individual the whole compass of human qualities."

It was not until Kean triumphed as Shylock at Drury Lane in 1814 that the world fully woke up to him. He had laboured for nine grinding years in the provinces, in pantomime, burlesque, equestrian stunts, and he did not in the least share Tate

William Henry West Betty (1791-1874) who was promoted at the age of thirteen as "The Young Roscius" and became a cult within months. He "retired" before he was twenty and made an unsuccessful comeback a few years later.

Mander and Mitchenson Theatre Collection

Wilkinson's stolid regard for the virtues of the country theatres. While still in an uncertain position at Drury Lane, he appealed to the manager: "Am I to be *cast again* into the provinces?'" It was a fate almost worse than unemployment.

Crabb Robinson records having seen Kean for the first time on 7th March, 1814, just a month after his first resounding success as Richard III. Richard remained Kean's most popular part. After the Drury Lane performance, Crabb Robinson entered in his journal: "He played Richard I believe better than any man I ever saw . . The expression of malignant joy is the one in which he surpasses all men I have ever seen. And his most flagrant defect is the want of dignity." Dignity was not, however, one of the qualities Kean strove to acquire. Crabb Robinson refused to be carried along with newspaper eulogies of Kean's genius: he did not believe that the actor would even reach the height of his profession. He began to distrust the little man's demonic representation of mental passion underlying physical suffering in the great death scenes, insisting that "the man who has received a mortal wound of which he is to dye in five minutes is a mere animal". In perhaps his most perceptive comment of all he said Kean's treatment of passion resembled strong likenesses in bad paintings. Two years later, Crabb Robinson met Kean face to face in the stiff artificiality of a London drawing room and scarcely recognised him—he was so taciturn. As always, it was the "fine eye" which compelled attention, the only Keanlike feature displayed by the otherwise stiff, quiet, awkward refugee from the glare of the stage.

Kean's interpretation of Timon of Athens in November, 1816, confirmed Crabb Robinson's doubts about Kean's soundness. "I begin to be tired of Kean," he wrote, "he too is a mannerist—Having seen his starts and convulsions—The protruded lip, the glancing eye, the shaken fist etc etc a few times the wonder ceases to astonish—And there is no pretence for delicacy of refinement in the delineation of strong passions."

It was very much longer before audiences experienced the same disenchantment. Women were hysterical about him and a few strong men were known to exhibit similar symptoms. Kean's sister-in-law, Susan Chambers, an admittedly partial spectator, wrote to a friend in 1816: "My dear Margaret, I wish you were here to see the numerous letters of congratulation and visits on the same that is pouring in every day. The house is quite a fair! To see him in the last act I think you would never get over it. Mrs Glover got into strong hysterics and many ladies fainted. It has brought 2 thousand pounds to the House."

Kean had revivified acting to an astonishing degree. He was the anthesis of the very proper Kembles and his style, for all its faults of excess, was undoubtedly the most controversial thing to seize the stage since Garrick pioneered the new naturalism. Before Kean's first Drury Lane season was out, his salary was doubled to £20 a week. As his biographer Giles Playfair records, there were now provincial engagements which he would be free to fulfil during the summer vacation and for which he would be paid, as a star among stars, 50 guineas an appearance, plus the receipts from a clear benefit night.

Managers found a man of Kean's originality, unconventionality and fire difficult to keep in check but even harder to dispense with. The man Sir Walter Scott called a "copper-laced, twopenny tearmouth, rendered mad by conceit and success" had become an idol. On his benefit night on 12th June, 1820, immense crowds battered the doors of Drury Lane before the theatre opened. People rushed into the boxes and the pit as if crazed. When they were in, they stewed in severe discomfort, compacted to such solidity that if they moved, they moved as a mass. An eye witness, James Winston, records in his diaries that the throng poured over the iron railings into the hall of the theatre, knocking down one of the box check-takers. In ten minutes, every corner of the house was full. Soon, Kean began to behave like the demi-god he had been created; he began to make his own rules. Some nights he demanded two private boxes, one for his wife and one for his mistress. Occasionally he was paid in advance. He failed to turn up for rehearsals, even for performances, and when he did arrive he was either late or drunk or both.

Kean's conduct during plays gave the management endless but helpless anxiety. Women were admitted to his dressing room to be "stroked" during the intervals and while he attended to one, two more would be waiting. "I went up to Kean's dressing room, where I found him scraping the colour off his face," wrote Alfred Bunn, the rascally London manager, "and sustaining the operation by copious draughts of cold brandy and water." Bunn surmised that if Kean's servant had brought him a simple glass of *eau sucre* without adding a considerable quantity of *eau de vie,* Kean would have "broken every bone in the varlet's body".

In 1819, Kean's brilliance was shadowed by the encroachment of his first serious rival—William Charles Macready—ironically an actor he had encouraged with his own applause. Two more disparate men could hardly be imagined in the top rank of the same interbred profession. Macready, who had a streak in him which was an amalgam of the pure and the puritanical, found something "irredeemably disgusting in the life and character" of Edmund Kean. Kean considered Macready equally distasteful. They were the Gladstone and the Disraeli of the early nineteenth-century stage. William Hazlitt's description of Macready went to the root of their deeply antipathetic natures. "He has Talent and a magnificent voice, but he is, I fear, too improving an actor to be a man of genius. That little ill-looking vagabond Kean never improved in anything."

Macready hated the provinces indiscriminately. He loathed the tedious, uncomfortable journeys, the mean, fit-up stages, the cramped begrimed dressing rooms, the second rate inns and the tenth rate players he was forced to endure as his supporting cast. In fact Macready, for whom the theatre was such an unremitting striving after personal perfection, hated the stage itself. Until his farewell performance, his children were never permitted to see him act in public. "What a calling is this," he would exclaim typically, "how deeply I feel the degradation of belonging to it, which yet for my dear children's sake I will endeavour cheerfully to pursue . . ." Such attitudes quickly set him apart. Crabb Robinson called him a gentleman who displayed none of the usual objectionable qualities of his profession: sensible, well-informed, a respecter of himself and others. Macready did not need to tour the provinces to recapture lost self-esteem. He did not rely on Bath, Bristol, Norwich or Plymouth to burst his ears with applause but he was well aware of the additional revenue his tours would bring him and his quickly increasing family.

William Macready visited Norwich in 1828, 1835 and 1845. One night during the first sojourn he so maltreated his opposite number in the throttling scene in "Virginius" that John Smith, one of the manager's sons decided to take the precaution of preparing himself for the next encounter with a great wad of cotton wool and towelling round his neck—to Macready's "measureless indignation". Smith was not the only one to resort to an appropriate gesture of self-defence when Macready seemed in danger of injecting a dangerous amount of realism into his performances. Fanny Kemble, the spirited actress who became his leading lady at the Princess's Theatre, Oxford Street, in the 1840s, said he prowled about the stage in every direction like a caged tiger. In "Macbeth" she alleged that he pinched her black and blue; in "Othello" she was "frightened to death" by his menaces and his roughness and wondered if she would escape alive. On one occasion he broke her little finger. "I got through Desdemona very well as far as my personal safety was concerned," she confided after a particularly intense performance, "for though I felt on the stage in real hysterics at the end of one of those horrible scenes with Othello, Macready was more considerate than I had expected."

Mary Ann Goward as Margaretta in the popular musical farce "No Song, No Supper" at Ipswich Theatre on 19th June, 1824. This charming, if slightly romanticised portrait of the Ipswich-born actress's debut was taken from an engraving by John Smart junior of Ipswich, and it used to hang in the vestibule of the Lyceum Theatre in Carr Street. In 1929 Miss Goward married the diminutive actor Robert Keeley.

Suffolk Record Office, Ipswich

A star of an altogether different stature joined the Norwich troupe briefly in 1816. He was "the young Roscius", formerly a child prodigy called William Henry West Betty. He was born in 1791 and had begun acting at the age of eleven for between 50 and 75 guineas a night. At thirteen he was breaking all box office records. By the time he reached East Anglia he had had his day: he was twenty-five, and had already retired from the stage at seventeen and returned. At Ipswich in 1816 he played the title role in John Home's "Douglas" and had also appeared as Sir Edward Mortimer in the hoary old stock piece "The Iron Chest". In his diary of 16th January, Green of Ipswich wrote: "In the evening to the Theatre with Mrs Fonnereau's order to see Master Betty in Norval. Perfect in stage deportment and histrionic trick but affected, elaborate and with a whining declamation; not one trait of genuine genius."

Betty had in his extreme youth been over-promoted by unscrupulous theatrical friends. Bettymania, as it was called, broke out like a fever but it was short-lived. John Green's straightforward judgement of this unfortunate, manipulated young man perfectly suggested the elaborate sell of which Betty had been the puppet. The girlish-looking boy actor had acquired a certain stagecraft under his hothouse tutelage, but he had never been worth the name of genius. By the time he made his debut with the Norwich Company, audiences were no longer worshipping at the shrine of virtuoso youth. Master Betty, the beautiful boy with shining blue eyes and fair curls, was developing into an effeminate, if likeable, young man. He was even getting stout.

If only for its curiosity value, however, his name was still a modest money-spinner at provincial box-offices. With a pathetic desire to make the most of his reception, he wrote from Ipswich: "I play tonight Friday Saturday here and I leave upon Sunday for Norwich when I am engaged to Act for 6 nights. I know you will be pleased to hear I was received last night with every mark of approbation from a crowded audience."

So great was the fortune that Master Betty had amassed as a child actor, that he was able to retire from the stage for a second time, when he was thirty-four, and live for the remaining fifty years of his uneventful life on his vast earnings as a child prodigy.

Joseph Munden, the celebrated comedian, had the misfortune to be temporarily eclipsed while the Bettymania hullaballoo was at its worst. He followed Master Betty to Ipswich and Norwich in 1817, accompanied by the talented but long-faced Mrs Davison, of Drury Lane. A local newspaper report claimed that Mrs Davison had "very widely and freely declared her decided opinion that the Norwich and Ipswich Company is at present the best out of London".

The steady procession of established actors on leave from London was by now both a prop and a drain to the Norwich Company. Junius Brutus Booth came from Covent Garden in 1818, Charles Mathews in 1819, the gentlemanly Charles Mayne Young in 1820. In 1824 Mary Ann Goward, a pretty girl of nineteen, appeared as Diana Vernon in "Rob Roy" at Ipswich, her home town. Miss Goward was born in Orwell Place, Ipswich, in 1805. Her father was a brazier and tinsmith with a workshop close to the theatre in Tankard Street. At sixteen, she made her stage debut as Lucy Bertram in "Guy Mannering" at the Theatre Royal, Yarmouth. She married Robert Keeley, a diminutive but powerful actor who had spent some of his early career with the Norwich Company. Miss Goward's first London appearance was at the Royal English Opera House (later the Lyceum Theatre); later she acted at Drury Lane, Covent Garden and the Old Vic, returning to East Anglia as a star from the metropolitan constellation. On 11th October, 1827, she appeared with her husband-to-be in "Wild Oats", John O'Keeffe's gently satirical comedy of the life of a strolling player. Her part was the high-spirited, dizzy Jane and on the same evening she played Lucette in the new operatic drama, "The Shepherd Boy". Soon after this success, Robert Keeley and Mary Goward were married. By 1830 they were back on the Norwich stage in such parts as Tony Lumpkin and Kate Hardcastle in "She Stoops to Conquer". When Robert Keeley died in 1869 Charles Dickens wrote to his widow:

"You know, of old I hope, that no one among his many friends can have had a higher respect for him or a profounder admiration of his qualities as a great artist, than I have always had. Many and many a year ago I remember how I was impelled to write to him after seeing you both in "The Loan of a Lover" expressing the extraordinary pleasure I had had in that most charming acting. And but the other day—though before he was lost to us—when I was dining with Macready at Cheltenham we both at the same instant cited his Verges as one of the most surprising instances within our experience of the manner in which a great actor can absorb an apparently much greater part than his into his own without the slightest obtrusion of himself."

Mary Keeley never lost her allegiance to the town of her birth: as a very old lady she opened the Lyceum in Ipswich in 1887 and took a lasting interest in its theatrical fortune.

The roll-call of famous names to join the Norwich Company as guest performers ran on throughout the 1830s—Harriet Smithson, Madame Vestris, James Sheridan Knowles and Ellen Tree his wife, William Farren and "the first and only appearance of this extraordinary pianist"—Liszt. But it had become noticeable that the effort to fill houses by engaging "names" was not paying; worse than that, it was a loss-maker. The colossal sapping of funds to feed brief, dazzling appearances was not being recouped at the box-office. But by the time a true diagnosis had been made, star-seeking had both undermined the confidence of the company and sucked it dry financially.

There was a time when Mrs Midnight's Animal Comedians provided a rival attraction to straight theatre in the eastern counties. They performed at the Old Assembly House in Ipswich in November, 1753, the year this print was published. *Suffolk Record Office, Ipswich*

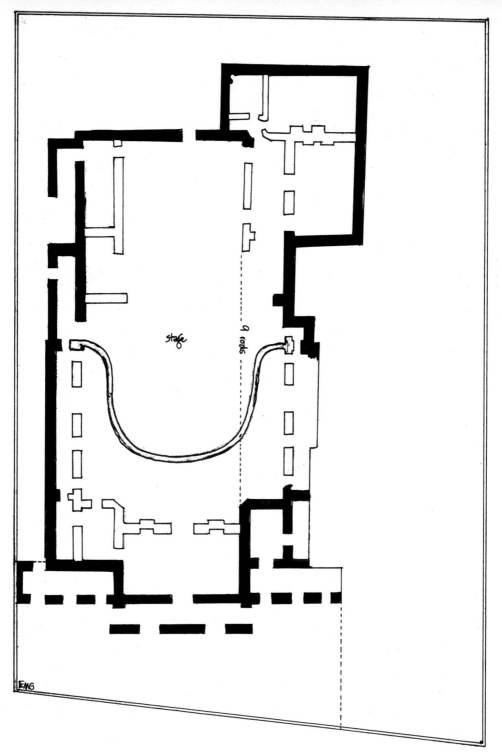

stage

9 rods

EMG

Plan of Bury St Edmunds **Theatre Royal as designed by** William Wilkins junior in 1819. It is the only provincial Regency theatre in its original structural form in the country today. The plan shows the traditional horseshoe shape of the auditorium. The building originally seated 780—360 in two tiers of boxes, 300 in the pit and 120 in the gallery. The galleries were lined with broken cork—one of the clues to the theatre's excellent acoustics.

Copied from the plan in the Suffolk Record Office, Bury St Edmunds

CHAPTER TWELVE

Bury St Edmunds; or,
Jewel of the Crown

"I need not say that the increase of sectarians, the change in the manners of the English which renders them less desirous of dramatic entertainments, added to the gradually increasing distresses of the times and the increase of the poor rates and parochial assessments must be severely felt. Under such circumstances, Bury, which used to contribute to the support of the other theatres which did not pay, but which we obliged to retain and keep open, at a loss, in order to give a respectable company constant employment scarcely now pays its expenses." William Wilkins, 1830.

ARCHITECTURALLY, the finest of the Norwich circuit theatres was built last, the only one to survive in use as a theatre to the present day. Bury St Edmunds Theatre Royal was the work of William Wilkins the younger. Built in 1819 in Westgate Street, it both crowned and ended the Norwich company's spate of theatre construction. Everything about it suggested that it was to be the final burst of enterprise before the decline of theatrical patronage and the threats of a troubled industrial age. Wilkins lavished exceptional care on its design, creating a miniature temple of drama, confident but not showy, bold yet intimate. He designed a stage larger than the stages in any of his other theatres—a full ten feet deeper even than the auditorium. The green room was almost the size of the seating area and two tiers of boxes were arranged in sweeping arcs, each box with its own door. At full capacity, the boxes accommodated 360 people, behind them ran the gallery for 120 and it was possible to pack 300 into the pit. Bury theatre embodied a proprietor's dream and an architect's fancy in one.

In the usual manner, the building was financed by subscriptions of £100, each subscriber receiving a silver (non-transferable) ticket for any performance he cared to witness for the rest of his life, in addition to five per cent interest on his shares. (This was later considered a rather too generous arrangement and the privilege was curtailed.) But the subscribers had no right to interfere in the theatre's concerns.

Bury had earned every brick of its gemlike Regency playhouse for its support for drama had been unflagging both before and after the formation of the Norwich Company of Comedians. The *Suffolk Mercury* records many fairtime visits by "Tollet's Company of Comedians at the Shire House" from 1723-1725, noting D'Urfey's "The Fond Husband; or, The Plotting Sisters" as popular fare, together with John Banks's "Virtue Betrayed; or, Anna Bullen" and "Oroonoko". After Tollet's death in 1725 the way seemed clear for other contenders. Powell's Puppet

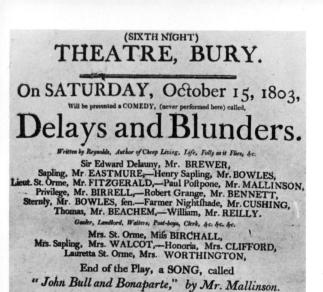

Playbill from Bury St Edmunds dated 1803, when actors were still using the Market Cross as a theatre. Their visits were timed to co-incide with Bury Fair. Mr Mallinson's song "John Bull and Bonaparte" is an example of how the players responded to the threat of Napoleonic invasion—usually with a mixture of patriotic zeal and frivolity. "Bon Ton" was a hardy old farce which the Norwich comedians produced as a regular "afterpiece".

Suffolk Record Office, Ipswich

Show from Bath aimed to divert "the Quality and Gentry" every evening during the races in May, 1725. Under the leadership of Tollet's successor, Green, the Tollet players reasserted themselves, introducing dancing, new scenes, allegedly the most celebrated tragedies and comedies of the realm and "a good band of musick". They made use of a huge theatrical booth in the Abbey Gardens.

The "Duke of Grafton's servants" from Norwich had called on Bury during its great fair from as early as 1728, and with such rewards that the town remained a prominent circuit stop until well into the nineteenth century. The Clothiers' Hall in the upper storey of the Market Cross was meticulously fitted out as a theatre for the players in 1734 and the opening season there was so popular that when the Company had completed its Colchester season it backtracked to Bury to perform a number of bespeaks.

West Suffolk's gentry, arriving with their carriages and two postillions, mingled with folk from surrounding villages who had tramped for several miles to join the crush of the gallery. They were offered the most up-to-date pieces in the company's repertoire, from "The Beggar's Opera" to the latest obscure afterpieces adapted to suit the locality. Occasionally, the comedians visited Bury twice a year—a luxury shared only by Norwich—since their welcome was assured by coveted bespeaks and persuasive box-office receipts.

Although by the 1770s Bury Fair was reputed to be no more than a frivolous reflection of its former self, the Norwich players still rode successfully on the back of the festivities, reaping their custom from the great concourse of entertainment-seekers. In his *Year Book* of 1773, Hone reported: "This fair is now become rather a Place of Amusement than a temporary Mart, as most of the Merchandises now brought thither are chiefly Articles of Luxury and Curiosity." It had become a resort for gingerbread sellers and cheap jewellery, for family reunions and scandalmongering on a magnificent scale. So long as amusement remained a popular commodity in itself, the players had no cause for complaint.

"Retired as I am at present from the scandal and tittle-tattle of Bury", wrote E. Mills in 1772 to his cousin Mary Hanson, "I cannot precisely inform you of the Company you may meet (at the fair) . . . Lord and Lady Montfort (of Horseheath) are to be there; at present I have heard of no more titles but I make no doubt but what there will be a brilliant appearance." The previous year he had referred superciliously to "the noise of the Sadler's Wells Company and a few mouthings of the Norwich Roscii".

After Mary married Sir Thomas Gery Cullum, she penned her own account of Bury's fashionable pursuits, the smart, crowded assemblies, the new plays. "Two nights are always good ones," she wrote in 1779, "for what fine folks we have in Town goe those nights and that brings numbers of other people *to see them*, so between *seeing and to be seen* there is a great number gathered together."

Among that number were one or two of the Norwich Company's traditional rivals, some of whom set themselves up in competition both at Stourbridge and Bury fairs. Mrs Sarah Baker (daughter of Mrs Wakelin who had brought the Sadler's Wells repertoire to Stourbridge Fair) brought the famous Lewy Owen to Bury in 1774. Owen was billed as the most celebrated clown out of London and he drew a damaging amount of patronage away from the Norwich players that season. Richard Griffith the manager did his best to be philosophical about it but poor houses frustrated him: "No wonder," he remarked, "that thefts and drunkenness and distress so abound when people go to booths instead of theatres, and prefer seeing a mountebank stand on his head, to an able tragedian in the character of Hamlet." The slight loss of revenue was doubly unfortunate since only a few months earlier the annual rent of the Market Cross theatre had been increased from £45 to £80 in recognition of the corporation's improvements there.

Griffith was a resilient character and not easily desolated by a bad season. He found time, as always, to pursue his favourite pastime of angling and conducted elaborate fishing parties for favoured members of the company whenever the weather held good. John Bernard has left a vivid picture of the pleasure-loving actor-manager being assisted with his float and bait, grasping the rod in immaculately white-gloved hands and adopting a number of elegant poses more suitable to a tragedian than an angler. While waiting for the elusive bite, Griffith would at intervals break off to take snuff from a brilliant box, or to sample cold fowl and punch from his well-stocked basket. The actors, and Robert Bowles in particular, teased Griffith as far as they dare, occasionally further than was good for their careers. Whether the sport under way was shooting or fishing, they were ever alert to an opportunity to make him the butt of a practical joke. Eventually Bowles probably overstepped the mark for he was dismissed, apparently for insubordination.

But fond as the company was of mocking Griffith, they seemed to have a fundamental respect for his performances and his managership. A poem published in Norwich in 1767 summed up the general feeling:

"'Gainst Griffith, tho' In comedy renown'd;
What infinite objections have been found!
But then by whom? By none, the Bard replies,
Who're over-candid, or who're over-wise.
Oft has his name, the ridicule been made
Of men, whom malice prompted to degrade."

By 1778, the Norwich Company had so found favour with the Bury public and even won over the authorities that Robert Adam the architect was engaged to remodel the Market Cross as a theatre proper and to enclose the cornstead below. The expense was met by the local aristocracy, including £500 from George, second Earl of Bristol. The theatre is described in *The Suffolk Traveller* (*1829*) as "no mean specimen of his taste and architectural skill. The body is of white brick, but the ornaments are of freestone".

The redesigned theatre served the town and company well but by 1819 it was becoming shabby and William Wilkins II believed the patrons deserved something better. The theatre was more profitable than many others on the circuit and yet it was the one on which least had been spent. The extent to which Wilkins was now sealing his acquisitions and improvements is evident from the hefty insurance policies he took out in March 1818—£1,000 each for the Norwich and Ipswich theatres, £2,000 for the new theatre at Barnwell and £2,500 for Colchester. Communally used wardrobes, scene shapes, printed books, manuscripts, plays and music books were insured for £400, and scenery, machinery and theatrical props for £600. The following year, Bury's new Theatre Royal in Westgate Street contributed to the insurance load by £1,000 and at the same time Wilkins covered his imposing detached brick house at Cambridge for £2,000.

Wilkins reached an agreement with Bury corporation to pay a £20 annual rental for the new playhouse—providing it was fully licensed. He would not tolerate competitors and insisted that the Adam theatre should not be licensed for plays but converted into a public room at a cost of £300. He wanted to be left at liberty to "construct a theatre of ample dimensions and elegance corresponding to the other public buildings of the place". At first, Wilkins thought he could raise £4,000 by 40 shares of £100 each. He would take ten shares himself and offer the corporation 20 of the remaining 30. But costs spiralled to £5,000 and in September, 1819, he wrote to his solicitor, James Borton of Bury: "I have laid out so much money that I must admit 36 ticket holders." By August of the following year he had £5,000, having contributed £1,400 himself and gathered the remainder from 36 shares of £100 each. The corporation in the end did not take any shares. Wilkins's annual charges were £200 a year of which £180 went in interest to the subscribers and £20 to the corporation. The interest on his own shares was £70.

George Colman the younger's comedy "John Bull; or, An Englishman's Fireside" was chosen to open the playhouse on 11th October. Unaccountably, the whole first night was a damp squib. "The only novelties we have seen in the dramatic corps," carped the *Bury and Norwich Post*, "are a Miss Phillips and a Mr Williams. If the former takes the place of Miss Dawson, the public will have reason to rejoice, though her introduction to us in farce enables us only to remark, that we wish she would make use of that compass of voice, those varied tones required to express the varied feelings; and that she would uniformly so deepen her accent as to relieve us from its puerility." The newspaper's reporter managed to summon a few complimentary words about the interior of the theatre, commending the "good taste" of the

The interior of the Theatre Royal, Bury St Edmunds, taken from the stage in 1977. *Richard Burn*

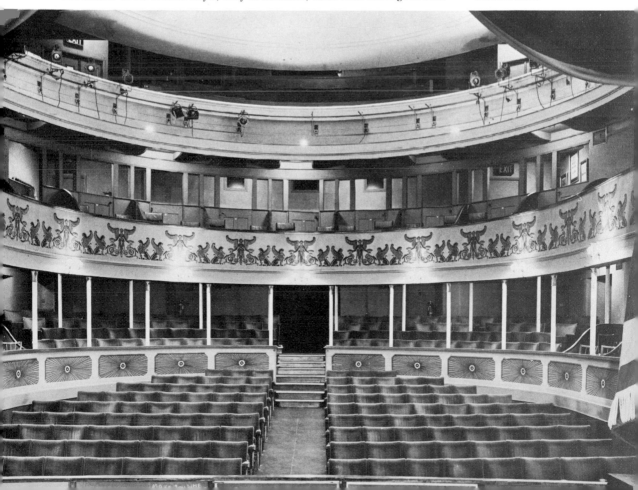

proscenium arch, the "advanced" scenery and the double tier of boxes. The lighting, however, did not do justice to the sphinxes and genii ornamenting the upper circle, and the gold cornice and rich vermilion lining of the boxes were "lost in sombre shade".

Bury St Edmunds theatre came to life just as the tide in the affairs of theatres was on the turn. The signs were still difficult to discern and nothing as easily diagnosed as decline could be made out from the early danger signals. The Norwich Company gradually found itself striving harder for full houses, pegging salaries and cutting back on its less profitable towns. James Smith, the new actor-manager under Wilkins, found himself the heir to hard times. Sir Thomas Gery Cullum wrote to his son in 1822: "Bury Fair is now over but neither I nor your mother were at one assemble or one play. The Wednesday evening, only 10 or 20 made their appearance by the dim light of two or three candles and consequently all was darkness very soon. Friday night was sufficiently crowded, though upward of 100 less than last year. Monday night the company were nearly the same as usual. The Play House had very thin Houses as the expression is, except on the nights of bespoke plays."

The same year that Macready appeared for a four-night stand in Bury (as Virginius, William Tell and Othello), the town was also host to Monsieur Gouffe, an "ape-man" with astonishing facility for climbing walls and suspending himself from the ceiling. Gouffe was to play the Brazilian ape in a melodrama tailored to his peculiar skills called "Jocko, the Brazilian Ape". Managers and showmen had begun to seek the lowest common denominator of popular entertainment and there was a prophetic irony in the fact that the country's greatest tragedian should have his audience-drawing powers measured against those of a creature who could "make a descent from gallery to stage, suspended only by three fingers, and holding two flags".

In temporarily depressed times, Bury had subsidised other less well patronised circuit theatres. By the late 1820s the shift in theatre-going habits was universally felt and Bury theatre scarcely paid its way. A realist in business matters, William Wilkins admitted to one of the Bury shareholders, Robert Rushbrooke, in April, 1830:

> "It is, I am sure, quite unnecessary to insist upon the great depreciation of Theatricals in general, but more especially of the property in provincial theatres. Induced by the flattering appearance of prosperity, I have been induced to embark very considerable sums in adapting the houses of the Norwich company to the more advanced state of society, and where the expenditure has not been made from my own pocket I have incurred weighty obligations to effect this purpose. At Bury, *in the piping times of war* the little theatre was one of the most productive and the most inconvenient in the circuit and I was naturally stimulated to render it more worthy of the town of Bury and its important neighbourhood. I could not do this without some considerable increase in rent or some equivalent expenditure, but this sacrifice I considered due to the patronage bestowed on the theatre."

In financial matters, Wilkins was a prosy pleader. His long, eloquently-delivered preambles generally meant only one thing: either that he was going to have to ask for extra revenue to keep the theatres afloat or reduce interest rates. In this case, he went on to suggest that the Bury shareholders should accept a drop in the interest they received on their shares. A similar expedient had had to be resorted to at King's Lynn, he argued, and the proprietors had agreed to accept three instead of five per cent for their 100 shares. "I do assure you with the greatest sincerity," urged Wilkins, "that a contemplated reduction will not benefit me, but my tenant [James Smith], from whose rental of all the theatres I have been obliged to make a 35 per cent reduction which will not enable him to carry on the business unless I can obtain, in addition, reductions in the rents of all the theatres—which is now my object."

Wilkins had decided to make his cap-in-hand approach to the Bury governors first because he had usually found them amenable. A liberal example from them, he hoped, would induce the other proprietors to follow suit. But the generous men of Bury were as much victims of economic stringency as theatre proprietors. They would not comply. The ensuing struggle so wore Wilkins down that it aggravated a latent illness. In 1831 he wrote from his sickbed of "the depressed and ruinous state of Provincial Theatricals" and although he himself was for the time being *hors de combat* he continued to issue advice about how to smooth the "contending animosities". Money was siphoned from his handsome architectural practice into the faltering theatrical concern year by year. Sick, weary and gout-ridden, Wilkins continued to fight for better terms but it was left to his brother, Henry, to pursue the theatre committee for their sympathy and their concessions and bear the brunt of their irritation. William Wilkins died on his sixty-first birthday in 1839 at his home "Lensfield" in Annesley Place, Cambridge, and was buried in Corpus Christi chapel which he had built.

The exterior of the Theatre Royal, Bury St Edmunds, today.   *Richard Burn*

Miss S. Booth was a Covent Garden actress paid handsomely to make a brief appearance with the Norwich company. By contemporary standards of beauty a "petite comedienne", Miss Booth drew full houses in Ipswich during the 1819 summer season. In February of the same year she had played at Norwich in the wake of Eliza O'Neill. *Suffolk Record Office, Ipswich*

CHAPTER THIRTEEN

Denouement; or,
The Struggle for Survival

"The wretched state of Theatrical Property throughout the whole kingdom is well known to everybody through the public press, and here in Norwich it cannot have escaped your own individual observation; I need not therefore tire you with farther observation on that point. It is sufficient for you, and you may congratulate yourselves on having hitherto escaped the general ruin, which has attended almost all others. But that you have done so is not owing to any local advantages such as the patronage of the citizens or the neighbourhood of Norwich; that the Contrary is the fact you all must know: It is owing to the high and honourable character of your late Tenant who, enabled from the resources of an extensive and lucrative profession has for the last Ten years paid your dividends from no other funds; and although this heavy loss has been sustained by him without complaining, it nevertheless weighed heavy on his mind and overthrew a naturally strong constitution; it so aggravated a disease (not otherwise fatal) that it brought him to his grave, worn out by mental anxieties, much more than by weight of years."
Henry Wilkins, 1840, addressing the Norwich proprietors as his brother's executor and trustee.

JUST sixteen years after William Wilkins the elder had rebuilt Norwich Theatre Royal in the classical style, his son William, architect of Bury St Edmunds Theatre, began to press for another wholesale renovation job at Norwich, this time to renew the dilapidated roof and stage. He broached his set of proposals at a special proprietors' meeting on 15th August, 1817, offering at the same time an alternative plan for an entirely new theatre built from money raised by the creation of new transferable tickets and the redemption of the old silver tickets. Of the two schemes, there was little doubt about which most appealed to Wilkins the architect. Ten days later, the new theatre proposal was the one which was backed but it was not until 22nd April, 1825, that the details were finalised. Wilkins ill-advisedly took the 30 new silver tickets upon himself to dispose of as he saw fit; he was impatient and hoped that his decisiveness would set the building work in motion after the eight years' delay.

The house was finally opened on Easter Monday, 1826, with "The School for Scandal" and "Youth, Love and Folly" by Dimond. David Webster Osbaldiston, who left for the London stage a few weeks later, was the leading man. He was later to become manager of Covent Garden, where Macready dubbed him "That very ignorant and incapable man". By way of celebration, Wilkins threw a party for 150 invited guests in the Green Room, ending with a dance on the stage. The press lavished praise on George Thorne for his scenery; praise on the enterprising patentee; and even fuller praise on the players. It was as though, entering a troublesome decade for the theatre generally, Norwich had patrons and goodwill enough to dodge the first few warning pebbles of the landslide.

Abruptly in the following year, however, all praise stopped and the Norwich Company suffered the most prolonged and vituperative period of public castigation it had ever experienced. The critical faction had as its mouthpiece a small twice-weekly penny sheet called the *Norwich Theatrical Observer* which in its brief life (it survived for only 42 numbers) managed to sling enough mud for some of it to stick. The *Observer* was run by Dr A. F. Fayerman and took as its guiding principle: "Nothing extenuate, nor set down aught in malice" from "Othello". The first issue appeared in February, 1827, announcing its chief aim as "the reformation of long existing abuses which have been tolerated for years past in the Norwich management and to make the Drama what it has not been—pure and legitimate". Fayerman's opening attack was directed at the Cibber's hugely popular comedy "The Provoked Husband" which in the mouths of the local company had become a travesty of its London self, he insinuated. Fitzball's nautical drama with music, an audience-pulling stock piece called "The Pilot", offended because the singers could not sing: "We must say, as our duty enjoins, that the singing throughout this piece was the vilest concert imitation of cats on the housetop in a frosty night's serenade we ever heard." The *Observer's* eye was everywhere: audiences as well as players were submitted to the same severe scrutiny—and the theatre's peace-keeping forces were not immune either if they were seen to be lax or incompetent. "What are the Mayor's Officers about," demanded the *Observer* shrilly, "that they cannot or will not preserve decent order in the Gallery and Slips? Some person threw half an orange on the stage, which struck Mr Balls on the face."

In the main, the *Observer* was not carping for carping's sake. The company, while no worse and probably a good deal better than companies in other provincial centres, had certainly slid from its earlier excellence. There was a reluctance to "get up" new plays for the new season and some of the ones which were introduced inevitably reflected the impoverishment of creative writing for the stage. Popular theatre had begun to exclude quality folk—who would now rather see and be seen at the opera—and the circuit playhouses exhibited a great deal of wear and tear from the messy, uncouth habits of sections of their audiences. If there was, as Fayerman detected, "a degree of niggard parsimony which corrodes and destroys everything it touches" in the Norwich management, the reverse side of the coin showed a havoc-making element in pit and gallery which was a positive discouragement to lavish spending on decor and front-of-house facilities.

The *Observer* argued that it made for confusion to admit playgoers after eight o'clock at half-price; that some of the most talented actors were being overtaxed; that "ticket nights" were a disgrace to the theatre. Ticket nights were usually awarded in the best (i.e. early) part of the season to bill-stickers, constables and others on the fringe of the theatre as a way of filling the house. Players' benefits were suspended on ticket nights "until the latter part of the season at a time when all the spare money has been gathered in by these ticket-takers and when the long days induce the playgoers rather to seek the sweetness of the summer air, than to encounter the unhealthy climate of a Theatre".

On 5th May, the *Observer* pitched itself into a personal assault on William Wilkins, accusing him of cultivating one overriding ambition—money-making—and of giving preferential treatment to the manager James Smith and his son George. The accusations were supported by two examples—the ill-lit state of the playhouse with its unfinishing ceiling, and the monopoly of complimentary tickets allotted to Smith and his kin. As many as 40 or 50 tickets a day were said to be issued to his friends, a method of "buying up the audience" which was immediately seem as depriving worthy actors of their dues, forcing them to "stoop to low, debasing means for the purpose of selling a few Tickets, haunting taverns and pothouses; exposed to the gross ribaldry of the unfeeling and the ungenerous". Those who refused to demean themselves in this way, it was argued, might well have to pay the manager £10 or £15 for the use of the house with no change for themselves from a benefit night. Actors were leaving the company as a result, the *Observer* alleged, and it would soon be impossible to keep anyone of eminence in the profession.

Later in the month, the popular English ballad opera, "Love in a Village" by Isaac Bickerstaffe provided another point of dispute. Twenty-two of the 42 songs were cut out in one performance at Norwich and others interpolated without regard for character or plot—a practice so common at the time that all but the most conscience-torn of purists had ceased to complain. The afterpiece "White Lies" "went off languidly from the dull state of the audience". The *Observer* was evidently pleased with its own iconoclasm and announced that it would persist "fearless of consequences" in its criticism for as long as necessary.

Under the cloak of pseudonyms, ostensibly like-minded correspondents contributed letters to the editor. Wilkins again came under fire. In a letter signed "Agricola" published on 26th May, 1827, in the 28th number, he was carpeted for incompetence and cupidity. The attack echoed almost thought for thought the open letter Fayerman himself had addressed to "W. Wilkin" in an earlier issue.

"The fault lies not with the supporters but with the conductors. The building erected by the former, is an ornament to the city, but the management of the latter, would disgrace even the boards of a strollers barn . . . within the last ten or eleven years, the company has seldom or never returned to Norwich without the loss of some favourite actor; no sooner does an actor begin to rise in any degree of favour with the audience, than he disappears like a Meteor."

Miss Maria Foote, a "great star" from London followed close on Macready's visit to Norwich and her four nights there in 1829 drew big audiences. But despite the combined attractions of Macready, Miss Foote, Miss Paton and Madame Vestris, all in 1829, the *Ipswich Journal* noted: "The taste for theatricals appears to be on the decline here as well as at other places."

Suffolk Record Office, Ipswich

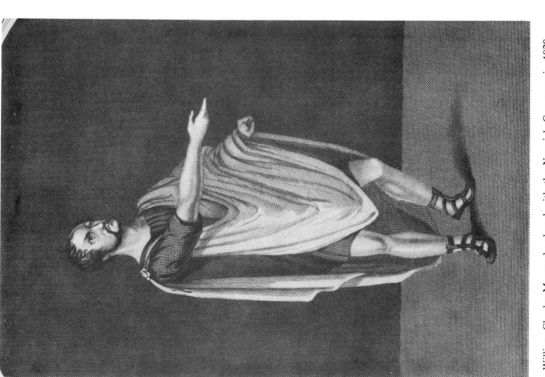
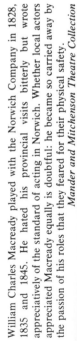

William Charles Macready played with the Norwich Company in 1828, 1835 and 1845. He hated his provincial visits bitterly but wrote appreciatively of the standard of acting in Norwich. Whether local actors appreciated Macready equally is doubtful: he became so carried away by the passion of his roles that they feared for their physical safety.

Mander and Mitchenson Theatre Collection

It was predictable that the *Observer* should also turn a tired and withering eye over the kind of plays and interludes which the Norwich Company had in its repertoire. The new pieces were deemed low, tasteless and lifeless—which in strict literary terms was true, but which failed to take into account the change in public taste from vigorous to sentimental drama. Charles Dibdin, struggling in one of the minor London theatres, conceded that although for the most part contemporary entertainment was of absolutely no literary value, it nevertheless "faithfully reflected the romantic dreams, the robust humour and the patriotic pride of the vast new popular audience that was turning to the theatre for its recreation and delight".

The season after Fayerman's most trenchant attack on the Norwich Company, the theatre embarked on a programme of star billing which brought a temporary injection of new spirit but became a serious drain on funds. In 1828, Macready played in Norwich for four nights but stayed in the city for seven. He took the title roles in "Virginius" (18th March), "Macbeth" (20th March), "William Tell", a part he detested (22nd March), and "The Roman Father" (24th March). To a defensive, somewhat demoralised company and an unadventuring public his presence was a tonic. It marked the beginning of a procession of London actors to the circuit—Madame Vestris, James Sheridan Knowles, Ellen Tree, Miss Booth, Power, Kean, Charles Kemble, Mlle Celeste, Charles Mathews, John Braham—a procession which in time acted more like a slow poison than a tonic.

Braham was a popular tenor who sang with the company first in 1832 and then in 1843—by which time he was an almost septuagenarian Guy Mannering and sang to empty boxes. Although still curly-headed and vestigially handsome, Braham was past his best. Crabb Robinson had heard him twenty years earlier in his heyday and noted: "His trillers, shakes and quavers are like those of all other great singers, tiresome to me, but his pure melody, the simple song clearly articulated is equal to anything I ever heard . . . indeed, I think Braham a fine actor while singing—And he throws his soul into his throat, it is true, but his whole frame is awakened, his gestures and looks are equally impassioned." Crabb Robinson did not pretend to any musicological prowess but he recognised in Braham's voice a beguiling attractiveness and warmth which delighted him in "a sensual way".

The star attractions quickly proved more than the slender revenue of the company could bear without damage. Audiences increasingly restricted their patronage to star nights and became thrifty with their support for the home company without big names. Once more, William Wilkins forced his gloomy observations on the Norwich proprietors. In the best of times, he maintained, the theatre had been a loss-maker but it was slipping into ruinous decline. In 1827 he had persuaded the proprietors to release him from the obligation to leave scenery and property to the value of £800 at the end of his lease, explaining that he had spent £6,000 on the new theatre and had no hope of recouping more than £2,000 on the old. (The minute absolving Wilkins of this obligation was not, however, signed—an omission which led to acrimony and frustration later on.) In 1830 he still had the problem of making a profitable disposal of the former site, an anxiety which increased his disillusionment with theatrical projects. He wrote from his home in Weymouth Street, London:

> "A few years ago, misled by the official statements of the Ministers as to the increasing prosperity of the Country and urged by some of the most respectable of the inhabitants of Norwich that a new Theatre better adapted to the prevailing taste of the times and approaching an elegant place of public amusement would be encouraged by the Norwich public, I was induced to expend a very considerable sum amounting to near £5,500 on the property belonging to the Norwich proprietors. Of this sum I have only received £1,100 from the Silver Ticket holders."

He deeply regretted the new building project of 1826, and he was not alone. London patentees had been among the first to feel the box-office slump and to restrain themselves from speculative projects. Charles Dibdin wrote (too late) of how he saw things on 1829:

> ". . . nor is this, I imagine, the time to erect additional theatres, in either Ireland or England; since, from the great increase of those who abstain altogether from Playhouses; the necessities of the Times, which debar as vast number of others from visiting them; and the very destructive extent to which the system of gratuitous admission, which crowds them nightly and unprofitably, is carried; theatrical property is, undoubtedly, become as precarious as it is peculiar; and there evidently appears a decline of dramatic taste in the public, in accounting for which, perhaps, the increased size of the Theatres Royal, and the high prices of admission, may in addition to two of the preceding causes, be very forcibly urged . . ."

Wilkins possessed no such antennae. Through bad advice, through ignorance or through slack judgement, he had overreached himself and the magnanimous gesture of taking the silver tickets on himself to dispose of at leisure had rebounded on him to the tune of £4,000—"while the Norwich proprietors [i.e. The Norwich Company, Wilkins's lessees] whose property it is," he complained, "have not contributed one single shilling although their property has been increased in its intrinsic value by the exchange of an Elegant and substantial new building in place of a ruinous old barn".

It was an elaborate preamble to a prosaic request for a reduction in the £600 annual rent. His father, Wilkins claimed, had tripled the value of the Norwich theatre, acting out of sheer benevolence. Allied to the early philanthropic speculation was a firm business motive which his father had passed on to him in undiluted form. What is more, most of the Wilkins family had shares in the theatre, including some of the women. It is not hard to see how the role of patentee, which the Wilkinses wore cheerfully and importantly enough in flourishing days, had become burdensome to them, particularly at a time of general economic crisis.

William Wilkins argued that the increase in the value of money would ensure that the proprietors would not be the losers if they agreed to lower the rent, since a dividend of £13 or £14 in 1830 was equal to what £19 or £20 had been previously. Besides, a reduction from £600 to £400 could mean the difference between sinking or swimming.

The committee was in a generous frame of mind. They agreed the reduction from 1830-1833, and then extended their leniency for a further year. The reprieve, though temporary, was quickly effective, but proved to be the signal for new star engagements at fees the theatre could ill afford. In fact it was argued that some provincial theatres were paying London actors better than their own managers. The controversial Covent Garden manager, Alfred Bunn, told Charles Kemble (whom he had tried to engage himself): "When I consider the present state of dramatic affairs in our country, the manager must be desperate who gives more, nor can I think of any theatre capable of

Charles Kemble, brother of John Philip and Sarah Siddons, was engaged for a few nights at many of the East Anglian theatres during the 1816 tour. At Ipswich, under Colonel Vernon's bespeak, he had a particularly strong supporting cast from the local company. *Suffolk Record Office, Ipswich*

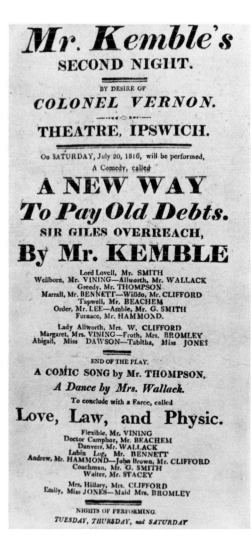

Mr. Kemble's
SECOND NIGHT.

BY DESIRE OF
COLONEL VERNON.

THEATRE, IPSWICH.

On SATURDAY, July 20, 1816, will be performed,
A Comedy, called

**A NEW WAY
To Pay Old Debts.**
SIR GILES OVERREACH,
By Mr. KEMBLE

Lord Lovell, Mr. SMITH
Wellborn, Mr. VINING—Allworth, Mr. WALLACK
Greedy, Mr. THOMPSON
Marrall, Mr. BENNETT—Willdo, Mr. CLIFFORD
Tapwell, Mr. BEACHEM
Order, Mr. LEE—Amble, Mr. G. SMITH
Furnace, Mr. HAMMOND.

Lady Allworth, Mrs. W. CLIFFORD
Margaret, Mrs. VINING—Froth, Mrs. BROMLEY
Abigail, Miss DAWSON—Tabitha, Miss JONES

END OF THE PLAY.

A COMIC SONG by Mr. THOMPSON,
A Dance by Mrs. Wallack.

To conclude with a Farce, called

Love, Law, and Physic.

Flexible, Mr. VINING
Doctor Camphor, Mr. BEACHEM
Danvers, Mr. WALLACK
Lubin Log, Mr. BENNETT
Andrew, Mr. HAMMOND—John Brown, Mr. CLIFFORD
Coachman, Mr. G. SMITH
Waiter, Mr. STACEY

Mrs. Hillary, Mrs. CLIFFORD
Emily, Miss JONES—Maid Mrs. BROMLEY

NIGHTS OF PERFORMING.

TUESDAY, THURSDAY, and SATURDAY

affording more than £30 for three nights per week, with the chance of doubling it by paying six nights." The Norwich manager *was* bordering on desperation. Macready was taken on in the spring of 1835 at well over the odds by Bunn's reckoning. The actor wrote on 8th April: "Received a letter from Mr Smith of Norwich, offering to share after £15 per night, which I accepted." On the 20th he recorded in detail the performance of "Hamlet", going through every act in the play minutely. It was a thin house. He observed tartly: "I might find an excuse for my inability to excite the audience in the difficulty of ascertaining where the audience was." He dissected his own performance with religious application, as though needing to fault himself to reach eventual perfection. Considering Macready's capacity for being his own inquisitor and judge it is not surprising that he was frequently explosively angry at a lack of perfectionism in others. Rough, incompetent country actors appalled him but he was tolerably happy with the standard of the Norwich players. In his *The Chronicles of an Old Playhouse* Bosworth Harcourt underlines the significance of Macready's temperate entry in his journal during the Norwich visit—not one actor is abused for crassness or stupidity.

Macready's exacting standards were not the only ones by which the Norwich Company measured up well. In 1832 Crabb Robinson had been pleasantly surprised by their performance in "As You Like It" at Bury St Edmunds and wrote in his journal on 10th November: "One Gill played Touchstone with great spirit and no extravagance. Even the gods seemed to feel and relish the seven degrees of rising to a challenge." Mason pleased him, Mrs Cramer made a respectable Rosalind, Wood a good Orlando. "The company is really quite respectable", he added.

Indeed, by the demands and expectations of the day, there was very little amiss in the company itself or even its repertoire. Where poor drama was billed, or stunts introduced to spice the evening, or animals brought on to the stage, it was not because the players had abandoned the purer forms of legitimate drama but because spectacle of a brasher kind was demanded. The *Suffolk Chronicle* was uneasy about the trend. The old favourites among the actors seemed played out, the newcomers were not sparkling enough. "We wish the manager would either muster up a little more pluck, or abdicate," the paper said tetchily. "Last season there was certainly an appearance of improvement; the house [Ipswich], which was miserably fitted before, was cleaned and repainted . . ."

Perhaps coincidentally, the abdication hint was followed soon after by the resignation of manager Smith after twenty-five years. "Jockey Smith", as he was known, was one of the circuits' most colourful and courageous characters. Fastidious to a fault, he dressed, so popular accounts go, in a well-brushed, tight-fitting coat, knee breeches and silk stockings. He wore a white cravat, surmounted by a rubicund, clean-shaven face and heavy wig. "Mr Smith might be seen standing daily near the Box Office of the Theatres at the hours when the tickets could be taken and places secured. He was a man of good manners and dined with the first families of the various towns," says H. R. Eyre in his manuscript books of the Ipswich theatre. Each night

Smith would position himself at the pay entrance, gold buckles at his knees and on his shoes, his hair powdered and in his hand a fine-topped cane. In 1839, at the age of sixty, he retired to King's Lynn, possibly hoping that his son George would be able to hold the theatre firm in dangerous times.

The other major change of personality in 1839 was brought about by the death of William Wilkins II. Henry Wilkins of Bath, his brother's executor and trustee for his widow and children, addressed the Norwich proprietors in a familiar vein. For the benefit of new listeners, he rehearsed the old aggravations between patentee and committee, the personal sacrifice on behalf of the theatre which had brought his brother to an early grave. The by now hopelessly unprofitable Norwich theatre was a millstone of which William Wilkins had been determined to rid himself by allowing the lease to run out without application for renewal. He rented Colchester theatre— also a financial disaster—where losses one season were likely to be so high that George Smith thought it less crippling to pay the rent and not visit the place than to play there and lose money a worse way. By comparison, the three freehold theatres in the circuit—Bury St Edmunds, Ipswich and Barnwell—were productive and likely to prove more so without the incubus of the others. According to Henry Wilkins, his brother had resigned himself to the inevitable drop in his family's shares if separated from the "really profitable" three theatres; but if he could have sold them for their original cost of £100 he would have done so.

"That our family are shareholders to the extent they are, is a very fortunate circumstance for you," he lectured the gathering. "This alone had induced me to stand forward to *prevent* such loss to the family of my late brother." The loss-making Norwich and Colchester theatres could not be kept open at even a nominal rent without the support of Bury, Ipswich and Barnwell; the Wilkins family shares could not be sold in a climate inimical to any kind of theatrical venture. Henry Wilkins therefore decided to deviate from his brother's intention of cutting off Norwich Theatre Royal and he publicly invoked the help of God in choosing a more dangerous course for the greater good of the Norwich playgoing community. He was, he said, quitting "a long and cherished retirement from the cares of life" to do so.

His proposal was to surrender the leases of Norwich, Yarmouth and Colchester theatres and to take out a new 30 year lease which allowed him the power to determine the conditions on 1st June, 1845, and on any subsequent 1st June. The rent was to be £400 a year. The arrangement would give him the right to make an annual review of his position and, if necessary, to pull out altogether at 12 months' notice. The Norwich proprietors had again been bailed out: they resolved tersely to "accept the liberal proposals of Mr Wilkins".

On 14th October, 1842, five men were appointed trustees of Norwich, Yarmouth and Colchester theatres, with the job of executing a new lease of all the theatres to Henry Wilkins of Bath and Jacob Murphy of Dundalk, Ireland. They were Norwich businessmen and professionals—John Warden Robberds, William Cooper, Carlos Cooper, John May Robberts and Henry Rix. Within a short time, the William

Wilkins III, a barrister, was in charge. But the times were sour and unpropitious and William Bushby Wilkins, who had been a minor when his father died, was soon aware of the albatross which had been hung about him. Three years later he was writing in tones more despairing than those of either his father or grandfather: "What I earnestly wish is to be quit of a concern which harrasses my life out."

As Tate Wilkinson had remarked prophetically fifty years earlier: "Theatres in general should be under the controul of an actor of judgment, experience, good nature etc. and though we have instances of gentlemen of property being managers they in general have found that money does not flow out like a spring well."

Elizabeth Cobbold (1767-1824), poet and Ipswich lady of letters. She was head of a local circle of writers and corresponded enthusiastically with the local literati. Mrs Cobbold had a penchant for writing prologues and epilogues for theatrical productions, some of them execrable. She prefaced Monk Lewis's gothic piece "Castle Spectre" with verses ending:
"Cheer our best hopes, our chilling doubts dispel,
Smile on our Spectre's merits, we implore ye,
And prove our Terrors all phantasmagoria."
Suffolk Record Office, Ipswich

CHAPTER FOURTEEN

The Broken Circuit; or,
In the Midst of Decadence

"The next year will be an awful one for Country Theatricals as everybody will go to London to see the Exhibition and take away all their tin. If the theatres are in the market I will come to Norwich and see the Committee." Charles Gill, 1850.

MOST convenient of all the theories summoned to account for the Norwich Company's demise and the wasting disease which affected country theatres generally, is the coming of the railways. For sheer neatness and simplicity the explanation that theatre-goers were able to travel by train to larger centres of entertainment in the 1840s and 1850s is appealing; but it will not do. The new era of industrialism and consequent move to the towns, certainly hastened the break-up of country circuits, but their links had already been proved too weak to take the strain of public disaffection. As early as the 1820s signs of change were showing—both in London and the provinces. Gimmickry and spectacle were being introduced to draw audiences who had tired of the familiar ingredients of comedy, tragedy, second-rate opera and farce. Animals and human freaks were drafted in to give the seasons a fillip. Playbills became strident, both in appearance and content, in directly inverse proportion to the entertainment they advertised. It was a general rule that the larger the letters, the heavier the exclamation marks, the more impoverished the fare.

The short-lived *Norwich Theatrical Observer,* for all its vituperative radicalism and occasional wrongheadedness, accurately diagnosed some of the symptoms of decay in its review of "The Winter's Tale". The play was opened to a wretchedly thin house in May, 1827. It was full of jarring elements and inconsistencies.

"I no longer wonder that the manager is obliged to have recourse to Melo Drama and Spectacle", wrote Omega, "for the legitimate Drama has, since the perversion of public taste, become so complete a drug, that were it not for *The Pilot, The Dumb Girl of Genoa* and other pieces of a nature equally flimsey, I doubt if the Treasury would be able to meet its weekly demands. Everything in this world has its rise and fall—the Stage certainly attained its height of glory during the reigns of Kemble and of Siddons; they have passed away, and their successors have as certainly done all in their power (by introducing burlesque in the place of sterling Comedy, and bombast and rant in the place of Tragedy) to degrade our national Theatre, as their illustrious predecessors did to advance it—there is an old adage, 'things at the worst will mend themselves', and as the Norwich taste for Theatricals cannot well be worse than it is, I hope that, too, will mend; the only consolation left is, it cannot be much worse, unless they insist on the manager's treating them with a Bull Bait or a Duck Hunt between the acts; this alone is wanting to complete their barbarism."

The *Observer* rightly wrote it off as a puppet show age, the age which put cheap diversion before legitimate drama. Before the critical sheet choked to death on its own spleen it ventured to voice moral judgements: women were driving coarse bargains with their managers for "exhibiting their persons to gaping curiosity, after every recent degradation of character"; harlotry was flaunted in every box; melodrama was condemned out of its own mouth by the slang of the kitchen and the stable.

Although the Norwich managers made a courageous attempt not to lower their standards, popular pressure could not be ignored in the face of poor takings. The consequences of compromise screamed from the towering black type of the playbills. In 1833 the burletta "Giovani in London; or, The Libertine Reclaimed" is billed in absurdly overblown terms as "the Comic Extravaganza Entertainment in Two Acts, comprising a grand Choral, Satirical, Tragical, Comical, Operatical, Melodramatical, Pantomimical, Critical, Infernal, Terrestrial, Celestial, one word in all—'Gally-maufricalollapodrical', Burletta Spectacle". Pieces such as "Wizard Skiff; or, The Tongueless Pirate Boy!" or the "romantic and interesting drama 'The Travellers Benighted; or, The Bleeding Nun of Lindenburg'", were part of the new repertory alongside bowlderised versions of "Hamlet", "Romeo and Juliet" and the best of Sheridan. In 1837 Andrew Ducrow arrived with his horses, one of them encased in a bull's hide for the stunt "Bull fight"; and in 1845 Ipswich audiences applauded the sleights of Mr Bernardo Eagle, "great wizard of the South".

There was nothing newly outrageous about trundling animals onto the stage but the frequency of their appearances threatened to turn theatres into menageries or hippodromes. From the heyday of Philip Astley's London in the 1770s circus audiences had been encouraged in equestrian drama and some theatres were fitted up with a moving section in the stage rather like a roll-top desk on which the horses galloped, in the opposite direction, without actually plunging into the wings. Alfred Bunn retaliated when attacked for introducing equestrian acts with: "It is perfectly true that I have resorted to quadruped performances," he said, "owing to the total want of attraction in biped ones." Bunn tended to impute his own fairly mercenary interest in drama to playgoers, maintaining that theatres were supported not from any intrinsic love of the art or profession practised in them, but "from extraneous excitement held out to us as a temptation to enter them". Not far below his ample surface, Bunn preferred spectacle to serious drama and it was only a matter of time before his outspokenness on the subject put him at loggerheads with the aesthete Macready, later to become Bunn's rival manager in London. Both men clung to and mistrusted the theatre—but for profoundly different reasons. On one of his Norwich engagements, Macready was asked his opinion about the desirability of the stage as a profession. The actor growled. "Sir," he said, "I would sooner see a son of mine coffin'd at my feet than that he should take to acting and the stage." But Macready was a paradox: he loved drama and hated the stage.

The first 1845 season opened in Norwich at the end of January and ran for two or three weeks. The much longer second Norwich season began in April with an address from Mrs Smith, the manager's wife:

"Six years are past since first, with spirits high,
We launched our barque beneath a cloudless sky."

She had unwittingly provided the first couplet of what was to develop into an elegy on the county theatres. The Norwich Company was now severely depleted, and the survivors had agreed to take a reduction of a quarter of their salaries; houses were thin, resulting in a loss of £26 on the summer season. Finding he could no longer make the circuit pay, Smith in desperation entered into a new agreement with W. B. Wilkins to take a share of a clear one-fifth of the receipts on nights of more than £10—in lieu of an annual rent. This was a mere holding operation, totally inadequate to the crisis. In a pathetic farewell address to his last audience Smith declared:

"I have witnessed the drama in its high and palmy state. I have seen its gradual decline until at length it has become even the shadow of its former self. Many and varied have been the causes assigned for that decay—the increase of dissent fanaticism on the one hand, errors of judgment on the other, reduction of prices the third."

Boxes were now slashed from 4s to 2s 6d; upper circle from 3s to 1s 6d, but without making any significant difference to the regularly thin houses. It was the worst season he or anyone else had ever known.

Side elevation of Ipswich Theatre, Tacket Street, after it was enlarged in 1888. The roof was taken off and the walls carried up 10 ft higher. A high pitched mansard roof (centre) replaced the old hip roof and new flies and a "grid" floor made the stage one of the most versatile in the provinces.

Suffolk Record Office, Ipswich

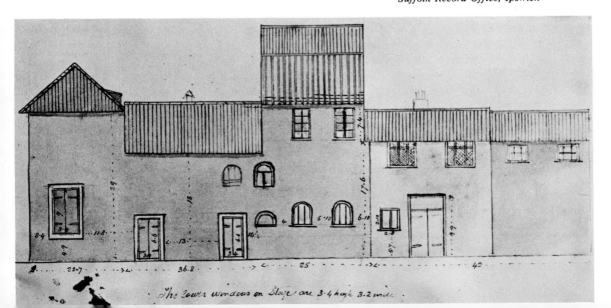

George Smith was unfortunate enough to have to preside over the company's decline but he had not either occasioned or precipitated it. He was a useful personification of catastrophe, however, and the proprietors were not above using him as a whipping boy. Smith began to plead in self-justification, putting his case in the poignant terms of a man not only down on his luck, but the victim of uniquely punishing events. "You will remember," he told the proprietors, "the last season in Norwich of 1845 was under peculiar circumstances, and I had not the opportunity of making it so profitable as it might otherwise have been, from the uncertainty which attached to the *latter* part of it, being doubtful which way it would terminate or whether I should be allowed to open the theatre at all; that uncertainty you will naturally allow tended to crib a man's energies, and prevented his making engagements which otherwise he might have had the opportunity of doing.

I will only add that if you can *fairly* do anything to further my interest in the matter I shall feel bound in gratitude to make you all and every return it may be in my power to do."

There was no reprieve. The company's loss of ground was too complete for the committee to extend either sympathy or support to the man who had been managing the theatre while audiences and profits seeped inexorably away. Smith went.

Wilkins was unwilling to sell the theatre, believing it would fetch next to nothing. He settled on an offer for the circuit from William James Achilles Abington, a barrister, member of Cambridge University and for three years lessee of Southampton Theatre. "I really expect Abington will do great things," wrote Wilkins, "He has spirit and confidence in himself, a very good actor and judge of acting. He is a *Gentleman* and likely to be popular with the respectable position of the inhabitants. He will follow a new system with, I expect, a totally new Company." This is in fact what happened; without any loss of continuity in performances, the old Norwich Company ceased to exist. In its place a touring company was developing with a different and much less firm band of actors.

For the sake of holding on to a dwindling group of theatre patrons, W. B. Wilkins supported the shareholders in their proposal to have the Norwich theatre redecorated. He saw the importance of keeping up appearances. "It doubles our chance—If the theatre is to be retrieved, now is the time, when we have changed the management and changed the system, and this is a change that should be forced upon everyone's attention the moment he enters the Theatre, by some great unmistakable outward and visible sign of it. This the proposed new decoration would be. It would having [sic] a *thriving* look, which always tells, and would put a new aspect on affairs, do away with old associations of failure and discontent and leave the question of *success* to be decided on its own merits." The proprietors agreed to £100 for re-decoration. The changes in the management were obvious to all, but the changes in the system were not so easily discerned. They amounted to a break with the tradition of a regular, salaried, circuit-touring theatre company and the substitution of a loose group of actors who were not bound by contract and had no firm allegiance to Norwich. Loyalties were cut and the new regime was characterised by a rapid succession of managers with little interest in the company outside profit-making. W. J. A. Abington does seem to have taken over the circuit from love of his profession and a desire to mend the Norwich circuit's fortunes but his reign was not a success.

By June 1846 the post of manager was again vacant and the former manager, George Smith, now under some financial strain with a large family to support, begged the proprietors to consider him for the lesseeship again. John Judd Sharpe, one of the governing body, wrote of the strong feeling in Norwich that Smith should be returned and given another chance to prove what he could do, before any of the Wilkins' nominees were considered. Smith lost, but his supporters claimed they would set him up in a rival theatre. He suffered the final humiliation of being refused a benefit night.

The new manager was T. D. Davenport, a showy man well versed in his job both in England and America. He had Wilkins's support and the outgoing manager thought him the "only proper person for the circuit". He had been a former manager at Portsmouth where it is said that, after auditioning Charles Dickens for his company, he advised the young man to stick to writing. Dickens is popularly supposed to have modelled Vincent Crummles in *Nicholas Nickleby* on Davenport, and Ninetta "the phenomenon" on his daughter Jean, in a form of mild retaliation. *Nicholas Nickleby* was first published in monthly parts in 1838-39, by which time Davenport's excessive manipulation of his daughter's career was well under way. On 26th October, 1837, father and daughter had appeared for a three night engagement at King's Lynn. Mr Davenport, "of the Theatre Royal, Haymarket", presented "the celebrated Miss Davenport, 10 Years of Age, styled by the Public Press the most astonishing and first Juvenile Actress of the day who has again been received with UNBOUNDED APPLAUSE". There were no bounds to the manager's exploitation or the public's curiosity. In four nights at Lynn the girl performed 33 characters— men, women, maids and matrons—danced seven dances and sang 16 songs. Her totally incongruous repertoire included the title role in "Richard III" and Sir Peter Teazle in "School for Scandal". Dickens may not have used Davenport's company alone as his model for the Crummleses but he would hardly have needed to embroider the manager's unscrupulous presentation of his infant phenomenon for his picture of Ninetta. Ninetta was all too real.

Considering his own background and that of the company's troubles it was not to be wondered at that Davenport met an unharmonious atmosphere at Norwich. W. B. Wilkins, the reluctant patentee, and the proprietors were still battling uneasily for their own as much as for the theatres' interests. Wilkins claimed that he had had to spend £200 of his own money on improvements at Norwich Theatre Royal and to do so had been forced to sell one of the shares which his family held in the theatre. With the spectre of his family's theatrical losses before him, he announced that he would relinquish the theatres, "being utterly unable to stand the expense and the harrass-ment of carrying them on any longer". He offered the scenery and stages in lieu of

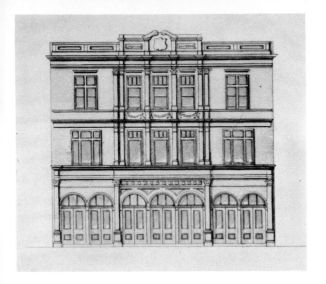

The architect Walter Emden designed Ipswich Lyceum. This is his plan of the front elevation which suggests a wedding cake elegance quite at odds with the actual no-nonsense exterior of the theatre in Carr Street. Mrs Keeley opened the Lyceum in 1891.

Ipswich Museums

rent and told the proprietors: "I only hope that whoever undertakes it after me will be able to make it answer better for you and at a less cruel loss to himself than he who now addresses you."

His letter was treated as absurd. The committee investigating his claims delved into their records and came up with a startling omission: a memorandum agreeing that Wilkins should be paid up to £500 at the end of his 30-year term as patentee, for all he had personally expended on Colchester theatre, had not been signed. Moreover, the 1828 minute absolving his father of the need to leave £740 16s 9d worth of property in the theatres when his lease expired was not signed either. The proprietors argued, on this evidence, that no claim could be sustained against them. On the contrary, Wilkins could be faced with a bill for dilapidations, but they trusted that some amicable adjustment could be made. Wilkins was incensed. In a letter to a shareholder, Richard Rackham, from 89 Chancery Lane, dated 30th May, 1846, he vented his exasperation and anger:

"Mr. Davenport's offer for your theatres is contingent upon his obtaining Cambridge and Bury. Mr. Poole [Charles Poole, who became manager at Ipswich in February, 1846] has no great wish for anything but Ipswich and has agreed to act in the matter as I choose. I have purposely delayed signing any agreement with respect to these last-named houses till I should see in what spirit the Norwich shareholders were prepared to meet me. If I have reason to consider myself harshly dealt with, I shall sever the circuit and put my shares up to auction, leaving them to find a tenant for themselves. I am prepared for a sacrifice, it is no new thing to us in the matter of Norwich Theatre where £4,000 of my father's money is buried in a desperate attempt to better the property of his fellow shareholders as well as of himself; *without return—without even thanks* for the good intention he displayed.

For myself, I have spent two years of vexation and harrassment of which the other shareholders have shared nothing, but are not only unprepared to share the loss incurred by striving to the last to make the property answer at a rent twice too high, but even strive to evade the repayment of sums advanced upon the faith of their resolutions. I am led to these observations by the Report of the Committee which I have only this morning received which purposing as it does to claim everything and to yield nothing, I *must* resist to the uttermost. Surely it is a farce to talk of an *amicable adjustment* upon the basis of such a report.

". . . I write warmly upon this subject for I feel so—I am wounded and disappointed—I feel that where we have been called upon to make allowances and sacrifices we have made them, and when we in turn find ourselves in a position to claim if not the forbearance at least the sympathy of others we have to fight for our own bare rights, step by step—

"I say, Mr. Rackham, that the Norwich Theatre has brought us *to the ground*, it has destroyed our prospects and embittered our lives and I have no hope so bright as being before long quit of that and Theatricals altogether.

"You are considerably younger than I am, you are on the spot and may perhaps if you take a leading part in its direction manage to make it answer the purpose of yourself and your co-proprietors better than I could do. I hope you will. I am, dear Sir,

Yours very truly
W. B. Wilkins"

Ipswich Lyceum, Carr Street, the town's last purpose-built theatre. It survived for just forty-five years and when it closed in 1936, Ipswich was without a regular theatre for nearly a decade.

Devastating in its disillusionment, its frankness and its weariness, this outburst is the final comment from Wilkins to survive. It is a semi-private letter, addressed to one of the young proprietors with whom Wilkins had no personal quarrel and, being unofficial, it has a strength and directness which his formal representations to the governors lacked.

The grisly business began of assessing the monetary value of the theatres in the dissolving circuit. Joseph Stannard and William Spelman drew up an inventory which showed that "dilapidations in the several theatres" amounted to £317 10s. The value of machinery, scenery, furniture, fixtures, gas fittings (introduced with such eclat only a decade earlier), wardrobes, library and music was estimated at £1,024 2s 6d. The stages, excluding traps, were put with nice precision at £101 1s 3d. A Prodigious library of musical scores for pieces with anything up to 12 parts, plus a pair of kettle drums and a gong, came to £129 5s 6d.

All the circuit playhouses seemed to be in tatters. At Colchester, the floors of the passages to the boxes, pit, staircases and slips all needed renewing. The ceilings were mottled with damp and peeling plaster; walls and broken glass were in need of repair; windows had to be replaced and tiles made good if the place was to be weatherproof. Yarmouth was in an even sorrier state: floors, ceilings, doors, shutters, chimneys, were all in a bad way and the outside woodwork had begun to rot from lack of repainting. At Norwich appearances were little better. By December, 1847, there was a real urgency about the repairs, especially to the dangerous south gate. The Theatre Royal was declared near to "ruinous delapidation".

In the scene rooms were noted "a quantity of set pieces and Roll Scenes for the Country Theatres, the whole very old and in bad condition". Among the stacked wings there were 12 woods, 12 chambers and 12 gothic scenes, all in reasonable order. But the streets and gardens had seen better days. Quantities of tunics, silk "trowsers", togas, Hussar dress, fur pelisses, plush breeches, Scottish kilts, embroidered waistcoats, military and naval uniforms, the trappings of kings and cardinals, Chinese dresses, leopard skins, "ghost dresses", breastplates and bedgowns amounted in their uncared for heaps to a mere £149 6s. The entire complement of scenery and machinery was valued at £331 19s. Davenport had taken on a circuit at the end of its road. Morally and materially, it was closer to bankruptcy than it had ever been. Even its goodwill was ebbing away.

The Wilkins trustees did not have a great deal with which to comfort themselves. Their property at Colchester had been put at £129 6s; at Yarmouth £156 11s 6d; and at Norwich £487 6s 9d. With a total of £160 16s worth of costumes, £116 3s 6d worth of books and music and £74 of gas paraphernalia, the assets stood at an unimpressive £1,128 3s 9d. Dilapidations alone amounted to £1,589 1s 6d. "The present moment is a crisis in the Theatrical Affairs," said Wilkins defeatedly, "and it behoves us all to act with caution."

Box office receipts at Great Yarmouth were as low as £6-odd some nights; at

Colchester they were unmentionable. Colchester briefly came to life during the four-night attraction of the Bedouin Arabs but lapsed again into apathy the moment regular drama returned. Colchester's 1847 season yielded only £238 in total. On 1st December, Mr Clarance's benefit brought in £17, of which Clarance took £3 15s. A few days later, 100 pit tickets were given away. It was not until the precocious Miss Davenport's benefit night came round that her father could take any pleasure in the normally gloomy business of counting the night's takings. On 10th December the total receipts were £42 14s—£16 7s for Miss Davenport, £26 7s for her father. Just 20 years earlier the humblest actor in the Norwich Company could have expected £45 from a benefit and James Smith, as manager, would have netted £140 with ease.

Even the Norwich proceeds were falling in this melancholy season . . . £180 in the summer season of 1847 was a humiliating reward for many weeks' toil and £438 from December to January, 1848, hardly covered salaries. Right from the beginning, Davenport had his back against the wall. In May, 1847, he was fined a nominal sum by a bench of Norwich magistrates for assaulting a man who was selling tickets outside the theatre for less than the regular prices of admission. Davenport alleged that by these "ticket nights"—a system he said was allowed in no other town—the former manager had lost £6,000 in 20 years. Davenport was heard sympathetically but the incident, as a symptom of desperation, said much for the state of morale in the theatre.

Davenport soon realised that he was not equal to the odds at Norwich and its struggling satellites. He relinquished managership to the tragedian Charles Dillon in 1848 and died two years later in America where he had gone with his daughter to seek audiences more receptive of their talents. Dillon's interregnum did not even last a year.

Similar changes and uncertainties were bedevilling efforts to keep Ipswich theatre afloat. Charles Poole, the manager there, was reduced to "actively catering for public amusements" with performing dogs as well as what he called "the ordinary drama". In 1847, Thompson of Drury Lane took over but the new man did nothing to allay the fears of the *Suffolk Chronicle* about the way things were going. "Never perhaps in the history of local theatricals, has the Ipswich stage exhibited a greater failure . . . the pieces performed have been from the lowest range of the acting drama", the newspaper criticised. "In the midst of decadence various expedients have been resorted to for the purpose of 'drawing houses'—for example, an actor in clown's costume rode in a washing-tub drawn by four geese on the River Orwell." No doubt because of its generous bar facilities (drinking could go on as long as an actor remained on the premises) the theatre kept unwarrantably late hours and added to this objection was the more serious allegation that some of the performances were an outrage to public decency.

In 1848 Poole was back for the summer season and he and Davenport competed for the licence. Davenport was the victor, securing "the entire old

Norwich Circuit" for five years but departing for America almost immediately afterwards. Those who cared about the loss of the old company's strengths and values saw in each managerial change new hope of recovery but each time they were disappointed. The *Suffolk Chronicle* fondly believed that "we are about to return to the good old days".

Joseph Holt, known as Joseph Clarance to the public, took up the ailing circuit in 1850. He was a decent comic actor but possessed none of the sinew needed by any manager taking over affairs at this deeply unpropitious juncture. The new Drury Lane management was openly poaching from provincial companies "so as to secure a monopoly of all the more efficient favourite actors" and putting the viability of country theatres more in jeopardy than ever. Clarance and his sub-lessee, Baynton Rolt, had a rough passage. In 1853 they were threatened with legal action under the Dramatic Authors' Act for not submitting playbills for scrutiny to the Dramatic Authors' Society. Clarance replied that he kept no file of playbills and claimed honestly if impertinently that he found he could run his theatre more economically by making private arrangements with authors unconnected with the society to use their plays.

The proprietors were forced to call on their solicitors to try to extricate themselves from the embarrassing position Clarance's unconventionality had placed them in. "Mr Clarance is a comical fellow and rather a favourite here," they wrote irrelevantly. "We should be glad to save him any unnecessary expense and trust that whilst we are trying to make arrangements with you for him all proceedings in the action will be stayed, of course, without prejudice."

Still the circuit was unable to retain its managers. The next man who seemed as if he would get his fingers burned was the comedian Charles Gill. He had made soundings about the theatres some years previously but his interest waned when he heard that he would have to supply £600 for rent and leases. Nor did he know enough about the circuit to be convinced that it was, or could be made, a paying proposition. He had ended by exclaiming to an acquaintance in 1850:

> "Clarance has lost up to the present period £200—the bonus which he gave for the theatres—and old Davenport now requires either £200—or £150—bonus for *Bury, Cambridge* and *Ipswich*—independent of the Rent—don't you wish he may get it—*I pity the poor devil who takes them.*"

Gill himself became that poor devil in 1854-55, evidently buoyant this time about his chances of making the theatres pay.

He set about restoring the old pattern of the circuit and made it one of his first jobs to refurbish the disreputable playhouse at Ipswich. He was generally thought to be "the right man in the right place" and, having himself lambasted "the late execrable systems of management" he was bound to do better. Gill went into the project with his old friend William Sidney and together they revived some of the money-spinners of the past—"The Hunchback" by Sheridan Knowles, "Deaf as a

Post", "Jane Shore", "Rob Roy" and a sizeable Shakespearian repertoire. His obituarist in 1895 claimed that Gill was "inveterately opposed to the touring system and prophesied bankruptcy for all who went into it, and a speedy return to the old stock seasons".

Whatever their aspirations, Gill and Sidney were too late to claim honours. In all but name, the Norwich circuit had snapped; the company of regular comedians had, all but for a few retainers, dwindled and dispersed, some to London, some to other companies and others simply to the haven of retirement; the old order had vanished—and only now, with the damage done, did the persuasions of rail travel consolidate the new theatre-going habits in a way which was bound to starve small playhouses.

In 1840 the long-mooted idea of a railway between Norwich and London had been revived but it was not until 1845 that the first passengers were able to make the journey. The London-Cambridge-Norwich-Yarmouth route was not in operation until 1849 (only later did the route to Norwich from London via Ipswich gain favour). In 1849 a cheap second-class return fare from Norwich to London was 10s. Third class return cost 7s 6d. Wealthier patrons had long since started to seek their pleasures farther from home and this new mobility soon spread through the social strata. The worst that could happen to the circuit had happened long before East Anglia entered the age of steam. All that the railways did was to write *finis*, to a uniquely prodigal century of theatrical development in East Anglia, to a remarkable band of players and to audiences who took their pleasures simply and at home. Theatrical property had become a losing proposition and there was no incentive to build new theatres until touring companies, later in the century, helped revive theatrical prosperity in the provinces.

A few months before the dissolution of the Fisher circuit late in 1844, Mrs Chapman, opening her benefit night at Bungay theatre, recited a few brave, prophetic lines at the front of the stage. They were, in one sense, an acknowledgement of defeat but they expressed, too, a simple belief that so long as there was life there would be theatre:

> "Of all its hopes the Drama is not reft,
> There are still some staunch supporters left;
> The love of harmless pleasure is not fled,
> The Muses only sleep, they are not dead . . ."

There seemed little justification for even this muted statement of optimism. The only thing which made her hope remotely realistic was the unequalled century of theatrical tradition sustained by two sets of players—Fisher's remarkable family circuit and the Norwich Company of Comedians. The present day theatres of Norwich, Ipswich, Bury St Edmunds and Colchester are the torch-carriers of those early companies.

APPENDIX I

Fate of the Norwich Circuit Theatres

Barnwell: Rebuilt 1816. In 1874 was still being referred to as "The Theatre". In 1878 became the home of a mission and was known as "Theatre Royal, Barnwell Mission". By 1922 was converted to "Old Theatre Royal, King's College Club for Boys". The first mention of the building as "Festival Theatre" (a title it holds now) was in 1926-27. From 1951 to 1960 it was used as a store for a local telecommunications firm. In 1962 the Cambridge Festival Theatre again took it over—this time as a workshop and wardrobe of the Cambridge Arts Theatre.

Bury St Edmunds: Gave world premiere of "Charley's Aunt" in 1892. Modernised in 1906. Succumbed to financial anaemia in 1925 at the time of cinema competition. Became barrel store for Greene, King, the brewers. Re-opened 1965 to seat 400. Now National Trust property.

Colchester: Theatre Royal burned down 1918. New playhouse built in the mid-twenties, with a cinema screen behind the proscenium arch. Robert Digby and Beatrice Radley set up repertory company in 1937 in former art gallery. New hexagonal Mercury Theatre opened 1972.

Great Yarmouth: Theatre Royal demolished 1929. Regal cinema built on site.

Ipswich: Theatre Royal closed 1890, passed to Salvation Army 1891. Lyceum opened in Carr Street to replace it. In use until 1936. Former lecture hall in Tower Street (Poole's Picture Palace) opened 1947 as theatre. New purpose-built theatre planned at Civic Centre.

King's Lynn: Remains of Georgian Theatre in St George's Hall existed until the mediaeval guildhall was rebuilt 1949-51. Theatre Royal, built 1815, remodelled 1904. Destroyed by fire 1936. New theatre built in same site. Opened with film show in 1938.

Norwich: Manager Fred Morgan reconstructed Tacket Street theatre in 1894. Destroyed by fire 1934. Third and present Theatre Royal built on same site in 1935.

Stourbridge: Site where Stourbridge Fair was held now shrunken to Stourbridge Common. Chesterton, Barnwell and Stourbridge overrun by suburban Cambridge. Some of the fair's ancient names remain— Garlick Row, Oyster Row, Mercers Row; so does the Leper Chapel, close to Barnwell Junction station. The Reverend Thomas Kerrick paid £160 for the chapel in 1816 and saved it from destruction. He conveyed it to the university; the university in turn conveyed it to Cambridge Preservation Society, its present owners. Services held there occasionally.

APPENDIX II

The Fisher Tradition

Charles I   Resigned company management 1842. Went to Glasgow as scene painter at Theatre Royal there.

George   After collapse of circuit in 1844 went to live in King's Lynn as private tutor and violin teacher. Wrote *A Harmony of the Gospels* but could not afford to publish it. Died in Norwich in reduced circumstances in 1864.

Charles II   Leading actor with Norwich Company until its collapse. Carried on family tradition in America, from 1861-1872 was member of Wallack's Theatre in New York, then joined Augustus Daly's stock company. At sixty married 20-year-old Josephine Shaw in 1876. "The sunshine streamed upon the bride with her delicate girlish figure robed in pale *cafe-au-lait* silk and her brown hair crowned white flowers as she came out of the picturesque church on the arm of the portly well-built gentleman, whose silvery hair floated in the pleasant breeze."

David III   After leaving Glasgow, made first appearance in London at Princesses Theatre, Oxford Street. Played with Charles Kean. Attracted attention of Queen Victoria at performance at Windsor in 1850. Acted occasionally at Norwich theatre. Joined Ben Webster in 1859 at Adelphi. Left stage briefly to give solo musical performances in Hanover Square Rooms. Joined Drury Lane. Last appearance was at Lyceum in 1884 as Sir Toby Belch. Died 4th October, 1887, in Camden Town.

David IV   Had first stage part as babe in arms. Father tutored him in theatre. Acted with Mathews, Phelps, Sothern, Charles Kean. Was Osric to Henry Irving's Hamlet. Joined D'Oyley Carte Opera Company.

Chronological Table—The Norwich Circuit of Theatres

White Swan becomes home of Norwich company	1730		
	1734	William James becomes manager	
IPSWICH THEATRE, Tankard Street, built	1736	Title Norwich Company of Comedians coined	
	1741	DAVID GARRICK makes stage debut in IPSWICH	
White Swan, Norwich, refurbished	1747		
NORWICH THEATRE built by Thos. Ivory	1758	THOMAS IVORY (1709-1779) becomes proprietor	
	1759	Richard Hurst manager	*PATENTEES*
	1760	WILLIAM HENRY CROUSE acting manager	THOMAS IVORY 1758-1768
COLCHESTER THEATRE built	1764		
	1766		
Multiple proprietorship initiated; Royal Patent	1768	IVORY gives up sole proprietorship	
NORWICH THEATRE repaired and refurbished	1771	CAPT. WILLIAM IVORY assumes patentee role	
	1772	Fund for decrepit actors founded at Norwich	
KING'S LYNN THEATRE built	1776		CAPTAIN
GREAT YARMOUTH THEATRE built	1778	ROBERT ADAM remodels BURY ST EDMUNDS theatre	WILLIAM IVORY
	1780	GILES LINNETT BARRETT becomes manager	
STOURBRIDGE FAIR added to Circuit	1782		
	1785	ANNE BRUNTON makes stage debut	GILES LINNETT BARRETT 1784-88
	1788	SARAH SIDDONS (1755-1831) in Norwich	
		JOHN BRUNTON becomes manager/lessee	JOHN BRUNTON 1788-1800
	1800	WILLIAM WILKINS I becomes lessee	
NORWICH THEATRE remodelled by Wm. WILKINS I	1801	JOHN CLAYTON HINDES actor/manager	
	1802	Four die in STOURBRIDGE theatre accident	
NEW IPSWICH THEATRE built by Wm. WILKINS II	1803		WILLIAM WILKINS I 1800-1815
STOURBRIDGE theatrical booth demolished	1807		
	1808	Wm. WILKINS II takes over BURY theatre	

BARNWELL THEATRE, Cambridge, built	1809		
NEW COLCHESTER THEATRE built	1811		
	1813	Lease renewed to Wm. WILKINS I for 30 years	
NORWICH THEATRE has facelift	1814	Critics v. Players battle at IPSWICH	
NEW KING'S LYNN THEATRE built	1815	Wm. WILKINS II takes over	
	1816	MASTER BETTY in IPSWICH	
	1817	JAMES SMITH becomes NORWICH manager	
	1818	ELIZA O'NEILL and EDMUND KEAN with circuit	WILLIAM WILKINS II 1815-1839
BURY ST EDMUNDS THEATRE built by Wm. WILKINS II	1819		
	1821	MARY ANNE GOWARD'S debut (MRS KEELEY)	
NEW NORWICH THEATRE built by Wm. WILKINS II	1826		
	1828	WILLIAM CHARLES MACREADY in NORWICH	
	1835	WILLIAM CHARLES MACREADY in NORWICH	
	1839	GEORGE SMITH becomes NORWICH manager	
	1840	Wm. WILKINS III takes out lease for 30 years	WILLIAM WILKINS III 1839-1846
	1842		
NORWICH CIRCUIT CURTAILED	1843		
NORWICH CIRCUIT BREAKS	1845	WILLIAM JAMES ACHILLES ABINGTON manager	
	1846	T. D. DAVENPORT manager	
	1848	CHARLES DILLON manager	
	1850	JOSEPH (HOLT) CLARANCE manager	
	1853	BAYNTON ROLT manager	
COMPANY changes from stock to travelling	1854	CHARLES GILL/Wm. SIDNEY managers	

APPENDIX IV

Chronological table—The Fisher Circuit of Theatres

	1785	DAVID FISHER I joins NORWICH company
	1786	DAVID FISHER I joins SCRAGGS's COMPANY
	1788	DAVID FISHER II born
	1790	ELIZABETH FISHER born
	1792 ⎱	DAVID FISHER I takes over management
	⎰	CHARLES FISHER I born
	1793	GEORGE FISHER I born
	1794	HENRY FISHER born
	1808	HALESWORTH TRACT battle
	1809	WILLIAM SCRAGGS dies; son takes over
WELLS-next-the-SEA THEATRE built	1812	FISHER-SCRAGGS partnership dissolves. DAVID FISHER I founds NORFOLK and SUFFOLK COMPANY of COMEDIANS
WOODBRIDGE THEATRE built	1814	ELIZABETH FISHER (wife of DAVID I) dies
EYE THEATRE built	1815	HENRY FISHER dies
EAST DEREHAM THEATRE built	1816	DAVID FISHER III born CHARLES FISHER II born
SUDBURY THEATRE rebuilt	1817	
? THETFORD THEATRE adapted	1818	DAVID FISHER II's debut at DRURY LANE
BECCLES THEATRE built	1819	
SWAFFHAM THEATRE built	1822	
? NEWMARKET THEATRE built	1824	
LOWESTOFT THEATRE built	1827	GEORGE FISHER I leaves company
NORTH WALSHAM THEATRE built ⎱	1828	
BUNGAY THEATRE built ⎰		
	1831	DAVID FISHER II leaves stage
	1832	DAVID FISHER I dies
ASSIZES move to NORWICH from THETFORD	1833	GEORGE FISHER II born
THETFORD THEATRE CLOSES	1834	GEORGE FISHER I leaves stage after brief comeback
	1844	FISHER CIRCUIT COLLAPSES
	1845	DAVID FISHER IV born (WALTER DAVID)

BIBLIOGRAPHY

Ashton, Geoffrey and Mackintosh, Iain. *The Georgian Playhouse,* Catalogue of the Hayward Gallery exhibition, 1975.

Bernard, John. *Retrospections of the Stage,* London, 1830.
Bibliotheca Topographica Britannica. xxxviii; The History and Antiquities of Barnwell Abbey and of Sturbridge Fair, London, 1786.
Boaden, James. *Memoirs of the Life of John Philip Kemble,* 2 vols., London, 1825.
Bolingbroke, L. G. *Players in Norwich,* Norfolk Archaeology, vol. xiii, 1898.
Bostock, E. H. *Menageries, Circuses and Theatres,* London, 1927.
Brown, Eluned (ed.). *The London Theatre (1811-1866) Selections from the Diary of Henry Crabb Robinson,* Society for Theatre Research, 1966.
Burley, T. G. *Playhouses and Players of East Anglia,* Norwich, 1928
Bury and Norwich Post.
Bunn, Alfred. *The Stage: both before and behind the curtain,* 3 vols., London, 1840.

Cambridge Chronicle.
Cambridge Journal.
Campbell, Thomas. *Life of Mrs Siddons,* London, 1834.
Carver, James. *The Norfolk and Suffolk Company of Comedians and the Fisher Family,* a paper read before the Norwich Science Gossip Club, March 10, 1909.
Catalogue Raisonnee of Mr Mathews's Gallery of Theatrical Pictures, 1659 to the present day, 1833.
Charke, Charlotte. *A Narrative of the Life of Mrs Charlotte Charke,* London, 1755.
Chase, William, *A Compleat History of the Famous City of Norwich to 1728,* Norwich, 1728.
Cibber, Colley. *An Apology for the Life of Mr Colley Cibber,* London, 1740.
Clarke, William S. *The Irish Stage in the Country Towns, 1720-1800,* Oxford, 1965.
Collier, Jeremy. *A Short View of the Immorality and Profaneness of the English Stage,* 1698.
Conolly, L. W. *The Censorship of English Drama 1737-1824,* The Huntington Library, 1976.
Cooper, C. H. *Annals of Cambridge,* Cambridge, 1852.

Davies, Thomas. *Memoirs of the Life of David Garrick,* 2 vols., London, 1784.
Dibdin, Charles. *Memoirs of Charles Dibdin the Younger,* Society for Theatre Research, 1950.
Dibdin, Thomas. *Reminiscences of Thomas Dibdin,* London, 1827.
Donohue, Joseph. *Theatre in the Age of Kean,* Oxford, 1976.
Duncan, Rev. John. *The Lawfulness of the Stage, enquired into,* 1787.

East Anglian Magazine. Various theatrical articles.
East Anglian Miscellany. Various theatrical articles.
Egan, Pierce. *Life of an Actor,* 1825.
Eshleman, Dorothy (ed.). *The Committee Books of the Theatre Royal, Norwich 1768-1825,* Society for Theatre Research, London 1970.
The Essex Review. Various theatrical articles.
Everitt, Alan. "Country Carriers in the Nineteenth Century", *Journal of Transport History,* February, 1976, vol. iii, No. 3.

Findlater, Richard. *Banned: Review of Theatrical Censorship in England,* London, 1967.
Findlater, Richard. *The Player Kings,* London, 1957.

Glyde, John Jnr. *The Moral, Social and Religious Condition of Ipswich in the Middle of the Nineteenth Century,* Ipswich and London, 1850.
Goodman, Walter. *The Keeleys on the Stage and at Home,* London, 1895.
Goodwyn, E. A. *A Century of a Suffolk Town — Beccles 1760-1815.*
Gosson, Stephen. *The Schoole of Abuse,* London, 1579.

The Halesworth Theatre Tracts, 1808.

Harcourt, Bosworth. *The Theatre Royal, Norwich: Chronicles of an Old Playhouse,* Norwich, 1903.

An Historical Account of Sturbridge, Bury and the Most Famous Fairs in Europe and America, 1773.

Jenkins, Elizabeth. *Ten Fascinating Women,* London, 1955.

The Jerningham Letters (1780-1843) Excerpts from the correspondence and diaries of the then Lady Mary Jerningham of Costessey and her daughter Lady Bedingfield.

Joseph, Stephen. *The Story of the Playhouse in England,* London, 1963.

Kenrick, Thomas. *The British Stage and Literary Cabinet,* 6 vols., London 1817-1822.

Kirby, John. *The Suffolk Traveller,* Woodbridge, 1829.

le Grice, E. C. *New Theatre Royal, Norwich: its past history and present story,* Norwich, 1946.

Lingwood, H. R. *Ipswich Playhouses: Chapters of Local Theatrical History,* Ipswich, 1936.

Loftis, John. *Sheridan and the Drama of Georgian England,* Oxford, 1976.

Mackie, Charles (ed.). *Norfolk Annals 1801-1850,* Norwich, 1901.

Macready, William Charles. *The Journal of William Charles Macready 1832-1851,* ed. J. C. Trewin, London, 1967.

Mander, Raymond and Mitchenson, Joe. *The Artist and the Theatre,* London, 1955.

Mann, Ethel. *Old Bungay,* London, 1934.

Misson, Henri. *Memoirs and Observations in his Travels over England,* London, 1719.

Mitchley, J. A. *East Anglian Theatre:* catalogue of an exhibition devoted to the history of the Players and Playhouses of Norfolk and Suffolk at the Castle Museum, Norwich, 3rd May — 3rd June, 1952.

Nelson, Alfred and Cross, Gilbert (eds.). *Drury Lane Journal: Selections from James Winston's Diaries, 1819-1829,* Society for Theatre Research, London, 1974.

Nicoll, Allardyce. *A History of Late Eighteenth Century Drama 1750-1800,* Cambridge, 1952.

Norfolk Chronicle.

Norwich Mercury.

Norwich Theatrical Observer. ed. A. T. Fayerman, 1827.

Parker, George. *A View of Society and Manners,* 2 vols. 1781.

Playfair, Giles. *Kean,* London, 1939.

Playfair, Giles. *The Prodigy: The Strange Life of Master Betty,* London, 1967.

Price, Cecil. *Theatre in the Age of Garrick,* Oxford, 1973.

Redstone, Vincent B. "Woodbridge Theatre and Fisher's Company", *Booth's Illustrated Almanack,* 1900.

Review in Verse of Performers from the Theatre Royal, Norwich, during the season at Lynn, of 1802, King's Lynn, 1802.

Richards, Kenneth and Thomson, Peter (eds.). *The Eighteenth Century English Stage,* London, 1972.

Rosenfeld, Sybil. *Strolling Players and Drama in the Provinces, 1660-1765,* Cambridge, 1939.

Rosenfeld, Sybil. "The Players in Norwich 1669-1709" in *Review of English Studies,* 1936.

Rosenfeld, Sybil. "The Players in Cambridge 1662-1800" in *Studies in English Theatre History,* Society for Theatre Research, 1952.

Rosenfeld, Sybil. "William Wilkins and the Bury St Edmunds Theatre", *Theatre Notebook,* vol. xiii, Autumn, 1958, No. 1.

Rosenfeld, Sybil. *The Theatre of the London Fairs in the Eighteenth Century,* Cambridge, 1959.

Rosenfeld, Sybil. "An Ipswich Theatre Book". *Theatre Notebook,* vol. xiii, Summer, 1959, No. 4.

Rosenfeld, Sybil. "St George's Hall, King's Lynn", *Theatre Notebook,* Jan.-Mar., 1949.

Roscius: Or, A Critical Examination Into the Merits of All the Principal Performers Belonging to Norwich Theatre. In the Last Season, Norwich, 1767.

The Secret History of the Green Rooms, 2 vols., London, 1790.

Snagg, Thomas. *Recollections of Occurrences: The Memoirs of Thomas Snagg,* London, 1951.

Southern, R. *The Georgian Playhouse,* London, 1948.

Southern, R. *The Victorian Theatre,* 1970.

Strictures in Verse on the Performances at the Theatre-Royal, Norwich, Towards the Close of the Season, 1799, Norwich, 1800.

Suffolk Chronicle.

Suffolk Literary Chronicle, 1837.

Suffolk Tracts "A Letter to the Dramatic Censor of the Suffolk Chronicle by B. P. Bellamy of the Theatre Royal, Norwich", 1813.

The Theatre. "The Old Circuits", April, 1880.

Theatrical Journal, vol. 5, 1844.

The Times leader, October 3, 1826.

Trewin, J. C. *Mr Macready,* London, 1955.

Troubridge St Vincent. *The Benefit System in the British Theatre,* Society for Theatre Research, 1967.

White's History. *Gazetteer and Directory of Norfolk, 1845.*

Wickham, Glynne. *Early English Stages Vol. II 1576-1660, Pt. i,* London, 1963.

Wilkinson, Tate. *Memoirs of his own Life,* York, 1790.

Wilkinson, Tate. *The Wandering Patentee.* 4 vols., York, 1795.

Winston, James. *The Theatric Tourist,* London, 1805.

Wood, O. I. and Mackintosh. I. "Theatre Royal, Bury St Edmunds", *Tabs,* vol. 23, No. 2, June, 1965.

Manuscripts

H. R. Eyre. Interesting Matter Relating to Scenery, Decorations, etc. of The Theatre Royal, Tacket Street, Ipswich, 1895 (from the Eyre Collection sale, 1904), Suffolk Record Office, Ipswich.

H. R. Eyre. *Theatricals in Suffolk.* The Inner Circuit or The Norfolk and Suffolk Company and also some of the Smaller Towns, 1891, Suffolk Record Office, Ipswich.

H. R. Eyre. H. R. Eyre's "Things Theatrical in Ipswich, 1895. The drama and theatres in Ipswich from the year 1296 to 1890", 7 vols. Suffolk Record Office, Ipswich.

H. R. Eyre. Playbills, Prints, Portraits and notes ("Hintlesham" vol.). Suffolk Record Office, Ipswich.

Elizabeth Cobbold Correspondence, Suffolk Record Office, Ipswich.

Leases, articles of agreement, indentures etc. relating to *Norwich circuit theatres and actors,* 1757 onwards. Norfolk Record Office, Norwich.

Contracts, conveyances, letters etc. relating to the building of *Bury St Edmunds Theatre Royal.* Suffolk Record Office, Bury St Edmunds.

Correspondence and deeds relating to the finances of *Bury St Edmunds Theatre Royal.* 1818-1846, Suffolk Record Office, Bury St Edmunds.

Burney Theatrical Portraits, British Museum.

Winston MS material in Birmingham Public Library.

Unpublished Theses:

R. G. Digby Chamberlain. *The Norwich Worsted Industry 1700-1850* (Colman and Rye Libraries of Local History, Norwich).

B. D. Hayes. *Politics in Norfolk 1750-1832* (Colman and Rye Libraries of Local History, Norwich).

Rex Stedman. *Vox Populi: the Norfolk newspaper press 1760-1900* (Colman and Rye Libraries of Local History, Norwich).

Fisher Collection: Letters, newspaper cuttings, salary books, notes (Private Collection).

R. P. Mander. Typescript article *"Two hundred years of theatrical history in Bury",* Suffolk Record Office, Bury St Edmunds.

Margaret Statham. Three typescript pamphlets on drama in *Bury St Edmunds and the Theatre Royal,* Suffolk Record Office, Bury St Edmunds.
Cullum Family Archives: Suffolk Record Office, Bury St Edmunds.
Letter from William Wilkins to Robert Rushbrooke, 1830, on the "great depreciation of Theatricals", Suffolk Record Office, Bury St Edmunds.

Bolingbroke MS: *Ladies Wardrobe, 1784* (inventory of costumes), Colman and Rye Libraries of Local History, Norwich.
Norwich Circuit: List of movements of the company and plays performed 1801-1817, Norfolk Record Office, Norwich.
Norwich Theatre: 1826-1850: List of plays etc. compiled by Norwich solicitor William Nicholas Harwen Turner, Norfolk Record Office, Norwich.
Diary of James George Zobel, glass stainer of Lady Lane, Norwich, 1827-1858, Norfolk Record Office, Norwich.

Maynard Collection, Cambridge Record Office.
Wilkins Correspondence, 1845-1846, Norfolk Record Office, Norwich.
Committee Book I, Theatre Royal, Norwich, 1768-1783
Committee Book II, Theatre Royal, Norwich, 1783-1825 } Norfolk Record Office, Norwich
Rough Committee Book, Theatre Royal, Norwich, 1825-1847
Miscellaneous theatrical receipts and correspondence (1845-50) relating to the *Theatre Royal, Norwich,* Norfolk Record Office, Norwich.

Playbills

British Museum collection of eighteenth and nineteenth century playbills.
Fisher Collection of playbills, property of Mrs Kitty Shaw and Miss Caroline Fisher-Carver.
Bolingbroke MS (1795-1855), Colman and Rye Libraries of Local History, Norwich.
St Vincent Troubridge collection of provincial playbills, recently given to The Enthoven Collection, Victoria and Albert Museum, by Lady Troubridge.
Theatre Royal Norwich (1769-1824) playbills, Colman and Rye Libraries of Local History, Norwich.
Ipswich Theatre: Playbills, prints and portraits ("Hintlesham" vol.), 1779-1832 with notes by William Booth, Suffolk Record Office, Ipswich.
Bungay Museum playbills.
H. R. Eyre's playbills of Ipswich Theatre, 1833-1838 and 1859-1890, Ipswich.
Cambridgeshire Collection playbills, Central Library, Cambridge.
Bury St Edmunds Theatre Royal playbills, Suffolk Record Office, Bury St Edmunds.
Norwich Circuit playbills (1799-1800) on microfilm, Colman and Rye Libraries of Local History, Norwich.

INDEX

Churchill

PAUL DOWSWELL

HODDER
Wayland

an imprint of Hodder Children's Books

© 2002 White-Thomson Publishing Ltd

Produced for Hodder Wayland by
White-Thomson Publishing Ltd
2/3 St Andrew's Place
Lewes
BN7 1UP

Other titles in this series:
Stalin
Kennedy
Hitler

Series concept: Alex Woolf
Editor: Philip de Ste. Croix
Design: Derek Lee
Consultant: Dr Nick Crowson,
 University of Birmingham
Picture research: Shelley Noronha,
 Glass Onion Pictures
Map artwork: Nick Hawken
Indexer: Richard O'Neill

First published in Great Britain in 2002 by Hodder
Wayland, an imprint of Hodder Children's Books

The right of Paul Dowswell to be identified as the
author has been asserted by him in accordance with
the Copyright, Designs and Patents Act 1988.

Quotations from the writings and speeches of Sir
Winston Churchill in this book are reproduced with
permission of Curtis Brown Ltd, London, on behalf
of the Estate of Sir Winston S. Churchill. Copyright
Winston S. Churchill.

British Library Cataloguing in Publication Data
Dowswell, Paul
 Sir Winston Churchill. – (20th century leaders)
 1. Churchill, Winston S. (Winston Spencer),
 1874-1965
 2. Prime ministers – Great Britain
 I. Title
 941'.082'092

ISBN 0 7502 3913 1

Printed in Hong Kong by Wing King Tong

Hodder Children's Books
A division of Hodder Headline Limited
338 Euston Road, London NW1 3BH

Picture acknowledgements: The publisher would like to
thank the following for permission to use their
pictures:
Camera Press: 4 (bottom), 8, 10, 11, 31, 39, 46, 57;
Hulton Archive: 22, 24, 25, 26, 27; Imperial War
Museum, London (Hodder Wayland Picture
Library): 17, 18, 35, 38, 40, 41, 42, 45 (top), 45
(bottom), 49, 58, 60 (top), 60 (bottom), 61 (top), 61
(bottom); Peter Newark's Historical and Military
Pictures: (imprint page), 9, 12, 14, 19, 20, 30, 34
(top), 34 (bottom), 36; Popperfoto: 5, 7, 13, 15, 16,
23, 32, 43, 47, 50, 51, 52, 53, 54, 55, 56, 59;
Topham Picturepoint: 4 (top), 28, 29, 37.

Cover picture: Camera Press (by Vivienne).

Contents

CHAPTER ONE

Early Life 1874-1900

Winston Churchill was born at Blenheim Palace on 30 November 1874. The upper class world he arrived into now seems impossibly glamorous and grand. Queen Victoria was on the throne, and Britain was approaching the height of her power as the world's greatest empire and richest nation. Victoria ruled over almost a quarter of the earth's population. Winston was born into a class that benefited most from this wealth and believed that it had a God-given duty and right to rule.

▼ Churchill's father, Lord Randolph Churchill.

Winston's father, Lord Randolph Churchill, was a prominent Conservative politician. He was a direct descendant of John Churchill, the first Duke of Marlborough, who had become a national hero. Blenheim Palace, a huge stately home, had been given to John Churchill in 1705 by Queen Anne, after he had led the English army to victory over the French king Louis XIV.

ANGLO-AMERICAN MARRIAGE

Lord Randolph had married a beautiful American girl, Jennie Jerome, early in 1874. The couple met on a yacht belonging to the heir to the Russian throne. Jennie, the daughter of a rich New York financier, had been swept off her feet and the couple became engaged after just three days, and married soon afterwards. He was 25 and she was 19.

Winston arrived seven months later. He liked to tell people that he had arrived early, as he was impatient to get on with life at Blenheim. Unfortunately his childhood was not a happy one, and would have crushed the spirit of a more sensitive child.

◄ Churchill's mother, Jennie, as a young woman.

LONELY CHILDHOOD

As was the custom at the time, upper class parents handed over the care of their children to nurses and nannies. Winston saw little of his parents, who were central figures in London 'society' – a fashionable, exclusive social circle of the richest, most influential people in the country.

So, almost from birth, Winston was brought up by a nurse named Mrs Everest. She was a large, kindly woman who gave him the affection he rarely received from his parents. He called her 'Womany', and in his memoirs he wrote of her with great affection: 'Mrs Everest it was who looked after me and tended all my wants. It was to her I poured out my many troubles...'

LORD AND LADY CHURCHILL

Winston adored his parents, as these two quotations from his memoirs show:

'We saw as children the passers-by take off their hats in the street and the workmen grin when they saw his big moustache.'

ON HIS FATHER'S FAME

'(She) shone for me like the Evening Star. I loved her dearly – but at a distance.'

ON HIS MOTHER

▼ Churchill in 1880. He is six years old. Standing with him is his aunt, Lady Leslie.

SENT AWAY

Winston, at the tender age of seven, was sent to a boarding school near Ascot called St George's. The school was run by a sadistic headmaster, who would beat boys with a birch twig cane until blood was drawn.

Churchill was a boisterous and arrogant child, and he was bullied by other boys. Fortunately, he was soon transferred to another boarding school. At thirteen and a half he went to Harrow, one of England's most prestigious boarding schools. His fellow pupils were the children of some of the richest and most powerful people in the country.

GOOD IN PARTS

Not all of his childhood was unhappy. Biographer Piers Brendon paints a picture of an energetic, cocksure youth, who was obviously drawn to the army life.

'He built an outdoor castle complete with moat and drawbridge and made a large catapult (chiefly used to shoot green apples at a cow). He liked to drill his cousins and his brother Jack... and revelled in the thrill of mock warfare as commander of his armies of toy soldiers.'

In later life Churchill liked to give the impression that he was a 'dud' at school. But while he was not a sparkling intellectual, he was already showing a gift for language that would serve him well in his future life.

PARENTAL WOES

Much of Churchill's correspondence survives, and some of the most touching letters he wrote were to his parents, who would rarely visit him at his school, and barely even wrote to him more than once a term.

LORD RANDOLPH CHURCHILL

Churchill's father was a larger-than-life character, who seemed to be bursting with energy. A brilliant public speaker with a flamboyant moustache, he rode around the corridors of Parliament on a bicycle. Young Winston adored him, and copied his style of dress and mannerisms. Lord Randolph had a meteoric career in politics. He rose to become Chancellor of the Exchequer by the age of 37. But after only five months in the job he resigned in a minor quarrel over military expenditure, and never regained political office.

As his time at Harrow drew to an end, Lord Randolph decided that Winston should join the army. This was a traditional career for the less academic sons of upper class families. Despite some success at school, Churchill's father was deeply disappointed by his son's conduct and progress. In one terrible, stern letter following Churchill's gaining a place at the officer training school of Sandhurst, he wrote: 'With all the advantages you had, and with all the abilities which you foolishly think yourself to possess... this is the grand result that you come up among the 2nd rate and 3rd rate class who are only good for commissions in a cavalry regiment.'

INTO THE ARMY

Following his father's stern disapproval Churchill blossomed at Sandhurst. When he graduated he was rated 20th in a class of 130, and was posted to the 4th Hussars Cavalry Regiment in 1895. In that year he had to grow up very quickly. His father had been suffering from ill health for several years, and finally died of a brain tumour in January 1895, after a long, difficult illness. He was only 45.

Churchill made his mark in the world with an extraordinary confidence. He had come from the very top level of British society, and he was determined to make the most of his social status and connections. His whole philosophy was to deal directly with the men at the top, and not to bother with the usually channels of communication through more junior officials.

His position as an army officer left him with a great deal of flexible free time. In 1895 five months of his year were set aside as leave, or time off. Intending to make a name for himself as a writer he set off, aged 21, to the Spanish colony of Cuba to cover a rebellion against Spanish rule. He also persuaded a London newspaper, the *Daily Graphic*, to publish any articles he wrote.

OFF TO INDIA

Soon after his return he was posted to India with his regiment. Life here was very dull, and Churchill spent much time reading to make up for his lack of study at Harrow. In 1897 he heard that General Sir Bindon Blood was mounting an expedition to the North West Frontier of India to put down a revolt by a tribe of Afghan mountain people called the Pathans.

Churchill knew Sir Bindon and begged to be allowed to come as an officer and war correspondent. Here he wrote stirring, patriotic reports for the *Daily Telegraph*, which

▼ Young Winston Churchill in the uniform of the 4th Hussars, while serving in India in 1896. The army would not contain his growing ambitions for long.

▲ Held captive by the Boers, Churchill stands forlornly in a prison compound in Pretoria, South Africa in 1899.

were later published as his first book – *The Story of the Malakand Field Force*.

As a tactic to gain Churchill attention it was a brilliant success. Both the Prince of Wales, and Lord Salisbury, the British Prime Minister, enjoyed the book.

THEN TO AFRICA

Churchill shrewdly used Salisbury's approval to get himself posted to another colonial hot spot – the Sudan, in Africa, where army commander Lord Kitchener was leading an expedition to reconquer the region after a revolt against British rule. Again Churchill travelled as an officer and war correspondent, and took part in one of the last cavalry charges in British history. During this campaign he fought with great bravery, and was lucky to have escaped with his life. Again, Churchill published a book of his experiences, *The River War*, which added to both his reputation and public profile.

OTHER AMBITIONS

But Churchill had never imagined he would stay in the army for long. He had always been fascinated by his father's life as a politician. As early as the summer of 1895 he had written to his mother to tell her that he was considering a career in politics ('It is a fine game to play.') Army life, he said, was character-building and extremely enjoyable, but he was certain that it would not be his life for ever.

He resigned from the army in 1899. Using his family connections he soon persuaded the Conservative Party to adopt him as a candidate, and stood at a

CHURCHILL'S BRAVERY

In action, Churchill always fought with great courage. He had no fear of death in battle and wrote to his mother: 'I am so conceited that I do not believe the Gods would create so potent [powerful] a being as myself for so prosaic [commonplace] an ending.'

by-election at Oldham in the summer of 1899. He fought a good campaign and was narrowly defeated.

Shortly after the election, more trouble was brewing in the Empire. In South Africa, descendants of Dutch immigrants, called the Boers, were rebelling against British control of the colony. Churchill immediately arranged to report for the *Morning Post*, and took the first boat out.

Travelling through hostile territory in an armoured train, Churchill and a squad of soldiers were ambushed. During the fighting that followed, Churchill was taken prisoner.

PRISON, ESCAPE AND FAME

Churchill was taken to Pretoria and held in a prisoner of war camp, where he spent his 25th birthday. He hated the life of a prisoner, and planned to escape as soon as possible. He got his chance soon enough, climbing over a wall at the edge of the camp at night. With great daring he bluffed his way out of Pretoria and on to Lourenço Marques in Portuguese East Africa. The escape made Churchill a nationally known hero. Finally he had achieved the kind of fame he felt necessary to launch him on a successful political career.

After his escape Churchill stayed in South Africa, persuading the British army there to let him serve in the South African Light Horse cavalry regiment. Here he continued both to report on the war and to fight in some of its most dangerous battles.

He returned to a hero's welcome and stood again as Conservative candidate for Oldham. Such was his reputation that even Joseph Chamberlain, the distinguished Conservative statesman, came to speak in his favour at an election meeting. This time Churchill won a convincing victory in the by-election, and so began a career in politics that would last for the rest of his life.

▼ The parliamentary hopeful. Churchill in 1899, when he stood as a Conservative candidate for Oldham.

CHAPTER TWO

Into Politics 1900-1914

In 1900 MPs (Members of Parliament) were not paid a salary. It was assumed that they would be wealthy people who would expect no financial reward for the privilege of ruling the country. Churchill's family were well off by most people's standards, but Churchill still felt he needed to make some money before he settled down into a life in politics.

So, almost as soon as he had been elected, he made the most of his new found fame and set off on a very highly-paid lecture tour of both Britain and the United States. When the tour was over he had made £10,000 from lecture fees and book sales (this was a lot of money then which he could live off for the foreseeable future). His income as a writer was to make him a comfortable living throughout his life.

▼ Suffragettes publicize their cause. The campaign for votes for women was only one of the great national issues that dominated British politics in the years before the First World War.

INTERESTING TIMES

The years before the First World War were turbulent times in Britain. There was great social unrest as trade unions fought for better wages and working conditions and suffragettes fought for women's right to vote. In Ireland, which was then entirely part of Britain, there was talk of civil war between the Protestant North and Catholic South, over the important issue of greater independence from Britain. There was great tension in government too, over the role and rights of the House of Lords. All of this took place against a backdrop of increasing anxiety about a major war breaking out in Europe.

LORDS AND COMMONS

The British Parliament contains two main chambers, the House of Commons and the House of Lords. In the 1900s, and still today, the Commons contained members who had been elected by the people of Britain. The Lords, though, contained members whose birth into aristocratic families gave them an automatic right to be part of the parliament.

The Lords could prevent government policies agreed in the Commons from being carried out. Many people felt that it was wrong for an unelected élite to block policies that an elected government wanted to carry out.

MAKING HIS MARK

Churchill was 25 when he became an MP. His fame and family connections made it certain that he would be noticed, and his career in parliament in the years before the First World War was quite phenomenal.

Just as he had packed an extraordinary amount into his life since leaving Harrow, so he now did as an MP. His gift with language meant that he soon gained a reputation as a memorable and effective speaker. Churchill made the most of this natural ability. He would practise his parliamentary speeches in the bath or in the garden of his mother's house. Here he would wander around speaking out loud to himself, and considering the effect of particular phrases.

But Churchill had a weakness too. He was not quick-witted enough to be a good debater, and when challenged and questioned by MPs who disagreed with what he was saying, he would visibly struggle. Earl Balfour, the Conservative Prime Minister, summed up his speaking style thus: 'heavy but not very mobile guns'.

▼ Churchill, in his late twenties, poses for a suitably serious political portrait. He quickly made his mark in the Houses of Parliament.

FREE TRADE V. PROTECTIONISM

Free trade is an economic policy whereby countries trade goods and materials with one another freely. Protectionism is an economic policy whereby imports (goods and materials from other countries) are heavily taxed.

Both policies have good and bad points. For example, free trade gives customers a greater choice, and the possibility of buying cheaper products from abroad. Protectionism on the other hand protects workers' jobs and factory owners' profits by deliberately making foreign goods too expensive to compete with home-produced goods.

▲ A poster supporting the view of protectionists. As customers stare into a shop window stuffed to bursting with foreign goods, unemployed men march by demanding work.

FREE TRADE

But four years into his Parliamentary career Churchill made the first of several extraordinary moves. The Conservative party were committed to supporting a policy of protectionism (see box), and wished only to trade with the countries in the British Empire. Churchill was convinced that free trade was the best economic policy. He became increasingly disillusioned with the Party he had joined and became an outspoken opponent of protectionism. Because of this, the Conservative Party became increasingly disillusioned with him. During one parliamentary speech he made in March 1904, many Conservatives walked out in a deliberate show of disapproval.

JUMPING SHIP

Churchill decided he had joined the wrong party. In the early 1900s, the two main parties in Britain were the Conservatives, who represented the British ruling class, and the Liberals who were more inclined to support other classes. The Liberals supported free trade too, and Churchill increasingly began to feel they were now his natural home.

So, in May 1904 he took the bold step of leaving the Conservatives and joining the Liberals. As a result, he became a hate figure among the Conservatives. But Churchill never really saw himself as belonging to one political party. He preferred to see himself as more of a national politician, someone who could appeal to all sections of British society.

The Liberals welcomed him warmly, especially when he attacked the Conservative prime minister Lord Balfour with great glee. Following a General Election in 1905, the Liberals became the ruling party and Churchill was rewarded with a post as a junior minister. He became Under Secretary of State for the Colonies.

▲ Churchill's wife-to-be, Clementine Hozier, pictured in the week before her marriage to him in 1908.

INTO GOVERNMENT

Given the chance to shine, Churchill seized his moment. He had a boundless energy and enthusiasm for his work which was infectious. In 1908, the Prime Minister Herbert Asquith promoted Churchill to the Cabinet (the highest level of government), giving him a job as President of the Board of Trade.

But Churchill instantly faced a setback. In a curious quirk of tradition, newly appointed ministers had to seek re-election, and Churchill lost his seat to the Conservatives, who fought a bitter, vindictive campaign against him. But shortly afterwards he was re-elected at Dundee. 1908 was quite a year for Churchill. Not only had he reached the very top level of government at the age of 33, but he also married. His wife, Clementine Hozier, would be a constant support for the rest of his life.

CLEMENTINE HOZIER

Churchill's wife came from a relatively humble background. Her mother was daughter of the Earl of Airlie, but her father was an insurance underwriter. Her own political sympathies were much more liberal than Churchill's. They had five children (one of whom died in childhood) and remained devoted to each throughout their lives. Churchill famously wrote in his biography: 'I married and lived happily ever after.'

military, relished the job. He was now in charge of the most powerful navy on earth. He loved the flamboyant uniforms he was expected to wear. He also greatly enjoyed the visits to ships, and trips aboard the huge Admiralty yacht *Enchantress*, the use of which came with the job.

By 1911 Churchill had become convinced that Britain would eventually have to fight a war against Germany. During the late nineteenth and early twentieth century, Germany had become the strongest country in mainland Europe. She was building a navy that was set to rival Britain's and was resentful of the colonies Britain, France and other European nations had gained for themselves, while Germany had almost none.

▶ Churchill dressed in the uniform of First Lord of the Admiralty, at the outbreak of the First World War. He would return to the job again, at the start of the Second World War.

16

MAJOR EXPENSES

Churchill saw his mission at the Admiralty as preparing the Navy for war. He began a major shipbuilding spree, and oversaw the largest naval expenditure in British history. He pushed though the decision to fuel ships by oil rather than coal, which made them both faster and capable of staying at sea for longer. He also created a 'War Staff' at the Admiralty, a committee which made proper planning for war much more efficient and effective.

These changes came not a moment too soon. By the time war came to Europe in the summer of 1914, Churchill had ensured that Britain's navy was both well prepared and still vastly superior in size to Germany's fleet.

Churchill greeted the outbreak of war with guilty enthusiasm. (He confessed in a letter to his wife that 'the preparations have a hideous fascination for me. I pray to God to forgive me for such fearful moods of levity.') He was in his element, but the war would bring him very mixed fortunes.

▲ The British Grand Fleet patrols the North Sea. Churchill's work at the Admiralty ensured that the Royal Navy entered the First World War as a highly effective fighting force.

CHAPTER THREE

The First World War 1914-1918

Britain entered the First World War as the richest and most powerful nation on Earth. Whatever the rights and wrongs of the British Empire, it had brought great wealth and influence to the country that Winston Churchill and a handful of other men now led. But the war was to bring many changes to the world and Britain's position in it. Churchill was to have a ringside seat at the beginning of the decline of his beloved Empire.

DASH TO ANTWERP

▼ Canadian troops in the trenches of the Western Front during the First World War. Men from Britain's empire volunteered for the war in their thousands.

Churchill's war began with an adventure straight from the pages of a story book. In October 1914, the German army had swept through Belgium and were threatening to overrun the port of Antwerp on the Belgian coast. Churchill rushed there himself, intent on organizing its defence. Under his direction, British and Belgian troops held off the German advance for a further week. This allowed

A NEW KIND OF WARFARE

The men who fought the First World War had the misfortune to be waging war at a time when the weapons of defence were far superior to the weapons of attack. Opposing armies faced each other in trenches defended by deadly machine guns and barbed wire. Such fortifications proved almost impossible for the ordinary infantryman to overrun. The war settled into a dreary stalemate, occasionally interrupted by an attack in which huge numbers of troops lost their lives.

British and French forces to prevent the German army capturing other important channel ports. But despite these successes, Antwerp still fell, and Churchill, who had risked his life to defend the port, was ridiculed by his political enemies.

THE WESTERN FRONT

After the initial German advance was halted, trenches were dug from the English Channel right down to the Swiss border. This line became known as the Western Front. Like everyone else of his generation, Churchill was not used to this kind of warfare. The battles he had fought as a young man were in open territory and usually involved a great deal of movement on both sides.

A CUNNING PLAN

Churchill was sure there was a better way of proceeding, and complained to colleagues: 'Are there not other alternatives than sending our armies to chew barbed wire in Flanders?'

Together with cabinet colleague David Lloyd George and other prominent military commanders, he devised a plan to save Britain from the deadlock of the Western Front. They intended to mount an attack against the Turks in the Dardanelles Straits and the tip of the Gallipoli Peninsula near to Istanbul in Turkey.

The idea was to open up a new battlefront to draw German troops away from the Western Front. It was also hoped that if Turkey could be knocked out of the war, then Britain and France would be able to ferry supplies and other aid directly to their Russian allies through the Black Sea.

At the Admiralty Churchill worked closely with Admiral Sir John Fisher, the most senior commander in the Navy. They had a difficult relationship, not least because Fisher was sure Churchill's plan to attack the Turks would fail.

▲ Admiral of the Royal Navy Sir John 'Jackie' Fisher, 1841–1920. Although he worked closely with Churchill, the two men had a very prickly relationship.

A British cruiser takes part in the ill-fated attack on the Dardenelles in 1915.

THE PLAN BEGINS

First, in February 1915, a naval attack was mounted by both British and French warships which were meant to bombard Turkish positions from offshore. This failed right from the start when several ships were damaged by Turkish mines. Despite Churchill's insistence that the attack should continue, the ships were immediately withdrawn by the commander in charge of the attack, Admiral J.M. de Robeck. Churchill was furious, but Prime Minister Asquith and other Admiralty colleagues all backed de Robeck's decision. Churchill was also heavily criticized for the attack by his political enemies, and Fisher added to the opposition against him by resigning in protest.

GOVERNMENT CHANGES

While all this was happening, the Liberal government collapsed and a new coalition government (made up of members of all the main political parties) was formed. The Conservatives had insisted that Churchill be demoted from his central wartime position as First Lord of the Admiralty. Instead he was offered the post of the curiously named Duchy of Lancaster, which had no specific responsibilities.

Here Churchill was to oversee further action in the Dardanelles. Although the naval assault had been a humiliating failure, it was nevertheless decided to launch a land invasion. This began in late April, and was a tragic failure. Nearly half a million British, New Zealand, Australian and French troops were dropped onto the beaches around Gallipoli where they met with fierce resistance from the Turks. Despite great determination and bravery by the troops, almost no progress was made beyond the seashore landing zones and the casualties were terrible – almost half the men who landed were killed or wounded.

CHURCHILL RESIGNS

As minister with overall responsibility for the Dardanelles campaign, Churchill was blamed for its failure, even though he had no power to direct the fighting. In the face of intense criticism he resigned from the government and volunteered for the army. He went to France as a lieutenant colonel in the 6th Royal Scots Fusiliers, commanding this battalion in both training and in the trenches.

During his time in the trenches Churchill contemplated the strange turn of events that had led him from the highest political office to the relatively minor position of a front line commander. Despite the excitement of being at war again, this was a low point in his life, and he even confessed that he would not mind if he was killed.

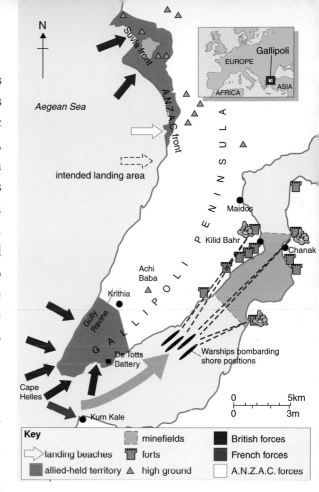

The Gallipoli peninsula stands at the entrance to the Black Sea. The narrow stretch of sea there is called the Dardanelles. Churchill and his colleagues hoped that a successful attack here would turn the war in Britain's favour.

CHURCHILL IN THE TRENCHES

Churchill looked forward to returning to life as a soldier, as some of his happiest times had been with the army during the Boer War. He frequently visited the trenches, and wrote to his wife of the excitement of prowling around no man's land (the wasteland between British and German trenches) under cover of darkness.

Churchill (on the right), looking suitably dogged, wears the uniform of the 6th Royal Scots Fusiliers, which he commanded. With him is his deputy, Major Sir Archibald Sinclair. The men were photographed in France in 1916.

BACK HOME

In June 1916, sections of the army were reorganized and his battalion was merged with other army groups, making his position as commander redundant. Churchill, who was still an MP, decided he could better serve the country by returning to the Houses of Parliament.

Much to his great disappointment he was not offered any role in government by Asquith. In December 1916 Asquith resigned and was replaced as Prime Minister by another Liberal, David Lloyd George. Lloyd George was keen to make use of Churchill, but the Conservatives in the coalition insisted he should be excluded from government.

There was some good news though in March 1917. A Government committee reporting on the Dardanelles campaign made it plain that Churchill, who was seen by the public as the man most responsible for its failure, was no more to blame than any other of his colleagues.

BACK IN GOVERNMENT

Lloyd George was determined that Churchill's talents should be put to good use. In July 1917, in the face of fierce Conservative opposition, he appointed Churchill to the central wartime post of Minister of Munitions. Here Churchill would be responsible for the manufacture of weapons and shells and bullets.

He made an impressive effort to improve the efficiency of the British munitions industry. Most importantly, he pushed forward the development of the tank. His presence at the ministry greatly speeded up the introduction of this new weapon, which would be used with great effectiveness in the final stages of the war.

Until the war ended in November 1918, he tirelessly worked to provide the armed forces with the weapons needed to defeat Germany. He regularly visited munitions factories in an effort to keep up the morale of war-weary workers. His job was a brilliant opportunity to show his worth, and Churchill was able to regain some of the prestige and respect he had lost following his fall from the Admiralty.

▼ Lloyd George leaving the Palace of Versailles after signing the Treaty of Versailles in 1919. Lloyd George's faith in Churchill ensured his political career would survive the disaster of the Gallipoli campaign.

CHAPTER FOUR

The Post-War Years 1919-1924

Churchill's success as Minister for Munitions was rewarded soon after the war ended. In January 1919, he was promoted to the prestigious cabinet post of Secretary of War in the coalition government. Here he now set about making drastic cuts in military spending. This would allow money to be spent on the task of rebuilding the nation, and creating 'homes fit for heroes' – which Prime Minister Lloyd George had rashly promised returning soldiers.

PROBLEMS IN FRANCE

One crisis which Churchill was immediately faced with was a revolt by British soldiers in France over demobilization – a military phrase meaning the return of troops to civilian life. Once the war had ended men who were not professional soldiers wanted to return home as soon as possible. The revolt happened because many men had to wait far longer than they thought was reasonable. The British commander-in-chief, General Haig, was keen to

▼ Churchill inspecting British troops in Cologne, Germany in 1919, shortly after the end of the First World War.

shoot the ringleaders of the protest. Churchill, who generally took a more generous view of such matters was not. 'Unless there was serious violence attended by bloodshed and actual loss of life, I do not consider that the infliction of the death penalty would be justified' he telegraphed to Haig. Churchill took steps to see that demobilization was fairly carried out, and within a month over a million men had been returned home.

OFF TO RUSSIA

But one area where his judgement was way out of step with popular feeling was in his decision to send troops to fight in Russia to support the Tsar (Emperor). In 1917, there had been a revolution in this huge, backward country. The Tsar had been deposed and Communist politicians had seized power. A terrible civil war was now raging between pro-communist government forces and 'White' Russians supporters of the Tsar, and other anti-communist forces.

Churchill immediately authorized the sending of British troops to Russia. What men who had just endured years of horror and deprivation in the trenches of the Western Front thought about being sent to fight a foreign war in the freezing north of Russia can only be imagined.

▼ British soldiers land in Northern Russia. Churchill's decision to send troops to intervene in the Russian civil war was unpopular with both soldiers and civilians.

CHURCHILL AND THE BOLSHEVIKS

Churchill, a member of the British aristocracy, had a total horror of communism, which was commonly referred to at the time as 'Bolshevism' – after the name of the Russian communist party, the Bolsheviks. He thought that this political philosophy, which believed the state should control and own all property and industry, would reduce human society 'to the level of an ant hill'.

BAMBOOZLED CABINET

Through sheer force of will, Churchill managed to persuade his reluctant cabinet colleagues to continue to send arms and soldiers to support the White Russians. British involvement in the war ended in 1920, but Churchill's enthusiasm for the campaign made him many enemies, especially among working class trade unionists and some Labour politicians who supported the Bolsheviks.

NEW POST

Churchill's unpopularity prompted another move. Prime Minister Lloyd George appointed him as Secretary of State for the Colonies. Here he had two major problems.

Firstly, there was the British controlled territory of Palestine in the Middle East. In 1922 he produced a White Paper (a government report outlining its intentions on forthcoming policy) on Palestine. This territory was increasingly being seen as a national home for the Jewish people, who were scattered throughout Europe and North America. The paper confirmed that the territory should become a Jewish national home, but also recognized that the Palestinian Arabs should have the right to live there.

Secondly, there was still the problem of Ireland, which was hovering on the brink of civil war, to sort out. Churchill engaged the notorious 'Black and Tans' (see box) to suppress Nationalist terrorist activity, and this caused much ill-feeling among the Catholic community. But, nonetheless, Churchill gave his full support to the new independent government of Eire, which now ruled all of Ireland except the province of Ulster, which remained under British control.

▼ Churchill (fourth from left, front row) photographed with Colonial Office civil servants and soldiers in 1921 when he was Secretary of State for the Colonies.

BLACK AND TANS

An auxiliary police force made up of British ex-soldiers, the Black and Tans took their name from the distinctive colours of their uniforms. When Catholic Irish nationalists attacked the mainly Protestant police, the Black and Tans reacted with brutal reprisals, randomly killing, and destroying the property of, Catholics.

▲ 'Black and Tans' photographed in Ireland in 1922 during a siege of the Irish Law Courts in Dublin.

ANOTHER FALL

Another problem was looming. After the war the territory of the Dardanelles in Turkey was declared a neutral zone, and a small force of British troops was sent to guard it. In the autumn of 1922, the Turkish government began to take steps to reoccupy this territory. Churchill and Lloyd George were both strongly opposed to this and threatened the Turks with all-out war if they should carry through this reoccupation.

As with the involvement of British troops in Russia, the idea of going to war over an issue of no real interest to the British people caused great concern. The coalition government, a hangover from the war, collapsed. Prime Minister Lloyd George was thrown out of office, as was Churchill and the rest of the Cabinet.

ELECTION DISASTER

An election was called. In the midst of all this upheaval, Churchill was struck down with appendicitis. His wife Clementine was forced to campaign on

A BAD YEAR

Churchill recalled the disastrous year of 1922 thus:

'Without an office, without a seat, without a party, and even without an appendix.'

his behalf. But such was Churchill's unpopularity that she was spat at in the street. He was defeated in his Dundee constituency by more than 10,000 votes. For the first time since a brief period in 1908, he was out of Parliament.

AWAY FROM POLITICS

Politics and power were his great passions, but Churchill was a man of many talents. His abilities as a writer and speaker continued to provide him with a very handsome income – which became necessary once he had lost his cabinet salary. His book *The World Crisis*, a history of the First World War written from a very personal perspective, did extremely well, and made him £20,000. Even if he had not entered politics, he would have undoubtedly have achieved some level of fame as an author.

▲ During the 1920s Churchill discovered a passion for painting. It remained one of his great joys throughout his life.

During this time Churchill also spent much of his time painting. His watercolours are considered to be pleasant rather than brilliant, but from this period onwards, painting turned into a lifelong passion.

CHARTWELL

With some of the money he made from *The World Crisis* Churchill bought and restored a sprawling wreck of a country home called Chartwell, in Kent. (He did not live at Blenheim as a cousin had inherited it.) His beloved nanny Mrs Everest had often talked about the beauty of Kent, and Churchill had felt a romantic attachment to the county since his childhood. Chartwell remained his country home for the rest of his life.

SPENT FORCE

Times were changing in British politics. The Labour Party, which represented working class people, and was supported and funded by the Trade Union movement, was growing increasingly popular. This popularity was being gained at the expense of the Liberal Party, which seemed to be a spent force. Churchill could now see no political future for himself in the Liberals. However, he detested the Labour Party – comparing its mild programme of social reforms with the excesses of the Russian communists.

After his fall from office in 1922, he increasingly began to wonder if his real sympathies, and political future, lay with the Conservative party. Despite feeling increasingly drawn to the Conservatives, he still chose to fight in the General Election of 1923 as a Liberal. This was mainly due to the Conservatives' decision to campaign for a protectionist trade policy (see page 12). He lost the seat by 4,000 votes. The Liberals' decision to support the new Labour Government which came to power in the election was the final straw. From here on, he severed his links with them.

His next attempt to re-enter Parliament was in 1924. He stood as an 'Independent Anti-Socialist' in a by-election at Westminster. This time he lost by a mere 43 votes.

BACK IN OFFICE

The Labour government fell in 1924 and another General Election was called in November of that year. This time Churchill stood in Epping, calling himself a 'Constitutional' candidate. He won a resounding victory, and Epping was to remain his seat for the next 20 years.

The new Conservative prime minister, Stanley Baldwin, was keen to make use of Churchill's talents. His party no longer supported the policy of protectionism, so there were now no political barriers between Churchill and the Conservatives. After the election, Baldwin asked Churchill to meet him, and offered him 'the Chancellorship'. Churchill assumed he was offering him the relatively unimportant post of 'Chancellorship of the Duchy of Lancaster'. When he realized Baldwin was offering him the job of Chancellor of the Exchequer his eyes filled with tears. He was back, right at the centre of British politics, in one of the most important jobs in Government.

▲ Churchill addresses a crowd of potential voters in the constituency of Epping during the 1924 election.

CHAPTER FIVE

From Chancellor To The Admiralty 1924-1939

Churchill's sudden return to the giddy heights of politics as Chancellor of the Exchequer was not a great success. Finance was not a subject that fired him with much enthusiasm. Nonetheless, Churchill still lent all his energy and imagination to the post, which he held for the next five years.

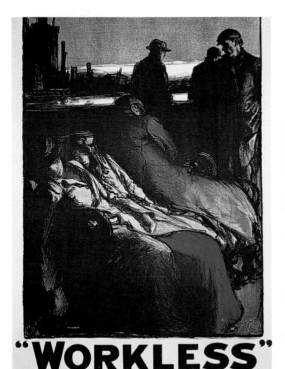

▼ A poster issued in 1924 by the Labour Party depicts the despair of unemployment – one of the great social problems of the inter-war years.

"WORKLESS"

GOLD STANDARD

His first act as Chancellor was to restore Britain to the Gold Standard (see box). The policy was a complete disaster because the British currency was rated too highly against other currencies. Because of this, British goods exported abroad became very expensive, and so sold less.

As a result, British trade and industry suffered a major slowdown and unemployment rose sharply. This caused a great deal of social unrest. Trade unions, fighting to protect the jobs and

THE GOLD STANDARD

This is a system of currency exchange between countries, which fixed a nation's currency to a set rate against the internationally agreed value of gold. In the 1920s it was thought to be a better method of maintaining the value of a nation's currency against foreign currencies than the system of fluctuating exchange rates which we have today.

wages of their members, organized strikes. Worst hit were the coal miners. As demand for coal dropped away, mine owners saw their profits decline. They tried to impose longer working hours and lower pay, but the miners went on strike in protest.

GENERAL STRIKE

The Trades Union Congress (TUC), an organization representing trade unions throughout the country, decided to call a general national strike in support of the miners. Churchill felt sympathy for the miners, but he was angered by the idea of a general strike. He thought this would be the start of a national revolution. He imagined a Bolshevik take-over and a bloody massacre of the aristocracy and the rest of the British upper class, which included himself and most of his closest friends.

His view of the situation was wildly unrealistic. The TUC were not bloodthirsty revolutionaries. They had even offered to safeguard supplies of food to cities during the strike. This idea was rejected by the government, which instead gave an army escort, complete with armoured cars and machine guns, to the convoys of lorries which delivered food to Britain's cities.

The British public were not inclined to revolution. In many other countries in such circumstances, bloody riots may have broken out. In Britain strikers and policemen even played football against

THE BRITISH GAZETTE

In the days before television, newspapers were the principal means of delivering news to the British population. All the national papers were hit by the strike, so Prime Minister Baldwin gave Churchill the job of editing a government paper. It was called *The British Gazette*, and it unashamedly presented the news from a very pro-government point of view. Churchill filled the paper with pompous and unfair propaganda, which presented the strikers in a very damaging light. His role here further increased the dislike that many working class people in Britain felt towards him.

▲ Stanley Baldwin, Conservative Prime Minister during the General Strike of May 1926, poses outside 10 Downing Street.

31

CHURCHILL AND THE EMPIRE

Churchill was a great supporter of the British Empire, and saw British colonialism as a force for good throughout the world. The British colony of India, especially, he considered to be the Empire's greatest asset. Like many people of his background and class, he had views about other races that would be completely unacceptable today. He thought that the exploitation of overseas colonies for their raw materials, and the use of their population as cheap labour, was Britain's natural right. He thought that the Asian and African people that Britain ruled over were inferior to white people, and incapable of running their own countries without the help of the British.

▼ Churchill with his wife Clementine on Budget Day, 15 April 1929.

each other. The strike ended peacefully after nine days. The TUC won none of its objectives, and the miners were eventually forced to return to work on lower wages and with increased working hours.

OUT OF OFFICE

Churchill's remaining time as Chancellor of the Exchequer was undistinguished. Although the government had triumphed in the General Strike, the ill-feeling this had generated against the Conservatives, and especially Churchill, resulted in a Labour victory in the 1929 General Election. Out of office Churchill fell out with the Conservative leader Baldwin, who did not share his almost hysterical fear of the Labour Party. When the Conservatives agreed to consider independence for India, Churchill distanced himself from the Party even further (see box).

OUT OF FAVOUR

The Labour government lasted only two years. In the early 1930s the whole world had been affected by the collapse of the powerful American economy in 1929. Unemployment and poverty were common. To combat this crisis in Britain, a national government was formed which included representatives from all leading parties. Churchill was not asked to join – he had made too many enemies in both the Conservative and Labour parties.

He was still a backbencher (an MP who does not hold senior office in his party), and, away from government, Churchill found more time for writing. Over the next decade he produced an extraordinary amount of work, both as an author and journalist. His first book from this period was a four-volume biography of his most famous ancestor John Churchill, the First Duke of Marlborough.

THE GERMAN THREAT

A visit to Germany to research some of the battles John Churchill had fought brought him face to face with the Nazi party. Churchill, who despised their anti-Semitic policies, was alarmed by this regime's threat to the peace of Europe. Surprisingly, he had initially been impressed by Hitler, whom he described as 'a cool well-informed functionary with an agreeable manner, and a subtle personal magnetism.' Throughout the 1930s, Churchill argued, in the face of fashion and government policy, that Britain should rearm to defend itself in the war he felt was sure to come with Nazi Germany.

APPEASEMENT AND DISARMAMENT

In the 1930s Churchill's pleas to rearm were out of step with political thinking on both left and right. Many people with left-wing sympathies favoured disarmament – wanting the government either to spend less money on, or get rid of, Britain's armed forces. They thought that the money saved could be spent on social services. The Conservatives favoured a foreign policy of appeasement. This was a policy that recognized that Germany had been treated unfairly at Versailles – the peace treaty that followed the end of the First World War – and should be allowed to regain territory that it had lost. Appeasement, as an alternative to war, was supported by many people in Britain for whom the horrors of the First World War were still a vivid memory.

▶ A Hawker Hart of the Royal Air Force in the 1930s. Churchill was deeply concerned that old-fashioned aircraft like this should be replaced with more modern ones before Britain had to fight another war.

He was particularly concerned about the strength of the Royal Air Force in relation to the German air force, the *Luftwaffe*. At the time it was predicted that bombers would be able to destroy cities with ease, and this would lead to mass panic among the population of a country at war. Churchill was particularly concerned that the RAF should have more aeroplanes.

▼ King Edward VIII making his abdication broadcast to the nation in 1936. He gave up the throne in order to marry Wallace Simpson.

EDWARD VIII

Churchill's reputation in the 1930s was not helped by his support for King Edward VIII. The English king wanted to marry an American divorcee, Wallace Simpson, much to the shock and outrage of the British public. Churchill felt that Edward should be allowed to do this. His stance made him even more unpopular with the public, and undermined his campaign for rearmament.

A NEW ROLE

In 1935, leading Conservative Stanley Baldwin again became Prime Minister, this time as leader of a National Government made up of all parties. Baldwin recognized Churchill's talents, but due to his unpopularity with MPs of all parties, was still not able to offer him a place in this government. He did, however, allow him to join a secret committee on air-defence research, which gave Churchill a vital role in strengthening the air force for its forthcoming battle with the *Luftwaffe*.

WAR LOOMS

Baldwin retired in 1937, to be replaced by Neville Chamberlain, a leading supporter of appeasement. In the late 1930s Hitler began to expand Germany's borders – first in Austria, then the Czech Sudetenland, then the rest of Czechoslovakia – and Churchill's worst fears were slowly realized.

Chamberlain recognized that his appeasement policy had collapsed when Nazi troops marched unopposed into Czechoslovakia. After this, rearmament in Britain finally began in earnest. Churchill considered the threat from Nazi Germany so great he even suggested making a defensive alliance with the hated Bolsheviks in Soviet Russia.

By 1939 the likelihood of a war with Nazi Germany seemed inevitable, especially when Prime Minister Chamberlain made an alliance with Hitler's next victims, the Poles. Throughout Britain there was a growing realization that Winston Churchill, political outcast and main supporter of rearmament, had been right all along.

▼ British Prime Minister Neville Chamberlain in 1938. His appeasement policy was a tragic failure, and he resigned from office a broken man.

CHAPTER SIX

Admiralty To Prime Minister
1939-1941

Hitler's armies invaded Poland on 1 September 1939. On 3 September Britain declared war on Germany. This was also the day Prime Minister Chamberlain brought Churchill back into the government. He was offered the post of First Lord of the Admiralty – the same job he had done so enthusiastically before and during the First World War. A week later Churchill received a letter from the American President Franklin Roosevelt, congratulating him on his return. It was to be the start of a highly significant political relationship.

▼ Complete with his trademark homburg hat and cigar, Churchill arrives for work on 4 September 1939, the day after he was appointed First Lord of the Admiralty.

PHONEY WAR

Churchill poured all his energy into the task of ensuring that the Navy was prepared and ever alert for whatever tasks awaited it. But the first six months of the war were strangely quiet. While the Germans concentrated on conquering Poland, both France and Britain held back. British bombers flew missions over Germany, but they dropped propaganda leaflets calling for an end to the war, rather than bombs. It was as if neither side wanted to provoke the other into violent action.

All this changed in April 1940, when Hitler's armies invaded Norway. This invasion coincided with a Royal Navy expedition to land British soldiers in Norway to help defend the country, and it was a terrible failure. Although Churchill was now in charge of the Navy, Chamberlain took the blame.

Then, the following month, Germany's troops swept through Holland and Belgium. Chamberlain, already terminally ill with a cancer that would kill him before the year was out, resigned. Lord Halifax, the Foreign Secretary, was his favoured successor. But all parties recognized that, because of his record of opposing Hitler, Churchill was the only man in Parliament with the credibility, determination and vision to lead the country in the terrible struggle ahead. On 10 May 1940, he became Prime Minister. He was 66 years old.

UNITED GOVERNMENT

Churchill's first task was to form a government that would unite all parties. At the head of this government was a war cabinet, which included two prominent Labour Party politicians, Clement Attlee and Arthur Greenwood. The uncompromising trade union leader and MP Ernest Bevin was brought into the government as Minister of Labour to be in charge of the nation's workforce.

This was a remarkable act of reconciliation on all sides. Despite the mistrust and enmity between them, the Labour politicians recognized Churchill's strengths and suitability as a war leader. Churchill, in turn, swallowed his dislike of the socialist Labour Party, and recognized the necessity of uniting the whole country in the struggle against Hitler. Forty years in politics had made Churchill a master of his profession. Throughout the war his

THE TOP JOB

'I felt as if I was walking with destiny, and that all my past life had been but a preparation for this hour.'

WINSTON CHURCHILL

'... The whole of Churchill's previous career had been a preparation for wartime leadership... he seemed to have been nursing all his faculties [abilities] so that when the moment came he could lavish them on the salvation of Britain and the values he believed Britain stood for in the world.'

HISTORIAN HERBERT G. NICHOLAS

▲ Churchill's war cabinet included Labour men, such as Attlee (second right, front row), Greenwood and Bevin (top row, first and second left).

▶ Throughout the war Churchill toured the bases of Britain's fighting forces on morale-raising visits. Here he inspects an RAF Bomber squadron.

government contained representatives of all the main parties, and remained united in their determination to defeat the Nazis.

INSPIRATIONAL FIGUREHEAD

The most obvious aspect of Churchill's leadership was his ability to inspire both his colleagues and the public. Nowhere was this more apparent than in his wartime speeches of 1940. When Churchill first spoke to Parliament as Prime Minister, he made a stirring call to arms, sombrely promising the nation: 'I have nothing to offer but blood, toil, tears and sweat.' This was the first of many ringing rallying cries that would stir the hearts of the people. In this same speech Churchill described his Nazi enemies as 'a monstrous tyranny, never surpassed in the dark, lamentable catalogue of human crime.'

A VIEW FROM ABROAD

'(Churchill) mobilized the English language and sent it into battle to steady his fellow countrymen and hearten those Europeans upon whom the long dark night of tyranny had descended.'

AMERICAN BROADCASTER ED MURROW

WORKING METHODS

As well as Prime Minister, Churchill also took the job of Minister of Defence. His war cabinet worked briskly and efficiently, and their decisions were swiftly acted upon. Churchill would always listen to his military chiefs and cabinet colleagues. If they were united on a course of action he would never overrule them, even if he disagreed with them. He was happy to delegate, but also intervened in any area he thought necessary.

Such was the enormity of the task ahead, that Churchill even pushed through the extraordinary measure of placing every citizen and their property and possessions 'at the disposal of the crown'. This meant that the government had the right to make use of any person and the assets, houses, factories and businesses they owned, to help Britain win the war.

WOOING A PRESIDENT

'No lover ever studied the whims of his mistress as I did those of President Roosevelt.'

CHURCHILL, ON HIS DETERMINATION TO FORGE AN ALLIANCE WITH ROOSEVELT

AMERICAN ALLY

Although Churchill was completely British in his cultural outlook and political loyalties, by birth he was actually half-American. Perhaps it was this that made him pursue an alliance with the United States so confidently. Churchill felt that America's support with, and best of all involvement in, the war would be crucial to Britain's success against Hitler.

President Roosevelt had watched the events in Europe with growing concern. But the American public, and many of her leading politicians, did not want their country to be involved in world affairs. This was a policy known as isolationism. Roosevelt, for all his sympathy and support of Churchill and Britain, felt that he could not involve America in the war against Hitler.

FROM BAD TO WORSE

The first year of Churchill's time as Prime Minister was one of the darkest in British history. Following their invasion of Denmark, Holland and Belgium, Nazi troops defeated France in six weeks. The remains of the British army, which had been fighting alongside the

▼ British troops returning from the French port of Dunkirk. The retreat from France prompted Churchill's famous 'We shall never surrender' speech.

French, had to be evacuated from the port of Dunkirk. Britain faced the horrifying prospect of a Nazi invasion. Churchill's power of oratory rose to the occasion. As the last British troops were ferried away from France he promised: '... we shall defend our island, whatever the cost may be. We shall fight on the beaches, we shall fight on the landing grounds, we shall fight in the fields and in the streets, we shall fight in the hills; we shall never surrender.'

A fortnight later he continued to prepare the British people for the sacrifices ahead with a speech that is still moving more than sixty years later. 'Let us therefore brace ourselves to our duty, and... if the British Commonwealth and its Empire lasts for a thousand years, men will still say "This was their finest hour".'

THE BATTLE OF BRITAIN

Before they could launch a seaborne invasion, Nazi generals had to ensure that their airforce controlled the skies over Britain. After all, a fleet of barges full of soldiers would be a vulnerable target for British warplanes. So began an aerial campaign that became known as the Battle of Britain.

The German *Luftwaffe* made a determined effort to destroy Britain's Royal Air Force. But the RAF's pilots, many of whom were from the British Commonwealth, or Poles

▼ RAF Hurricane fighter pilots 'scramble' (run to their planes) to attack incoming German bombers during the Battle of Britain in 1940.

and Czechs who had escaped from their defeated countries, fought with great courage. Almost one in three of the 1,500 RAF pilots who took part in the campaign were killed, but the *Luftwaffe* lost so many planes that Hitler called off his invasion. Again, Churchill had a rousing tribute to sum up his relief, and the gratitude the country felt towards these pilots: 'Never in the field of human conflict was so much owed by so many to so few.'

▲ Churchill's visits to bomb-damaged cities, such as here in Bristol, were remembered with deep affection by Britain's wartime civilian population.

THE BLITZ

Having failed to defeat the RAF, the *Luftwaffe* turned instead to a campaign of night-time bombing. Over the late summer and beyond, London and other British cities were subjected to heavy attack. It was during this period that Churchill is most fondly remembered as a great war leader. He made regular visits to bombed-out streets and factories in London and throughout the country. Photographs showing him wearing his old-fashioned bow tie, smoking a fat cigar, and making his trademark V-for-Victory sign, seem to sum up this era of British history.

GOOD NEWS

Alongside the British victory against the German airforce came another vital success. Although they could not offer direct help, the Americans were persuaded by Churchill to provide warships and other military equipment in exchange for bases in British colonies in the Caribbean.

In June 1941, came stunning news. While Britain lay undefeated to his west, Hitler turned his attention to the east, and launched the greatest invasion of all time against the Soviet Union. History would show that Hitler had fatally overreached himself, and this invasion marked the beginning of the end of his evil empire.

CHAPTER SEVEN

The Grand Alliance 1941-1945

A few weeks after the German invasion of the Soviet Union, Churchill sailed to North America aboard the British battleship HMS *Prince of Wales* to meet Roosevelt. The very real threat of attack by U-boat or enemy warplanes never dissuaded him from making such dangerous trips. Part of his charisma had always been the courage he showed in his willingness to expose himself to genuine danger.

The meeting was a tremendous success. Churchill met Roosevelt aboard the American battleship USS *Augusta* on 9 August. The two men got on well. It was a relationship that was to last for the rest of the war. Churchill was especially proud of his close personal friendship with Roosevelt. The American president, though, was more cautious. He liked Churchill, but he did not let his friendship interfere with what he considered to be America's best interests. (Churchill would find this out to his cost, when Roosevelt sometimes sided with the Soviet leader Stalin against him.)

The two men issued a declaration known as The Atlantic Charter, setting out the principles for which their two nations stood. Then Roosevelt and many of the crew of the *Augusta* joined Churchill aboard the *Prince of Wales* for a

▼ Churchill aboard HMS *Prince of Wales* in 1941 on the occasion of his meeting with President Roosevelt. He is seen here with cabinet colleague and friend Lord Beaverbrook.

EXCERPT FROM THE ATLANTIC CHARTER

'(Britain and America) respect the right of all peoples to choose the form of government under which they will live; and they wish to see sovereign rights and self-government restored to those who have been forcibly deprived of them.'

Sunday Service. Looking back, Churchill recalled how he was deeply moved by the sailors of the two nations mingling together on the deck, singing and saying the same common hymns and prayers.

PEARL HARBOR

By the end of the year, events would force Britain and America even closer together. On 7 December 1941, Japanese fighter-bomber aircraft attacked the American fleet anchored at Pearl Harbor, inflicting grave damage. Britain was also attacked by the Japanese. Over the next few months she lost many of her own colonial possessions in the Pacific, such as Singapore. But America and Britain were now fighting together in the Pacific as allies.

There was even more satisfying news to come in Europe. Germany had made an alliance with Japan in the 1930s. When Japan attacked America, Hitler also declared war on America. This was a puzzling move, as his alliance did not oblige him to do so. At a stroke, the question of whether or not America should join the war against Hitler was settled. Churchill was naturally overjoyed. This was the moment, he declared in his memoirs, when he knew the war would be won. 'Hitler's fate was sealed. Mussolini's fate was sealed. As for the Japanese, they would be ground to powder. All the rest was merely the proper application of overwhelming force.'

THE SAME BOAT

'Today all of us are in the same boat with you and the people of the Empire, and it is a ship that will not and cannot be sunk.'

ROOSEVELT, IN A CABLE TO CHURCHILL, ON 11 DECEMBER, THE DAY HITLER DECLARED WAR ON AMERICA

'I went to bed and slept the sleep of the saved and thankful.'

CHURCHILL, IN HIS MEMOIRS, ON THE NIGHT OF 11 DECEMBER

▼ American battleships burn at Pearl Harbor. The attack, which caused America's entry into the Second World War, sealed the fate of both Japan and Germany.

CHURCHILL AND THE SOVIET UNION

Churchill had very mixed feelings about Britain's alliance with the Soviets. On his visit to Moscow in 1942, he recalled: 'I pondered on my mission to this sullen, sinister Bolshevik State I had once tried so hard to strangle at its birth, and which, until Hitler appeared, I had regarded as the mortal foe of civilised freedom...'

TIES WITH RUSSIA

When the Soviet Union had been invaded, Churchill had immediately given his support to Stalin and the Russian people. With America now fighting with Britain, Churchill worked to forge closer ties with the Soviets. He had a vision of a 'Grand Alliance', with Britain, America and the Soviet Union all working together to defeat the Nazis. More than any other world leader, Churchill ensured that this alliance was a success by working hard to ensure that its three leaders co-operated together

In August 1942, Churchill visited the Soviet leader, Joseph Stalin, in Moscow. Stalin was keen for America and Britain to open a 'second front' against the Nazis in Europe, to take the pressure off his own army, who were suffering terrible losses. He was deeply angry when Churchill told him Britain and America needed to build up their forces before such an invasion could take place. Nevertheless, when he returned home, Churchill instructed his War Cabinet colleagues to do everything they could to help the Soviets.

CASABLANCA

The beginning of 1943 saw another meeting between Churchill and Roosevelt – this time in Casablanca in North Africa. British troops had just defeated German and Italian armies in North Africa and Churchill now pushed forward a strategy of attacking Germany and Italy from the south. The two leaders also agreed on a policy of unconditional surrender for Germany. This meant they would accept nothing less than the total defeat of the Nazis, rather than

Churchill on his travels. Here he is in Cairo in 1942 with US President Franklin Roosevelt (centre) and Chinese leader Chiang Kai-shek.

any compromise peace which might leave Hitler or other Nazi leaders in charge of Germany.

Churchill travelled a great deal in 1943. He visited British troops in the Libyan port of Tripoli, then went to Turkey and tried unsuccessfully to persuade the Turks to enter the war against Germany. In May he met the Americans again in Washington, and then again in August at Quebec in Canada. This time he was there to discuss plans for a seaborne invasion of France. Despite his age, his immense enthusiasm and drive seemed unstoppable. Another meeting with the Americans followed in the Egyptian capital, Cairo, in November.

'The Big Three': Stalin (left), Roosevelt (centre) and Churchill in Teheran in 1943. Unlike Germany, Italy and Japan, Britain, the United States and the Soviet Union usually worked together effectively as allies

THE BIG THREE

Then, most significantly, at the end of November, Churchill, Roosevelt and Stalin all met in Teheran, in Persia (now Iran). Dubbed 'The Big Three' by the press, they discussed the next stage of the war and what was to be done following their inevitable victory.

The meeting was not an unqualified success for Churchill. Roosevelt refused to see Churchill alone, although he had several private meetings with Stalin. It was the first indication that America and the Soviets regarded Britain as the

junior member of the three. Frankly, it was true. As a world power Britain was on the wane, and the Soviets and Americans were growing stronger. Churchill hoped that Britain would come out of the war with her Empire stronger than ever. But neither the Soviets nor the Americans were interested in helping Britain maintain her leading position in the world.

BREAKDOWN

After the meeting Churchill flew to Tunis. But before he could return to Britain he collapsed with pneumonia, and then had a heart attack. He was now 69, and slowly coming to terms with the fact that old age was creeping up on him. During his illness he told his daughter Sarah, who was travelling with him, 'If I die, don't worry – the war is won.' He returned to Britain by boat in mid-January to plot the next stage of the war – the invasion of France.

▼ Churchill, flanked by the US generals Eisenhower (left) and Bradley (right), tries out new weapons for the benefit of newspaper photographers prior to D-Day in 1944.

OPERATION OVERLORD

The invasion was to take place in Normandy and preparations were complete by late May. Now all that remained was to wait for a good weather report. Churchill was desperate to watch the D-Day landings off shore from a battleship, and it took the personal intervention of the British King George VI to persuade him not to endanger his life like this.

On the day of the invasion, 6 June 1944, Churchill again had to be dissuaded from visiting the landing zones. He crossed over to France on 12 June, six days after the landing. He was so close to the fighting that his ship, the destroyer HMS *Kelvin*, actually bombarded German positions inland from the coast during the voyage.

The Normandy landings were a tremendous success. By the end of

August Paris, occupied by the Germans since June 1940, had been liberated. By September over two million troops had crossed over from Britain to France.

RIFTS WITH STALIN

At Teheran Churchill had told Stalin that he wanted to ensure that all nations liberated from the Nazis should be allowed to choose their own form of government. It was a frank admission of his fear that the Soviet regime would impose its own form of communist government on the nations of eastern Europe, which its army would pass through on the way to conquer Germany.

He met Stalin again in Moscow, in September 1944, to discuss the post-war settlement in eastern Europe. The Polish government in exile in Britain was determined to remain independent of Soviet control and not give up any Polish territory occupied by the advancing Russians. Churchill tried to convince the Poles that their resistance would just lead to further bloodshed, but nonetheless still argued their case to Stalin.

Stalin was determined that his country would control the eastern European nations. But he was prepared to barter territories, and allowed Churchill to use the British army to put down a communist revolt in Greece.

YALTA

In February 1945, with the war drawing to an end, the 'Big Three' met again in the Crimean town of Yalta, on the Black Sea. Here Churchill tried again to convince Stalin to allow the Poles their independence, and schemed with Roosevelt to prevent the Soviets from overrunning too much of eastern

▲ American soldiers wade ashore during the D-Day landings on the beaches of Normandy, France on 6 June 1944.

STALIN ON CHURCHILL

Although they were usually civil to one another, Stalin did not trust Churchill. He once remarked: '(He) is the kind of man who will pick your pocket for a kopeck (penny) if you don't watch him.'

STALIN AND ROOSEVELT

'There was a time when the Marshal (Stalin) was not so kindly towards us, and I remember I said a few rude things about him, but our common dangers and common loyalties have wiped all that out. The fire of war has burned up the misunderstandings of the past.'

CHURCHILL, IN A SPEECH AT YALTA, 8 FEBRUARY 1945

'To the end he faced his innumerable tasks unflinchingly... In war he...raised the strength, might and glory of the great Republic (America) to a height never attained by any nation in history.'

CHURCHILL, TO THE HOUSE OF COMMONS, FOLLOWING ROOSEVELT'S DEATH, 17 APRIL 1945

Europe. However, the Americans were not prepared to support him. As at Teheran, it was increasingly obvious that the Americans and the Soviets were the two major players in the world. It was the last time Churchill and Roosevelt met. The American president died two months later on 12 April 1945.

THE WAR IN EUROPE ENDS

In the closing stages of the war Churchill continued to visit the front, especially when British and American troops crossed over the river Rhine and into Germany.

At the end of April, Hitler committed suicide, and Germany surrendered on 7 May. Churchill was mobbed by enthusiastic crowds in London and made a radio broadcast to the nation the following day. Here he generously paid tribute to the enormous suffering of the Russian army and acknowledged their contribution to the defeat of Hitler. He also reminded his listeners that the war was far from over, and that Japan had still to be defeated.

After six years of co-operating together in a coalition government, all parties were now keen to hold a General Election. Campaigning began immediately, and wherever he went Churchill was greeted by huge cheering crowds. Yet he surprised many people by launching quite vicious attacks on the Labour Party, with whom he had worked so closely during the war. Labour, led by the able Clement Attlee, put forward a policy of major social reform, including a welfare system that would provide free health care and generous pension and unemployment provisions.

Waiting for the results of the election was a drawn-out affair, as postal votes from soldiers overseas all had to be counted. As he waited to know whether or not he would be re-elected, Churchill departed for Potsdam, for a final meeting with the Russians and Americans, who were now represented by former Vice-President Harry S. Truman.

Halfway through the conference Churchill left to hear the results of the election. The news that greeted him was perhaps the most astounding he had ever heard in his life.

▲ Churchill greets jubilant crowds in London on VE Day – 7 May 1945.

▼ The map shows where Churchill met other allied leaders for important wartime conferences.

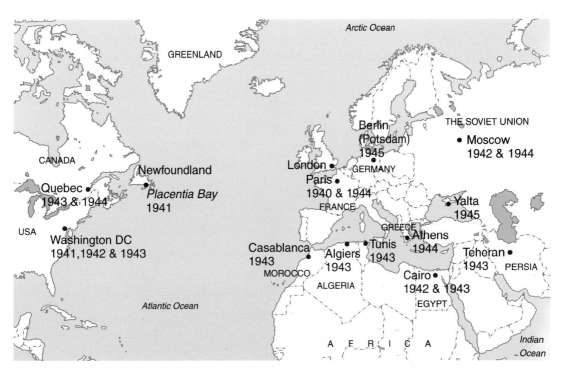

49

CHAPTER EIGHT

The Slow Decline 1945–1965

The Labour Party had won a landslide victory, with 393 seats against the Conservatives' 213, in a Parliament of 640. Churchill was flabbergasted and humiliated. He had led his country to victory, and this was his reward. It was one of the most astounding electoral defeats in British history.

There was a feeling in the country that people deserved some reward for the efforts and sacrifices they had made in the war. Unfortunately for Churchill, the British electorate thought the Labour Party's plans for social reform would provide this reward more effectively.

OPPOSITION LEADER

Churchill was still the undisputed leader of the Conservatives, but he was never comfortable in his new role as leader of the opposition (the head of the largest political party not actually forming the government). In his mind's eye he saw himself as a world statesman, travelling around the globe, and deciding the fate of nations with other towering figures in international politics. Debating welfare benefits with the 'abhorrent' socialists who now ran the country did not have the same glamorous appeal.

▼ The news of Clement Attlee's victory in the election campaign of July 1945 is greeted by Labour Party supporters in his local constituency of Limehouse in London.

In opposition he continued to press for close ties between Britain and the United States and talked of the 'special relationship' between 'the English-speaking peoples'. He also urged the European nations to set up a 'council of Europe', where they could work closer together. As a great believer in the might and right of the British Empire, he watched Labour's granting of independence to India and Burma in 1947 and 1948 respectively, with great disappointment.

ARTIST AT WORK

Aside from politics and writing, Churchill's great love was painting. He has been described as a 'gifted amateur', and had no illusions about the level of his talent. He once said: 'When I get to heaven I mean to spend a considerable portion of my first million years in painting, and so get to the bottom of the subject.'

OVER TO AMERICA

In 1946 Churchill returned to America, where he was greeted with wild enthusiasm. It was here on 5 March that he made a speech at least as famous as any of his wartime performances. At Westminster College, Fulton, Missouri, he spoke of the alarming deterioration in relations between the Soviet Union and America and Britain, now that their common Nazi foe had been defeated. Referring to the border that separated Soviet-held territory from the rest of Europe he said: 'From Stettin in the Baltic to Trieste in the Adriatic an iron curtain has descended across the Continent.' It was a brilliant image – sinister, ugly, secretive – that chimed in with many people's perception of Stalin's Soviet Union. Following this speech, it would become a stock phrase for the rest of the century.

▲ Churchill painting a view of the village of Camara de Lobos on the island of Madeira in 1950.

THE COLD WAR

The era following the Second World War and up to the collapse of the Soviet Union in 1991 has been called the 'Cold War'. During this time the Soviet Union (now Russia) and its allies, and the United States and its allies, were very hostile and mistrustful of each other. Although there was no fighting between these two great powers, both sides supported communist, or anti-communist, forces in other wars such as Korea and Vietnam.

IRON CURTAINS

Churchill undoubtedly popularized the phrase 'iron curtain', but he did not invent it. Journalist Ethel Snowden first used it in her 1920 book *Through Bolshevik Russia*. Hitler's propaganda minister Dr Joseph Goebbels had used the phrase as well in a speech in February 1945.

PRIME MINISTER AGAIN

Even in his late 70s Churchill was still keen to regain the centre stage he had lost in 1945. An election was held in Britain in 1950, which the Labour Party won by a very narrow majority of five seats. Another election followed the year after, and this time Churchill was returned to power with a small 26 seat majority.

Back in office Churchill once again concentrated most of his efforts on international affairs. He immediately visited President

▶ Churchill making history at Fulton, Missouri, in March 1946. Here he delivered a famous speech which popularized the term 'iron curtain' – referring to the division between western and communist Europe.

Truman in Washington to assure the Americans that British troops would support them in the Korean War, where the US army was fighting a hard battle against North Korean and Chinese communist troops.

Churchill was disappointed in what the Americans were prepared to offer him in return. The US were no longer willing to share their atomic weapon secrets with the British – a clear sign that they now regarded the British as very much a junior partner in world affairs. This situation remained the same when Truman was replaced by President Eisenhower in 1953.

POMP AND CEREMONY

1953 was a golden year for Churchill in many ways. His leadership of the British people during the war was recognized with a knighthood. He also received a Nobel Prize for Literature for his six-volume work *The Second World War*, which he had written during his time as opposition leader. The year also marked the coronation of Queen Elizabeth II which was just the sort of mighty traditional public ceremony he enjoyed so much.

Soviet leader Joseph Stalin also died in April of that year. Churchill saw his death as a golden opportunity for a new start, and immediately urged the United States to meet with the new Soviet leaders. 'At the worst the participants in the meeting would have established more intimate contacts. At the best we might have a generation of peace' he told the House of Commons.

RAISED TO THE ARISTOCRACY?

Following his knighthood, Churchill was also offered a dukedom. This would have entitled him to sit in the House of Lords. He turned this down, because he did not want to leave the House of Commons.

▼ Swedish ambassador Gunnar Hagglof presents Churchill with a cheque for £12,000 – his award for winning the Nobel Prize for Literature in 1953.

▲ Looking frail and distant, Churchill gives his famous V-for-Victory sign while fighting his final Parliamentary election campaign in 1959. He was 84 at the time.

But the year was also marred by a stroke, which Churchill suffered in June. Although he recovered, other strokes followed and he began to look and sound increasingly frail. From this period onward many of the responsibilities of his office were taken on by Conservative Party chairman Frederick Woolton, and Foreign Secretary Anthony Eden. On 5 April 1955, aged 80, he resigned as Prime Minister, but still remained an MP. In 1959, at the age of 84, he even fought and won another by-election.

Away from office Churchill continued to do what he had always done. He wrote a four-volume *History of the English-Speaking Peoples*, and painted. When his health permitted, he still travelled, staying in the grand homes and yachts of his circle of wealthy friends.

DEATH OF CHURCHILL

He died in London, on 24 January 1965, two months after his 90th birthday. His funeral, which he had largely planned himself, was a massive affair in keeping with his status as international statesman and Britain's great war leader. The service was held at St Paul's Cathedral in London and attended by dignitaries and politicians from all over the world.

After the service, his coffin was placed on a Royal Navy launch and taken along the River Thames to Waterloo Station. From Waterloo it was taken by train to Blenheim. Churchill was buried near Blenheim Palace, in Bladon churchyard, next to his father, mother and brother.

The tributes paid to him were lavish in the extreme. Perhaps one of the most touching came from his wartime deputy, and Labour opponent, Clement Attlee. Churchill had once described the mild-mannered Attlee with gleeful schoolboy spite as 'a sheep in sheep's clothing'. At his funeral Attlee described Churchill as 'the greatest Englishman of our time.'

◀ Churchill's funeral procession leaves Westminster for St Paul's Cathedral. The grandiose ceremony was a fitting end for one of Britain's greatest leaders.

Winston Churchill – Success And Failure

Winston Churchill led a long and complex life. After an unhappy childhood sometimes with, but mainly without, his adored but distant parents, he quickly established himself as a soldier and journalist of great bravery. The fame he gained opened doors that led to a rapidly successful career in politics. He was a junior minister at 30, and a cabinet minister at 33. During his time in the House of Commons he held many of the most important positions in government. But his term as Home Secretary and as Chancellor of the Exchequer were marred by failure. His second spell as Prime Minister was undistinguished. Perhaps his stint as wartime Prime Minister was the only Government position he held that was an unqualified success.

▶ The wartime leader – Churchill at his desk in March 1945. He wears his trademark bow tie and carries an ever-present cigar in his hand.

CHURCHILL'S HUMOUR

His writing, speeches and conversation were peppered with memorable, witty phrases. During the war, when President Roosevelt visited him in his apartment, he was astonished to see Churchill emerging from his bath, stark naked. 'The Prime Minister of Great Britain,' announced Churchill, 'has nothing to conceal from the President of the United States.'

CONTRADICTORY CHARACTER

His faults were transparent – he was undoubtedly a conceited boaster, and could be spiteful on a personal level. This sometimes worked against him disastrously – as his comments on his Labour opponents in the 1945 election showed. His enemies described him as unprincipled chancer, but others saw him as a wily pragmatist – willing to make whatever move best served the cause he believed in. For instance, Attlee, his Labour arch enemy at home, was his deputy during the war. Stalin, the tyrannical Soviet leader, was one of his principal allies in the fight against Hitler.

▲ Sir Winston Churchill addresses the US Congress in January 1952. He is fondly remembered by many Americans. President George W. Bush has revealed that Churchill is one of his heroes.

FAILURES AND SUCCESSES

Churchill's career until he first became Prime Minister had been a rollercoaster ride of success and failure. One historian, Robert Rhodes James, even entitled a biography *Churchill: A Study in Failure 1900-1939*. If Churchill had retired at 65 he would be probably be best remembered as a

TWO SIDES OF A COIN

'*... as an adult Churchill was dominated by a belief in his own uniqueness and destiny, combined with a marked lack of respect in other people and their views.*'

HISTORIAN CLIVE PONTING

'*In 1940 Churchill became the hero he had always dreamed of being... In that dark time, what England needed was not a shrewd, balanced leader. She needed a prophet, a heroic visionary, a man who could dream dreams of victory when all seemed lost. Winston Churchill was such a man...*'

HISTORIAN ANTHONY STORR

journalist and historian who had a mixed, but mainly unsuccessful, career in politics.

CLAIM TO GREATNESS

His success as a wartime Prime Minister is unquestionably his most convincing claim to greatness. His ability to inspire a nation during perhaps the darkest days in its history was extraordinary. One eyewitness recalls seeing people, who had just had their homes destroyed by bombs, leaping into the air and cheering madly when Churchill arrived to inspect the scene of devastation.

Churchill was also the principal architect of the 'Grand Alliance' between himself, Stalin and Roosevelt. Hitler's allies, Italy and Japan, had been

▶ Churchill's popularity as a war leader was unquestionable, and helped to wipe out much of the resentment that many working-class British people felt towards him before the war.

▲ Churchill, looking considerably less vigorous than he did during the war, relaxes with family and friends at Chartwell in 1951.

of little use to Germany. Churchill, more than any other war leader, ensured that Britain, the United States and the Soviet Union would co-operate with great effectiveness in their mission to destroy Hitler.

Like many men from his era and background, Churchill had political ideas and opinions that have not aged well. He was cruel about people with mental illness, thought black and Asian people were inferior to whites, and that the working class in Britain should have only limited political power. Yet there was a basic humanity in his character that is best summed up in a phrase from his book *The Second World War*: 'In war: resolution. In defeat: defiance. In victory: magnanimity. In peace: goodwill.'

CHURCHILL ON HIS WARTIME PREMIERSHIP

'*It was a nation and race dwelling all around the globe that had the lion's heart. I had the luck to be called upon to give the roar.*'

SPEECH GIVEN ON HIS 80TH BIRTHDAY, 1954

59

1874
30 NOVEMBER
Born Blenheim Palace

1886
His father, Lord Randolph Churchill, briefly becomes Chancellor of the Exchequer

1888–92
Educated at Harrow school

1893–98
Military training at Sandhurst and service in India and the Sudan

1895
Lord Randolph Churchill dies

1898
Publishes first book – *The Story of the Malakand Field Force*

1899–1900
War correspondent and serving soldier in South Africa. During this time he is captured by and escapes from the Boers

1900
Elected MP for Oldham

1904
Leaves Conservative Party and joins Liberal Party

1905
Under-Secretary for the Colonies

1906
MP for North-West Manchester

1908
APRIL
MP for Dundee.
Made President of the Board of Trade

SEPTEMBER
Marries Clementine Hozier

1910
Liberal Party wins General Election.
Home Secretary

1911
First Lord of the Admiralty

1915
Ill-fated Dardanelles campaign. Resigns from Admiralty

1915–1916
Goes to France to fight on Western Front

1917
Minister of Munitions

1919
Secretary of State for War

1921
Secretary of State for the Colonies

1922
Out of Parliament

1924
NOVEMBER
Elected MP for Epping.
Made Chancellor of the Exchequer by Baldwin

1925
Returns Britain to the Gold Standard

1929
Out of office as Baldwin's government falls

1931
Resigns from Shadow Cabinet

1939
Returns to government as First Lord of the Admiralty

1940–45
Prime Minister

1941
JUNE
Nazi Germany invades Soviet Union

AUGUST
Historic meeting with US President Roosevelt at Placentia Bay

DECEMBER
Japanese attack on Pearl Harbor brings America into Second World War

1944
JUNE
D-Day landings mark beginning of final campaign to conquer Hitler's Germany

1945
FEBRUARY
Meets Stalin and Roosevelt at Yalta

MAY
Germany surrenders. VE (Victory in Europe) Day

JULY
Churchill's Conservatives defeated in General Election by Labour Party. MP for Woodford and Leader of the Opposition

1946
'Iron Curtain' speech given at Fulton in USA

1948–54
Publishes volumes of The Second World War

1951
Elected Prime Minister again

1953
Wins Nobel Prize for Literature for The Second World War

1955
Steps down as Prime Minister

1959
Wins last election as MP

1964
Steps down as MP for Woodford

1965
24 JANUARY
Dies. Following State Funeral at St Paul's Cathedral is buried in Bladon churchyard, near Blenheim

1977
Clementine Churchill dies

61

Anarchist Someone who believes in the abolition of all governments

Anti-socialist Someone who opposes the policies of socialist parties, such as Britain's Labour Party

ANZAC Australian and New Zealand Army Corps

Appeasement Policy adopted by British MP Neville Chamberlain which accepted that the Treaty of Versailles was unjust and that Germany should be allowed to regain territory she lost after the First World War. A harsher definition is: to give in to the demands of a hostile nation in the hope of avoiding war

Aristocratic In the manner of an aristocrat, a person at the top of the upper class

Auxiliary Additional

Battalion A military unit made up of three companies

Bolshevik A Russian communist – the word was used as a critical term for any radical left-wing person

British Commonwealth An informal alliance of countries that were formerly part of the British Empire

Cavalry charge A charge by cavalry troops mounted on horseback

Cavalry regiment A group of troops who are trained to fight on horseback

Chancellor of the Exchequer A member of the British government responsible for the financial policy of the country

Civil war A war between opposing forces in one country (as opposed to between different countries)

Civilian A person who is not in the armed forces

Coalition government A government made up of members of different political parties

Colonial To do with colonies

Colony A country controlled by another country

Communist Someone who believes in communism – a political philosophy which holds that the state should control the wealth and industry of a country on behalf of its people

Conscript Someone who has been forced by law to join the armed forces, as opposed to someone who has volunteered to join up

Constituency A district and its voters, who elect a person to be their Member of Parliament

Deposed Removed from a position of power

Empire A collection of colonies controlled by a country

Financier Someone who borrows or lends money to businesses or countries

Fleet A collection of warships

Home Secretary A member of the British government responsible for law and order and immigration

Immigrants People from one country who come to live in another country

Infantryman A soldier who fights on foot

Insurance underwriter Someone who calculates risks and costs for an insurance company

Labour laws Laws dealing with the employment of people, such as what hours they may work and how much they should be paid

Leader of the Opposition In British politics, the leader of the largest political party which has not gained enough votes to form a government

Left-wing Someone or something which has socialist or communist political inclinations

Liberal Broadly speaking, a person who has political views which favour tolerance of others and personal freedom

Lieutenant A junior officer in the army

Magnanimity Generosity

Meteoric Literally meaning like a meteor, but used to describe a short, brilliant career

Militant Aggressive (in support of a particular political cause, for example)

Minimum wage The least amount that an employer should pay a worker

Munitions Shells and other ammunition, and also a general term for military equipment

Nationalist Generally, someone who staunchly supports their country; specifically with regard to Ireland, a Nationalist is someone who supports Irish independence from Britain, as opposed to a Unionist, who wishes Ireland, especially Northern Ireland, to remain united with Britain

Oratory The art of making speeches

Parliament The home of the British government, consisting of the House of Commons and House of Lords

Patriotic Showing great loyalty to one's country

Poignant Affectingly sad
President of the Board of Trade A member of the British government responsible for business, and in particular British exports
Propaganda Biased information, especially news, which puts forward the views of a government or political party in order to persuade people to think in a particular way
Right-wing Someone or something which has conservative or fascist political inclinations
Sadistic Literally, taking pleasure in cruelty, but also used to mean exceptionally cruel
Secretary of State for the Colonies A member of the British government responsible for Britain's colonies
Secretary of War A member of the British government responsible for the country's armed forces, especially during wartime
Social unrest Dissatisfaction in a country with a government, sometimes displayed by demonstrations or other protests, and even rioting
Socialist A supporter of socialism – a milder form of communism
Suffragette Someone who supported the idea that women should be allowed to vote
Totalitarian state A regime in a country, such as the Soviet Union or Nazi Germany, where the government has total control of people's lives and any form of rebellion is punished very harshly
Trade union A group of workers who have banded together, usually with the aim of persuading their employers to give them better working conditions or pay
Tyrannical Behaving like a tyrant – a leader who acts in an oppressive and unjust manner
Unelected Elite members of a society who exercise great influence, or even control, over a country, even though they have not been chosen by an electorate to do so
War correspondent A journalist who reports on wars, usually from the battlefield
Working class Section of society who are usually the least educated, and who usually do the least well-paid and most unskilled work

FURTHER INFORMATION

WEBSITES
The official Churchill home page will be found at **http://www.winstonchurchill.org** You may also like to try **http://www.churchill-society-london-org.uk/index.html** which is packed with detailed information about his life.

BOOKS
For older readers:
Churchill's official biographer Martin Gilbert has written a dense but readable single volume biography called *Churchill: A Life* (Mandarin, 1993)

For a more unsympathetic view try Clive Ponting's *Churchill* (Sinclair-Stevenson, 1995)

One very accessible and readable biography is *Winston Churchill A Brief Life* by Piers Brendon (Pimlico, 2001)

For younger readers:
Winston Churchill, H. Castor (Franklin Watts, 2000)

Winston Churchill, Fiona Reynolds (Heinemann, 2001)

FILMS
Young Winston, starring Simon Ward as Churchill, is a rip-roaring account of Churchill's early life, especially his escapades in South Africa. It was made in 1972.